SNOW JOB

SNOW JOB

MY LIFE IN THE MEDELLIN CARTEL

CARLOS STIER

Edited with an Introduction by
MICHAEL O'KANE

ANDALUS
PUBLISHING

INTRODUCTION

AFTER HE SHOT OFF A MAN'S FACE and beheaded a woman in Broward County, Florida, Carlos Stier started working as an informant for the Drug Enforcement Administration. His work led him to cross paths with another informant, Julio Diaz, a physician and Bay of Pigs veteran who had worked for both the FBI and CIA in matters deemed secret because they affect the security of the United States of America.

The two undercover operations collided, and after the FBI claimed that Dr. Diaz' work was not authorized, an indictment followed. In preparation for trial, Stier prepared a statement outlining his journey from drug trafficker to government informant. This statement was turned over to the defense in the Diaz case. The statement provides a prettified view history of Stier's involvement in the drug trade on behalf of Carlos Lehder, one of the leaders of the Medellín Cartel. The second or third generation photocopied statement was over two hundred typewritten pages long. Unlike digital copies, analog copies degrade when copied. Several portions of the statement are no longer legible. There are gaps in the statement showing redactions and penciled-in revisions, done presumably at the request of his DEA handlers.

The statement was filed with the court and made a part of the appellate record. For thirty years it has sat in archives in Miami, Florida.

Until today.

Like most former traffickers now working with the government, Stier claimed that his trial on State drug trafficking charges and a mandatory fifteen year prison sentence was his road to Damascus that led to his enlightenment and rejection of the drug business. Though he claimed to have fully switched sides, he cannot help taking pride in having smuggled thousands of kilograms of cocaine into the United States; he cannot help but describe his fellow lawbreakers with pride.

After he broke off ties with Lehder, Stier started selling kilogram quantities of cocaine in Broward County, Florida. One of the distributors who worked with him was a junior college student named Sandra Suarez. After the police found Sandra's remains in the trunk of her car in Broward County, their investigation quickly focused on Stier, the last person to have seen her alive. Stier was arrested and brought in for questioning. During police interrogation, he claimed that he had nothing to do with her murder, but freely confessed to having used Suarez to sell his cocaine. He also denied leaving her body in the trunk of a car in a parking lot he had previously chosen to consummate narcotics transactions.

The State of Florida initially charged Stier with Suarez' murder. However, at a probable cause hearing, the State judge found that the Broward County prosecutor, Michael Satz, had insufficient evidence to proceed to trial. At that point, using Stier's confession detailing his involvement in cocaine distribution, Satz brought cocaine trafficking charges against Stier.

During his trial in Broward County for narcotics trafficking, Stier saw that the evidence was against him. His confession had been recorded. His voice was on tape, played before the jury, talking about selling cocaine. Stier's lawyer, Fred Graves, warned him that conviction was likely. The prosecutor knew just as well as Stier and Graves did that Stier's defense case was not going well. Graves then approached the prosecutor and sought a plea agreement.

According to Stier, the prosecutor agreed to a deal in which probation was a real possibility,[1] as long as Stier was cleared of any involvement in Suarez' murder. Stier agreed to take a lie detector to prove his innocence. If he failed the test, Stier faced a mandatory minimum sentence of fifteen years' imprisonment under State statutes.

Stier failed the test. He was then sentenced to fifteen years in Florida State prison for drug trafficking.

~

One of the most notorious drug traffickers of the 1970's and 1980's was Carlos Lehder, a German-Colombian who became famous for very public—he ran for the Colombian senate—and ostentatious behavior. He made no secret of his fondness for Adolf Hitler and commissioned a statute of the Beatles' murdered John Lennon which featured a bullet hole.

Lehder did not go to university but completed his education at the Federal Correctional Institution in Otisville, New York, where he shared a cell with George Jung, a Boston marijuana trafficker who would later be portrayed by actor Johnny Depp in the Hollywood movie *Blow*. Lehder has yet to inspire a Hollywood film, but his notoriety has far eclipsed Jung's. For years he was targeted by the DEA as one of the most important drug traffickers in the world.

Most Americans would be surprised to learn that the DEA buys and sells illegal drugs. The DEA sells buys and sells drugs, permitting the owners of the illegal substances to make a profit. They may sell the drugs, letting what judges sometimes refer as "poison" onto the streets of the United States. The reason this behavior is legal is because the government permits the DEA to buy, sell and import drugs without fear of sanction. This is accomplished in order to catch and interdict non-government actors.

When the Bureau of Alcohol, Tobacco and Firearms lost control of firearms, including weapons of war, in the operation they christened "Fast and Furious," Congress was in an uproar because some of those weapons made it into the hands of Mexican drug cartels, the heirs to operations like Carlos Lehder's. No sleep is lost over that marijuana and cocaine that makes its way to the streets of the United States because American consumers want the very drugs the special agents are trying to interdict.

Ten American States have made recreational marijuana legal and thirty-three States have legalized marijuana use in one way or another. Despite these moves by a majority of American States and substantial voter demand, at a federal level the importation, cultivation and use of marijuana remains illegal.

∼

Carlos Stier's fate was sealed in part because of the accident of his Colombian birth and the fact that his boyhood friend was Carlos Lehder. His friendship with Lehder and knowledge of Lehder's operations would cause the DEA to give him a "get out of jail free" card that ultimately permitted him to walk away from a fifteen year state prison sentence, a punishment that was, as prosecutors like to say, inextricably intertwined with the murder of Sandra Suarez.

Part dowsing, part witchcraft, the polygraph's effectiveness as a law enforcement tool is based on the common-sense belief that a person will have a physical reaction when telling a lie. This hypothesis has never been proven. In short, a polygraph is like homeopathy, which itself is based on the placebo effect: if you believe that it works, it works. The government believes in the test's accuracy.

Polygraphs are used both by law enforcement and the intelligence community to determine the veracity of witnesses in the conduct of investigations. A CIA agent may lose his classified clearance and his employment if he fails the test. The same is true for police officers. When it comes to polygraph examinations, federal government agents are true believers. The DEA polygraphs potential witnesses. In the private sector, retail establishments subject employees to polygraph tests as a means of loss prevention. Polygraph evidence is inadmissible in federal court in every single federal circuit except one: the Eleventh, which has responsibility for South Florida, the site of Sandra Suarez' murder.[2]

As far as the DEA was concerned, by failing to "beat the box," Carlos Stier was proven to be a murderer. Nevertheless, they overlooked this fact and freed him in order to help build a case against Carlos Lehder.

~

The DEA's culture celebrates drugs seized, arrests made and assets forfeited. Stier was allowed to prove his worth to the DEA by becoming a field operative. After Stier was released from jail into the custody of two DEA special agents—which was no custody at all—Stier was permitted to pose locally and internationally as a trafficker.

Astonishingly, Stier worked under the name he had previously used when working for the Medellín Cartel. Stier had been expelled from Lehder's organization, not for killing Sandra Suarez, but for attempting to kill a trusted Lehder lieutenant in Broward County. Though Stier later claimed that *sicarios*[3] sent by the Medellín Cartel had killed Suarez in an effort to frame him, this did not stop him from using the same name he used while working with Lehder.

Stier returned to the Bahamas as he had often done for Lehder, but now at the behest of and directed by the DEA. There Stier renewed contact with the Treco family, Bahamians who had earlier facilitated Lehder's drug flights. Stier was an experienced supply-chain and logistics drug trafficker. He knew what was needed. He was good at his work.

Harry Treco was a respected member of a celebrated old Bahamian family but the DEA knew that if the price were right, he would assist the traffickers. Stier and Treco had worked together on drug importations. Treco arranged for police protection, jet fuel, manpower, security and transportation. By the time Stier became involved, the organization was responsible for over one hundred such flights. No flight ferried less than two hundred kilos of cocaine; sometimes the amounts were as high as five hundred kilos.

Harry's son, Robert, was part of the operation. He introduced Stier to Dr. Julio Diaz, a Miami physician who was also a drug trafficker. Dr. Diaz did not just lead a double life, he led at least four. In addition to physician and drug trafficker, add to his resume, soldier—he was part of Brigade 2506, the CIA-led invasion of the Bay of Pigs in 1961

He was also a spy.

Spies usually take care of their own. But not in this case.

Despite his career as an adventurer, Diaz was astonishingly naive. Or astonishingly truthful. There is no way to know for certain if Diaz was conducting undercover narcotics operations for the FBI. The FBI said no, and so Diaz was indicted for drug trafficking. The one hundred kilos he claimed to want to purchase were to be supplied by none other than Robert Treco and the murderer the DEA freed from jail, Carlos Stier.

What work Dr. Julio Diaz had done for the government as a spy was a mystery. The government would only admit that once upon a time, Dr. Diaz had been a spy. They would not say what he had done. Conveniently, his control agent was not available to testify. Instead the FBI sent three agents to Miami to testify that Dr. Diaz was indeed a spy, but his control agent had never told them anything about investigating narcotics trafficking.

This claim might have had some validity if the FBI had not in 1973 reversed a Hoover-era policy precisely in order to get in on the drug war. Hoover had prohibited his agents from getting involved in drug trafficking cases since the potential for corruption was so great. After the San Diego Mercury and revelations about Iran-Contra, the CIA's involvement in drug trafficking was an open secret.

When Dr. Diaz started working for the FBI, the agency was prohibited from investigating narcotics cases, a decision made by J. Edgar Hoover, to avoid corruption in the ranks and because of Hoover's rivalry with Harry Anslinger, his bureaucratic equal and the long-standing chief of another bureau, the Bureau of Narcotics and Dangerous Drugs, the forerunner of the Drug Enforcement Administration. L. Patrick Gray, appointed by Nixon to lead the FBI after Hoover's death, reversed the order. Nixon had declared a war on drugs to get people's minds off the war in Vietnam and was running around taking pictures with Elvis Presley, who was made an honorary special agent, and who, liked Anslinger, died while using the very drugs he publicly condemned.

Dr. Diaz made his claim against someone who wasn't there, who hadn't put anything in writing. Worse, Judge Federico Moreno, the trial judge in the Diaz case, restricted cross-examination into classified matters. Even the 11th Circuit Court of Appeals, the only polygraph-friendly circuit in the United States, felt that this had gone too far.

~

I broke my right arm the night before Julio Diaz' trial was to begin.

I had joined a group of friends for an evening of ice skating at the rink in Homestead. Ice skating is not a traditional Florida activity. The rink was to be blown away by Hurricane Andrew in 1992 and was never rebuilt.

I had grown up with hockey skates but the only skates available for rental at the Homestead were figure skating skates. These skates have a toe pick, or steps, cut into the front of the blade. I tripped on these and fell on my right elbow. There was some initial pain from the blow but I got up and tried to shake it off. I could still move my arm.

A member of our party was an orthopedic surgeon from Puerto Rico who always carried a gun. But he was off-duty, at least as far as his life as a physician. He wasn't interested in examining me but said, "if you wake up in the morning and it hurts like hell, it's probably broken."

In the morning, my arm hurt like hell. I improvised a sling and drove myself to the courthouse.

Julio Diaz and his co-defendants were there, along with the prosecution team and several DEA agents. In contradistinction to all other witnesses, DEA or FBI agents are permitted to sit at counsel table with the prosecutors. The reason for this is to "personalize" the prosecution, to create the illusion that the prosecutor represents the wholesome agent against those accused of crime sitting on the other side of the courtroom with the defense attorneys. Those who drafted the rules governing trials knew that it is all to easy for a juror to vote against the nebulous idea of "government" as opposed to voting for or against a real person.

This rule is all well and good, but the problem is that usually witnesses are barred from the courtroom until after they testify. The danger is that a witness will conform his testimony to that of another or even change his story. This rule, unfortunately, does not apply to government agents, so they can hear and see the cross-examination of other witnesses before they take the stand. This information can then be shared with later government witnesses.

As everyone found their places, Judge Moreno addressed me and asked me why I was not wearing a tie. I explained that I had broken my arm the night before and was not in a physical condition to defend my client. "You look all right to me," he said, "why can't you continue?" I explained that I am right-handed and could not write with a broken arm.

The judge asked how I had got to the courthouse that morning and I told him I had driven myself. He asked me how I had accomplished that, and I told him, "with difficulty." He then asked if I had taken any painkillers. I told him I had. He then asked if I had violated Florida law by driving under the influence of painkillers. When I asked for a continuance, he threatened to have the US Marshals take me into custody for a medical examination.[4]

Judge Moreno then asked my codefendant client, Robby Clavo, if he felt comfortable with proceeding with the trial despite my medical condition. Clavo said that he did not feel comfortable at all.[5] Judge Moreno reluctantly agreed to continue the case.

A few months later, my arm healed, Julio Diaz' case began. Having been threatened with jail once by the judge, I had to redouble my efforts to meet the government's case at every possible level. Otherwise Clavo would think that I was simply throwing the case in favor of the government out of fear. He was entitled to a defense. I would give him one.

∾

Historically, the trial of a matter by the presentation of evidence before a judge and jury is just one of the ways facts were determined.

The word "trial" historically encompassed ordeals such as putting a hand into boiling water, or being thrown fully clothed into a river. Since God protects the innocent, the accused would swim to the surface and not drown or withdraw his hand unharmed.

Up until the 1930's, trials of both civil and criminal cases were essentially trials by ambush. Because the results of these ordeals often had little to do with reality as well as being patently unfair, reforms were instituted. Prior to trial, the parties were obligated to identify the witnesses whose testimony they planned to rely on. The parties also had to exchange any documents they planned to use.

This exchange of evidence prior to trial is called "discovery." In time, discovery even came to include the opportunity to put questions to a witness under oath, outside the presence of a judge and usually in the offices of the lawyers or a court reporter though under general judicial supervision.

As a result of the liberalization of discovery, cases settled. A party who could see his opponent's evidence could weigh how that evidence would be seen by a jury. A plaintiff whose case rested on documents would have those documents examined and tested for authenticity and veracity by an opponent. Only a foolhardy plaintiff would proceed to trial after an unrebutted expert witness had questioned these prior to trial. The liberalization of discovery had as its consequence the narrowing of issues, the more efficient administration of justice and removed from the system those cases that should not have been filed or defended in the first instance.

While discovery reform was an unmitigated success on the civil side of the court, the reform was never implemented in criminal cases. Those accused of crime often had no idea who would testify against them at trial. They had no idea what documents would be used and whether these were authentic or not.

Not only the defense, but the forensic examination of the government's case had to be conducted at trial. Judges were loathe to grant continuances, and a 1912 death case out of Alabama said they didn't have to.

In time, the innocent were too often convicted and the courts, by now exposed to the efficiency of discovery in civil cases, let some of the reforms bleed into the criminal docket. The imposition of discovery obligations was rarely accomplished as a legislative matter. Instead, on a case by case basis, meager reforms were allowed to bleed through.

It took a Supreme Court decision, in the case of *Brady v. Maryland*, to establish the sensible requirement that the prosecution reveal evidence of a defendant's innocence. In *Jencks v. United States*, the Court permitted the defendant to see the previous testimony of a witness before the grand jury—but included the unworkable requirement that the testimony be turned over only after such witness had testified at trial.

In order to avoid mandatory recesses so that defense counsel could read what were often hundreds of pages of documents before attempting to cross-examine for inconsistencies, courts worked out a system where *Jencks* material was turned over after the jury was empaneled. So in addition to worrying about all of his trial duties—preparing, rehearsing and giving an opening statement, rebutting the prosecution's opening, arranging for the presence of witnesses, the defense was forced to stay up nights reading these hundreds of pages.

∼

I never understood why defense attorneys rush to obtain security clearances when handling a case involving classified information. My own experience with classified information goes back a long way. In 1980 on a fall afternoon in Chicago, I passed Edward Lee Howard in the hall of the Conrad Hilton hotel on Michigan Avenue. He had just finished one initial round of CIA recruitment interviews. He was hired but the Agency but later failed a polygraph and lost an assignment to Moscow. His wife helped him evade an FBI tail and he left the country. He wrote about these adventures years later after defecting to the Soviet Union.

In the early 1980's, the US Southern Command ran war games in Panama. The scenarios were fictitious, but as true to life as the planners could anticipate. The Berlin Wall had not fallen; the Warsaw Pact was a threat. The plan was to defend the Canal from an attack by a Maoist guerrilla army. Though there were no Maoist guerrilla armies in Panama, this practice for war was useful insofar as it exposed weaknesses in command structure, strategy and tactics.

In the war games, my role was to play the Administrator of the Panama Canal. Military personnel gave a cryptographic device that I was to keep on my person during the exercise. The device was contained within a black metal case about six inches long by an inch wide and half an inch thick. There were no markings other than a legend advising that the device belonged to the National Security Agency. At one end there was a strange connector, one that I hadn't seen before. In those days, personal computers were still in their infancy. Government offices ran dedicated Wang word processors and the Engineering and Construction division had just received an IBM PC-AT, a marvel with a key and a ten megabyte hard drive.

At the end of the war game, with the pretend Maoist guerrillas vanquished, they asked for the device back. I still wonder what it really was and what it could do.

As recent Wikileaks revelations show, classified information usually consists of information already in the public domain. At a foreign post, local newspaper articles are summarized, translated and then sent in a cable to the Secretary of State. You are unlikely to find the identification of the shooter behind the grassy knoll, a memorandum explaining what really happened on 9/11 or the real story behind the Israeli "art students" testing penetration techniques in the months before the attacks.

Before his death, Senator John McCain asked a group of intelligence princelings at a Congressional hearing about an article that had appeared in the Washington Post.

"Oh no," one princeling said, "we can't answer that. It's classified information."

"But it's in the newspaper," McCain pleaded, "can't we talk about it?"

"Oh no," chorused the princelings. "We cannot. It's classified."

Twenty years ago closed door sessions of Congress were rare. Now they are common. Information is kept from the public and doled out only to those special few, those who have accepted a clearance.

Those who, for better or worse, are now under control.

More than hiding secrets, classified information hides embarrassment. The philosopher and mathematician Norbert Weiner pointed out that it is a commonplace of human existence that we seek to hide what shames us.[6] What better way to hide an embarrassing secret than to classify it?

The problem is that at least three people always know the secret: the source; the person who prepared the classified document and the person who read the classified document.

~

One of the goals of government is to keep its own secrets. Every presidential administration and every federal agency worries about leaks. Vigorous efforts are made to try to stop leaks, but information has a way of finding its way to freedom.

In the 1970's, *Counterspy*, a newsletter linked to Philip Agee, a CIA defector, started identifying CIA spies working abroad. The CIA places its agents in foreign embassies in order to obtain diplomatic protection for its spies. This is to avoid embarrassing incidents and criminal prosecution when spies get caught.

One such incident occurred recently when a CIA spy in Moscow went to meet a Russian agent who he thought had turned against Putin. Unfortunately for the CIA, the Russian recruit was just as undercover as their own spy. When the Russian intelligence services arrested the American spy, he was wearing a red wig and carrying $130,000 in cash. Fortunately, the American spy was attached to the US Embassy and had diplomatic immunity. After the embarrassing press conference at which the failed secret recruitment was revealed, the cash and wig-carrying spy was declared persona non-grata and deported.

He was fortunate. After the identification of Richard Welch as a CIA officer, he was murdered in 1975. This led to the passing of the Intelligence Identities Protection Act ("IIPA"), making it illegal to publish the names of covert agents.

That law was the first to successfully censor an annoying newsletter—the First Amendment be damned—and laid the groundwork for Judge Hoeveler's prior restraint injunction against CNN in the Noriega case. *Counterspy* wasn't *The New York Times*, after all. On an aiding and abetting theory, the government could threaten any company that wanted to distribute *Counterspy* as well as deny them the use of the mails. Within a few years, the newsletter was effectively dead.

One might think that given the breadth of the First Amendment that it is illegal to enjoin a newspaper from publication in the United States. Once upon a time it was, but classified information has a way not only of engendering new rules but breaking old ones. It had been a long time since anyone had paid any attention to the IIPA, until that law was broken by the George W. Bush White House in an effort to discredit a CIA analyst. From time to time the IIPA has been threatened against any publication that might feel a need to report on CIA activities abroad.

The Classified Information Procedures Act (CIPA) is a much more frequently used cousin of the IIPA. Both laws were designed to prevent the unauthorized disclosure of classified information. Whereas the IIPA targeted the press, CIPA targeted the courts.

According to the US Attorney's Manual:

> "After a criminal indictment becomes public, the prosecutor remains responsible for taking reasonable precautions against the unauthorized disclosure of classified information during the case. This responsibility applies both when the government intends to use classified information in its case-in-chief as well as when the defendant seeks to use classified information in his/her defense. The tool with which the proper protection of classified information may be ensured in indicted cases is the CLASSIFIED INFORMATION PROCEDURES ACT (CIPA). *See* Title 18, U.S.C. App III."

A tactic used in the defense of those who possessed classified information was to threaten its disclosure at criminal trial. This tactic was given the name of "graymail." The government was concerned that its secrets would be spilled because trials were public, they were open to the public, and journalists or even foreign spies could attend to fill their ears with tales of classified embarrassments.

CIPA created a procedure by which a defendant who intended to reveal classified information in his defense had to give a notice to the government which could then seek a protective order prohibiting such testimony after a secret hearing before a judge that may or may not take place outside the presence of the defendant.

∾

The case against Dr. Julio Diaz was to be just another "reverse," that is, a drug bust where the DEA isn't taking drugs off the streets, but putting them on. This is a common drug enforcement tactic. It is not always a good idea.

Several years ago, near Gifford Lane and Day Avenue in Coconut Grove, a neighborhood in Miami, a young man was murdered. The murder was odd—it seemed to be a random killing in a neighborhood where murder was unusual. Before the murder, Gifford Lane seemed to be more trafficked than usual; that in itself was strange. A few months later, the drug police announced that they had set up a drug hole near that corner, selling drugs to all comers in an effort to glean intelligence and take users off the streets.

Their actions had the opposite effect. Their product was remarkably pure. The police had access to seized, high quality, undiluted Colombian cocaine. That brought buyers not just from all parts of the county, but from other counties as well once the news traveled. Because their purchases were not subject to the law of supply and demand, prices were low. The combination of low prices and high quality was irresistible. The murder occurred when a buyer tried to rip-off another buyer. Astonishingly, the drug police thought they were doing God's work by bringing murder to the neighborhood. Most assuredly they were not.

The residents were not canvassed before the police brought murder to the neighborhood. They were never asked. And if you think that it is hyperbole for me to use the word 'murder,' but remember that a person who aids and abets the commission of a crime is just as responsible as the person who pulls the trigger.

The intelligence community is divided into competing fiefdoms. Information is siloed and shared begrudgingly. The CIA doesn't trust the FBI and the FBI trusts no one. The DEA's remit is supposed to be limited, but they have no problem directing foreign relations in what should be the agency's limited sphere of interest.

What Carlos Stier didn't know was that "the doctor," Julio Diaz, whom he targeted for DEA Special Agent Michael McManus, already had a relationship with the FBI. Whatever Diaz did for the FBI involved national security. When McManus ran Diaz's name through DEA's NADDIS, the Narcotics and Dangerous Drugs Information System, this tidbit didn't turn up.

Neither Stier nor McManus had any idea that Dr. Diaz was a spy. But they would soon learn.

A federal narcotics arrest is not a board game. There is nothing genteel about it. Immediately before an arrest there is calm, which is then interrupted by the shock of screamed obscenities, assault and armed violence. The police threaten lethal force while waving their weapons. The effect is painful and disorienting. Add to the pain a collision of realities. It will be a while before the mind catches up with the new reality. The mind needs time to adjust to the violence done to your beliefs so you can accept the new reality.

In Dr. Diaz' case, the new reality was especially harsh. Stier was mostly real—a link to a reality that was disappearing, minute by minute. McManus was not a private plane owner from Colorado but a government agent. But how could he be? Dr. Diaz had asked him point blank if he were a government agent and McManus had laughed and denied it.

Federal agents, like George Washington in the children's story, are not supposed to lie. cannot lie. The FBI since its inception one hundred years ago has beaten the drum of their agents' truthfulness. It is widely believed that FBI agents cannot lie and must tell the truth. Agents laugh at this widely held misconception. Of course McManus had been lying. He was acting. Playing a role. Do agents go to drama school? Are failed actors recruited for police work? Dr. Diaz had spent a good deal of time around the FBI. He knew how to play a role. But McManus didn't know this.

Like Jim Carrey in *The Truman Show* finally realizing that his life was a television show and he was the only one who did not know that it was all a play, Dr. Diaz slowly came to the realization that while there was no cocaine and no drug deal. McManus was indeed, like him, a government agent. It would be a long time before Dr. Diaz would learn that for a cocaine arrest there need not be any cocaine, and that in the specialized world of the drug war, words without more are more than enough to sustain not only an arrest, but a conviction.

McManus and Stier knew that Dr. Diaz was a drug dealer. They had not sought him out or targeted him, at least initially. Their goal was to shut down Harry Treco and his operation. Dr. Diaz merely showed up. But once he involved himself he became a legitimate target.

Dr. Diaz was a smart man. His flaw was that he believed

himself to be smarter than people who were just as smart as he was. Stier couldn't believe Dr. Diaz' naïveté: why would anyone think that asking someone if they were an agent means anything? The answer is that Dr. Diaz had spent a lot of time with the FBI. Except for undercover operations, an FBI agent will always identify himself and show his credentials. Except, of course, when that agent is undercover.

After his arrest, Dr. Diaz was taken to the DEA office in Hialeah. The office is in a bland, featureless office park west of Miami International Airport. The open-plan office is a scene of lots of activity, with agents talking on the phone, moving around, people coming in and out—there is lots of movement. They answer the phone strangely. The three letters are never mentioned. Instead they answer with the number of their tactical units: "Group Five" is how they answer the phone if you call in.

When the agents are out on in the field the office is mostly empty. You could easily mistake the office for that of any successful business, except for the cage affixed to the wall, a cage with black bars and an unmovable bench. This is where prisoners are kept before they are delivered to the US Marshals.

In one notorious case not related to Diaz, on a Friday afternoon the agents were out in the field, and as it was the weekend, didn't return to the office. They forgot about the college student in the cage—he had been arrested for possession of a small amount of marijuana.

The US Attorney might not even prosecute the case but transfer it to State authorities. The threshold for a federal narcotics prosecution was a kilo of cocaine. Lesser amounts were usually, but not always, handled in the State courts.

Unfortunately, it was a three-day weekend. No one came back to the office until early the following Tuesday. The college student had been without water for almost four days. The Navy teaches its new sailors that after five days without water, death is inevitable. On the following Monday morning, the young man was barely alive.

After his arrest, McManus and the other agents eagerly offered a telephone to Diaz to see if he could call someone else in the narcotics chain, someone else who could be arrested. The standard speech contains a notice of how much trouble Diaz was in, how he could help himself by helping the agents, that they would make his assistance known to the prosecutor, and if he cooperated he might even get probation. Stier hung around to see if he might be needed, to see if he could lend authenticity to the call.

A person arrested is desperate not just to get out of the cage, but to get back to a familiar reality, to a world where a person is who he claims to be. Someone already familiar with tradecraft might be less eager. Castro had not treated the captured prisoners at *Playa Girón* with courtesy. He could not tell McManus about his activities for the government. Diaz knew that there would be time for a call. Meanwhile, he claimed that he was innocent.

I do not know when McManus learned of Dr. Diaz' work for the FBI. While he was in the cage, Dr. Diaz did not ask to call the FBI. He did not want to cooperate and instead said there was no one to call. Strangely, Dr. Diaz, the naive drug buyer, started acting like a soldier. Soldiers do not talk. But if he was a soldier, in whose army did he serve?

McManus took Dr. Diaz in handcuffs to the Metropolitan Correctional Center. At that time, the MCC was in West Kendall, close to MetroZoo. If a prisoner had a court hearing, he was awoken at four in the morning for court processing. The weekday traffic from West Kendall up 826 and east to 836 and downtown could take more than an hour if you did not leave by six-thirty. A prisoner transport bus crawling in traffic is an easy target.

Eventually the government built a a new facility connected by a Venetian Bridge of Sighs to one of the Miami federal courthouses in downtown Miami. The Kendall prison was re-designated as a prison for long-term offenders. In Italy Venetian courtrooms built for the Doge's justice are empty but to process the local casualties of the drug war three new courthouses have been built in Miami.

After being processed into the MCC, Dr. Diaz was held in isolation for a few days and given access to a telephone. Usually the first call is to family, because all they know is that you have disappeared. If you have an attorney, you can call him, but a person arrested for a crime rarely believes he will ever be caught and so has not made preparations for a legal defense. So there is no attorney to call.

It is a sad reality of the health care system in the United States that no matter how skilled a physician you are; you will be sued. Perhaps Dr. Diaz remembered the number of an attorney who had represented him in a civil case. A malpractice attorney could help him find a quality criminal defense attorney.

Or perhaps he called his Control. More likely, his Control agent had previously given him instructions not to tell anyone of their work, not to tell anyone—even other government agents, *especially* other government agents, of the work they were doing.

Even in the cage, Dr. Diaz knew that there was nothing to worry about. The arrest, the few days in jail, these were just inconveniences, the price that a soldier must pay.

US Magistrate's court holds morning and afternoon sessions daily, except for weekends. Federal law requires that a prisoner be taken before a federal magistrate "forthwith" after arrest. For this reason, federal agents always try to make arrests on Fridays so that they miss the court's last session so the prisoner sits in jail until Monday.

The idea is to punish the prisoner—a little—and expose him to never-pleasant prison life in order to convince him to cooperate, to identify other criminals and to plead guilty in order to receive a mild sentence.

I do not remember if Dr. Diaz had a private attorney when he next went to court. The prosecutor is entitled to a three-day continuance at that first appearance in order to prepare for a hearing to determine whether the defendant should be denied bond.

McManus had already filled out a form affidavit with a short narrative outlining Dr. Diaz' efforts to purchase a kilogram of cocaine. This is not a large amount for South Florida, which at that time was one of the country's main cocaine entry points. In any event, there was no real cocaine to put on the table.

In order to circumvent the Constitution's guarantee of bail, the prosecutor must prove that Dr. Diaz lacked community ties and presented a danger to the community. The law is written in such a way that danger is presumed if the drugs are over a certain amount, even if the cocaine was the fantasy, non-existent drug sold by Stier and McManus. In order to win a pretrial detention order, all McManus had to do was testify about the failed importation with Harry Treco. That McManus did. And so, Dr. Diaz was detained without bond.

A few days later, the prosecutor and McManus went before a federal grand jury and obtained an indictment against Dr. Diaz and others, his co-defendants. Another hearing was held before the magistrate so that Dr. Diaz could formally answer the charges by pleading not guilty, waiving the archaic requirement that the indictment be read out loud, requesting a trial by jury and finally, asking the magistrate to enter the Southern District of Florida's standard discovery order.

At that point, I was appointed to represent Robby Clavo. He was alleged to have been a part of Dr. Diaz' cocaine sales network. I don't recall if Dr. Diaz then hired his own attorney or asked the court to appoint the public defender.

Up until this point, Dr. Diaz was just another criminal defendant, one of hundreds processed by the South Florida federal court.

~

The FBI and the DEA in those days did not share information concerning their informants. The information was siloed. The FBI's reports were prepared on FBI Form 302; the DEA's reports were filed on DEA Form 6. These forms were not exchanged. The identities of the informants were not exchanged. The CIA and the FBI kept the names of their spies to themselves. Since 9/11 there is greater cooperation among agencies but the bulk of classified information remains siloed. At the level of street drug busts, the information sharing does not exist.

The Central Intelligence Agency is responsible for international spying. The FBI ran counterespionage operations in the United States and even investigated the CIA. For that reason, the FBI was "above" the CIA. The FBI had, to some extent, run spies internationally prior to World War II. Even after the CIA was formed out of World War II's Office of Strategic Security, the FBI held on to its Mexico City base of operations because Mexico City was rich place for spying activity during the war.

The CIA had authority over international operations and the FBI was restricted to domestic work. The Bureau was never happy with this state of affairs and felt that it unnecessarily restricted their counterespionage efforts. Leaving the Department of Defense out of the loop was an invitation to intrude: eventually sixteen agencies formed the United States Intelligence Community.[7]

McManus did the standard checks, but nothing turned up. In the meantime, Dr. Diaz was reaching out. "Deniability" is a hallmark of running spies. If you have diplomatic cover you claim that the spies are diplomats; before the CIA (supposedly) put an end to the practice at the request of legitimate journalists, journalistic cover was also popular. Even better was just denying that you had anything to do at all with the spy.

The spy relies on the agency to get him out of trouble, even to save his life; during the Cold War the exchange of spies in Berlin was commonplace. Using the criminal justice system against spies was dangerous. From the days of Nathan Hale, spies expected that they might be executed. But if you execute a spy you have nothing to exchange if one of yours is captured. And they will be captured. Using your criminal justice system against the Rosenbergs invites your target to use their criminal justice system against your agents. Because the criminal justice system has a logic and an inertia all its own, it is hard to slow down or deflect. If you can get the system off-script miracles can happen, but as long as the government's actors remain on script the inexorable end of the drama is preplanned.

The main job of the spy is to keep his mouth shut and not admit to anything, certainly not identify anyone or any evidence that would prove his intelligence work. So Dr. Diaz kept his mouth shut and reached out to his handler at the

FBI, hoping that in due course she would get him out of trouble.

For whatever reason she did not. This left Dr. Diaz without any recourse except to bring the matter to his defense attorney. McManus was not about to ask the US Attorney to dismiss the indictment. The DEA cares more about the pursuit of powder, even imaginary powder, than foreign relations. The agency's sole job is drug interdiction.

The CIA, of course, has other concerns. As the *San Diego Mercury* reported, the intelligence agency had no problem in letting the drugs go in order to obtain financial support for anti-Communist *contra* guerrillas in Nicaragua.

The case against Diaz was shaping up to be informant vs. informant, spy vs. spy. But McManus didn't know that yet.

Government informants are government contractors. They are not regular employees. They get no healthcare, no government pension or other fringe benefits. Instead they are paid based on the cases they bring in. If they don't bring in new matters, they don't get paid. Or their sentences don't get reduced. Time, in any event, is just another currency.

Regular government agents have to be careful to avoid entrapment defenses. Not that this is ever an easy defense, it is an extremely difficult defense to prevail. To succeed the defendant must be purer than Caesar's wife and few are. So the special federal agents let the informants, that is, the contract government agents, do the softening up, the convincing.

By the time the contract agent brings a case to the DEA or the FBI, the target is already enthusiastically involved, since the contract agent has been working months to convince him, to cajole him, to meet his objections, to pull him back in even after receiving final expressions of disinterest.

The jury usually never hears of any of these refusals to go along. They are never recorded, for the contract agents keep no notes. Instead, they go out into the street, "make a few moves" and make cases, guided only generally by the government. For this work the contract agents are handsomely rewarded. Usually murder is off-limits, but as we have seen with Stier, this is not always the case.

In his cell Dr. Diaz despaired when he realized that the FBI would not get him out of jail. As a spy he had betrayed many, just as Carlos Stier had done. He played a role, just as McManus had played a role. But now the FBI disavowed any knowledge of him, until Diaz threatened to make public what he knew. Diaz' control agent communicated this threat to her superiors, who communicated it up the chain to the US Department of Justice.

∽

During the Diaz and the Noriega cases I refused to accept a government clearance and access to government-provided classified information. My colleagues thought I was crazy. The *Miami Daily Business Review* attacked me. A federal judge sent law enforcement officers to find me so that he could interrogate me about "leaking" the location of a top secret National Security Agency facility—one whose location was shown on maps contained in the Canal Zone phone book.

Accepting a clearance means accepting government control and the last thing you want, when defending a client in a criminal case, is to be under the control of the government you are supposed to be fighting.

Two so-called[8] "court security officers" were dispatched to Judge Moreno's chambers in Miami, where outside the presence of the defendants and defense counsel, they told him that Diaz had in his possession information vital to the national security of the United States.

Dr. Diaz' attorney then filed a CIPA notice. This public document advised the court that that it was likely classified information would be made public at trial. The court security officers sent security clearance applications to all of the attorneys as well as the prosecutor, since not all federal prosecutors hold top secret security clearances.

The defense attorneys made the mistake of hurrying to fill in the forms in order to obtain a top secret clearance. There are roughly three regular levels of clearance: Confidential (grey), Secret (blue) and Top Secret (red). From time to time levels above "Top Secret" are created or discontinued. Dr. Diaz possessed information at the highest level.

Receiving a clearance permits the holder to view material classified at the level of the clearance. The background investigation is exhaustive. You must list all the addresses you have lived in for the past ten years. You must list if you have any relatives or family members who do not hold US citizenship. If you have traveled outside the United States, you must give the dates of each trip, starting with your first visit, and the reasons for each.

You must give five references. Understand that when the investigation is conducted, the agents assigned to the task will only ask your references if they can name five persons who know you. If any of your references cannot, the agents will return to you to ask for the name of another reference.

The agents may go through the motions of asking your references innocuous questions about you. But they assume that any information they obtain from these interviews will be useless, because they know you will only list people who will only say good things.

They do not want the good things. So they ask your references if they know you well. If they say "no," your reference is useless. If they say yes, they will ask for the names of at least five other people who know you. They will ask for the names of people you know to be enemies—or who might have a dispute with you. After all, if your references truly know you well, they should have some idea about such people. They will ask about your political views, if you drink to excess, if you stray outside your marriage, if you are in the closet, if you gamble, if you have *secrets*. Anything that could be used to blackmail you, that is what they want to know.

After conducting these interviews, the investigating agents will issue a report that you will never see. You are then invited in for a polygraph examination. You need to pass the polygraph to get the clearance. At the time of the prosecution of Dr. Diaz, defense attorneys were not required to pass polygraph examinations. It is not clear why, since the successful passing of a polygraph examination was and is a condition precedent for the granting of a clearance.

In the cases I have been involved in, defense attorneys who sought a clearance were not subjected to polygraph tests. Regular government employees were.

I do really not know why the defense attorneys all ran to obtain a clearance. Young boys love to create super-secret clubs and hideouts in order to reward their friends with membership while punishing others with exclusion. Part of it, I suppose, was due to curiosity; to see if the super-duper secret club would have you as a member. Calvin & Hobbes cartoons document this period of our childhood, but apparently the urge to join, to avoid the threat of ostracism, never really goes away.

The government can withdraw a clearance at any time and for any reason. There is no appeal. Once defense attorneys are cleared, the government can prevent them from speaking to the press, from writing books, blogging or posting on Twitter. By accepting a clearance, a cleared attorney agrees for the rest of his life to submit anything he may write to the government for review.

If the attorney fails to meet this obligation, there are both criminal and economic penalties. The only reciprocal obligation on behalf of the government is to let you review the classified information it has in its possession that it has deemed is relevant to the case. If you lose or violate the terms of the clearance in the government's sole judgment, the government can have you removed from the case.

To apply for a clearance is to submit to the government's control. You do not want to be subject to the control of the prosecutor while defending a criminal case. You do not want to personally be put in jeopardy because it will cloud your thinking and will prevent you from being as aggressive as you might otherwise be while defending your client.

It is not easy to resist peer pressure in these circumstances. All your fellow counsel will race to obtain a clearance; they will question your judgment. Reporters writing about the case will question whether you really know what you are doing. Feelings of self-doubt will creep in. The judge will urge you to go along. Resist them. The natural urge to see whatever extra classified information that would otherwise not be available—what if it is *Brady*,[9] that is, exculpatory material? —will at times be overwhelming.

If it is any consolation, you will not find anything that helps your client among the classified files that you might be permitted to see if you accept a clearance. There will be nothing. If there was truly exculpatory information, the prosecutor would dismiss the case. The prosecutor's access to the material might be a little better than yours, but not by much. Is he a CIA agent? Of course not. So he doesn't get to see what is in their files either.

The presiding judge will hold *in camera* proceedings—that is, proceedings inside a closed courtroom. Your client should be able to attend, but you will be asked to waive his presence. Pressure will be put on you to do so. If you do not —your clearance might be pulled and you will be off the case. All your client will be told is that you lost your clearance. Because you were so excited about obtaining the clearance in the first place, your client won't believe you if you try to tell him that a clearance really isn't needed for the defense of the case.

If you have been paid to represent him, you will have to give the money back. All of it. Fees paid for criminal trials are unlike fees paid for any other matter. They are paid in full and up-front at the time you enter your appearance on the day your client enters a plea to the indictment. Once you enter your appearance, the judge will rarely let you retire from the case, absent just cause. Not being paid does not qualify as a good reason.

Without a clearance, you will not be able to attend the secret hearings. This is not necessarily a bad thing. It's peer pressure again—all of your colleagues might agree to a continuance, but you cannot, for the simple reason that you are not there. If you survive pressure from your peers and prosecutor, you can nevertheless represent your client effectively without surrendering to the secret nation of spies.

If you have not accepted a clearance, things get a little more interesting, especially if your client doesn't really know if he is in possession of classified information or not. Hillary Clinton surely knew what classified information is, even if she didn't know that it made its way onto her unsecure email server. A CIA analyst like Aldrich Ames knew what classified information was—safeguarding it and not selling it to the Soviets—was his job.

Not attending the secret hearings and having to leave the courtroom or chambers when they commence slows down the conviction express train. It puts pressure on the government and tends to separate your client from the other defendants. It might even lead to a severance or a more favorable plea offer. Does the government really want to run the risk of having your client start talking about classified information from the witness stand? You haven't filed a CIPA notice, after all. The prosecutor has no idea what information your client has, if any at all.

The worst thing to happen for a prosecutor is if the carefully planned trial goes off-script. If some defense attorney suggests say, trying on a glove in front of the jury. Or forcing you to jump up and object furiously, or worse, having the court security officers jump up because the prosecutor is too slow even though they are not officially attorneys in the case. They have to prevent your defendant from blurting out something that *must not be revealed*. Like details of the failed secret CIA operation that the Cubans call *Playa Girón* and the Americans the Bay of Pigs or whether Senator Ted Cruz' father, Rafael Cruz, did in fact know Lee Harvey Oswald.

"Nothing to see here," the Warren Commission said, "move along now." Now Alice, do you really want to go down the rabbit hole in the middle of a criminal trial? Does a Cuban drug dealer in Miami possess classified information? Probably not. But you can never be sure, and in the case of Dr. Diaz, the presumption that national security was not involved was wrong.

~

After Diaz reached his Control agent, the case no longer was just a street level reverse sting involving an imaginary shipment of phantom cocaine. The FBI was now involved, because Dr. Diaz was telling the truth when he said that he worked for the FBI on national security matters. Otherwise the court security officers would have no reason to be there. Their involvement is eloquent evidence that Dr. Diaz was telling the truth.

And if he was telling the truth about matters vital to the national defense of the United States, could he be telling the truth when he claimed that he was investigating Stier and McManus, two narcotics traffickers he came across while working for the government of the United States, the same government that was prosecuting him? The solution was to claim that *this time* Diaz wasn't involved in a national security case.

Dr. Diaz did not know Michael McManus, special agent of the Drug Enforcement Administration. He only knew Robert Treco, an airplane owner who flew drug loads into the United States. This was the kind of valuable information the FBI would be interested in; the kind of information they would pay for.

The Bureau—the FBI that is—wanted in on the drug carnival. They had to start with the assets they had. It was time to play catch-up with the DEA. If Dr. Diaz could be entrusted with matters affecting national security, surely he could be entrusted with street level drug busts in Miami. At least, that's what Dr. Diaz said.

But with a CIPA notice in hand and secret testimony from three FBI agents, none of whom was Dr. Diaz' control agent and none of whom had personal knowledge of his drug activities, Judge Moreno ruled anything Dr. Diaz might say about the subject was prohibited and that his counsel could ask no questions about such matters before the jury.

So when he testified, Dr. Diaz could only give hints about his activities that affected national security. He couldn't testify in depth about his relationship with the FBI, because his FBI control agent didn't even bother showing up for his trial. Instead, the FBI sent three special agents who assured Judge Moreno that Dr. Diaz was not authorized to go out and work as a drug agent.

But that's not how informants work. The combination of denying Dr. Diaz the ability to discuss his real relationship with the FBI on national security grounds coupled with a ruling that Dr. Diaz had no authority to investigate drug cases destroyed Dr. Diaz' defense. The national security relationship between Dr. Diaz and the FBI corroborated Diaz belief that he was authorized by the FBI to go out and make cases, as long as he brought the cases back to the FBI for evaluation. In other words, he was doing exactly what Carlos Stier was doing, except perhaps that he was under less directed supervision by the official agents.

There are two kinds of informants. The first class includes those who have committed crimes and are now testifying against their confederates in the hope of a lesser sentence. The second kind, the evangelizing informant, makes cases at the pre-investigative state in the hopes of earning a paycheck from his government handler. There is a long history to this kind of work.

In the 4th century the Roman emperor Valerius made Constantinople his capital. He found that informants had run amok:

{the informers} were...the scourge of the people...Their careless or criminal violation of truth and justice was covered by the consecrated mask of zeal; and they might securely aim their poisoned arrows at the breast either of the guilty or the innocent...A faithful subject...was exposed to the danger of being dragged in chains to the court to defend his life and fortune against the malicious charge of these privileged informers.

10

Today, informants continue to run amok. No one doubts the legitimate need for law enforcement to prevent crime. But when crime is created, no one is protected and the real criminals are left to run free. From time to time the courts halfheartedly call for greater supervision of informants "at the pre-investigative stage." They did not do so in the Diaz case.

By forestalling any real inquiry into the relationship between Dr. Diaz and the FBI, by preventing testimony about Dr. Diaz' activities as an informant, without corroboration of any kind, the trial pitted Dr. Diaz' word against that of S/A Michael McManus.

&

"When Louis XVI was put on trial, he should simply have said that according to law his person was sacred, and left it at that. This would not have saved his life, but he would have died as King."
   —Napoleon Bonaparte[11]

The prosecution of General Manuel Noriega of Panama was another case tried in the Southern District of Florida under CIPA procedures. General Noriega, in effect the sovereign of

Panama, had been the head of that country's intelligence service for many years. General Omar Torrijos had preceded him in power. Torrijos had helped the Sandinistas when they threw out Anastasio Somoza in 1979. Torrijos had just signed two treaties under which the United States would leave Panama and turn over the Canal to the Panamanian government. Although Somoza had been supported by several American administrations, under the Carter Administration Somoza had become an embarrassment.

The Carter Administration took no action against Torrijos and looked the other way as he helped the Sandinistas. After Torrijos died in a plane crash, other members of the general staff of the Panamanian Defense Forces jockeyed for position. Eventually, General Noriega, the head of G2, the intelligence branch, came out on top.

Noriega had had a long relationship with American intelligence agencies. In the 1950's, Panama successfully infiltrated the 455th military intelligence operation at Ft. Clayton. Student unrest in 1964 and the Chicago Tribune's leaking of a proposed treaty internationalizing the Canal led to Omar Torrijos taking control of Panama in a 1968 coup. A coup against Torrijos in 1969 by Col. Amado Sanjur, who had counted on Torrijos' travel outside the country to effect his plan. What Col. Sanjur hadn't counted on was Colonel Noriega's loyalty to his commander. Colonel Noriega was the commander of Chiriqui province, on the border with Costa Rica and he controlled the airport in David, the provincial capital. An American pilot named Red Gray flew General Torrijos back to Panama, ending the rebellion. Noriega became Torrijos' chief of intelligence. When the Reagan administration turned back Carter's policies and asked General Torrijos for help with the Sandinistas, Reagan's request put the Panamanians in a difficult position. Not to assist the Americans would betray their new friends, the Nicaraguans. But the Panamanians had to work with the Americans for twenty years under the treaty. The solution was to help, but clandestinely. Noriega was in charge.

In those days, much was done clandestinely in Central America. When the Shah of Iran lost the Peacock Throne, the Carter Administration turned to Panama, and Torrijos arranged refuge for the Shah on Panama's Contadora Island. When legal proceedings threatened the Shah's safe haven, Torrijos, through Noriega, arranged for the dying Shah, Torrijos arranged for the dying Shah to be flown out of the country to Egypt without interference.

The Reagan administration turned to Panama for help with the contras. Once again, Panama was caught in a familiar, but uncomfortable place—the middle. To help the contras was to betray the Sandinistas. Not to help the contras was to disappoint the United States. An angry American government was not in the interest of Panama. The solution was to look away officially but assist discreetly. C-130 gunships were dispatched out of Howard Air Force Base to provide logistical support for *contra* ground troops. So heavy was the fighting that upon returning to Panama, the aircraft would often have to swap out their melted gun barrels

Eventually, Panama was put in the middle again: this time between powerful drug cartels and an American administration that was still fighting the War on Drugs. The accommodation Noriega made was to look the other way while the unlicensed pharmaceuticals flowed north. Why would Panama, a country of less than two million, believe it could stop the cartels when the United States, a country of 350 million, had miserably failed? The condition imposed on the cartel was that Panama was not to be a market for their product.

As head of Panamanian intelligence, General Noriega knew all about these secret stories, the unwritten secret histories that explain so many public acts.

∼

I had already been involved in the Noriega case for almost a year before the invasion of Panama in 1989. Ricard Gregorie, who was the initial prosecutor in the case, told me that if the case were dismissed against the General for political reasons that the case would be dismissed against my client as well. So there was really nothing for me to do. An invasion seemed unlikely: the United States had, after all, pledged not to invade Panama in the "other" Panama Canal treaty, the Treaty Concerning the Neutrality of the Panama Canal. US and Panamanian military conducted joint patrols. There were areas under each country's joint jurisdiction. The Panama Canal itself was operated by an agency that was bi-national in structure.

Before the invasion of Panama, one of Noriega's lawyers, Raymond Takiff, traveled to Panama City to meet with him. On his return, he held a briefcase up and loudly told the press that it was full of secrets that would be revealed if the United States were to try to invade, that Noriega "had the goods" on the United States.

Though Noriega didn't know it, at the time Takiff was working as a government informant. Whatever secrets were in the briefcase fell into the possession of the government as Takiff desperately tried to please his control agents by revealing what his client told him.

For political reasons, George H.W. Bush had to show that

he was tough. While Ronald Reagan pursued his acting career in California, Bush had been a fighter pilot and had been shot down by Japanese forces in WW II in the Pacific. Nevertheless, in those days, Bush ironically fought the political "wimp" factor.

As contemplated by the Panama Canal treaties, in January 1990, for the first time in its history, Panama was to lead the Panama Canal by appointing an administrator to run the Panama Canal Commission. Noriega's government had proposed a candidate.

A US-backed coup against Noriega led by Col. Moises Giroldi failed in October 1989.

Afterwards, the United States looked for an excuse to invade. There was a case against General Noriega only if you believed that law enforcement agents of another country are not privileged to act as do law enforcement agents in the United States. They found a pretext when a US naval officer tried to run a Panamanian Defense Forces roadblock. The US military admitted later that if a Panamanian officer had tried to run a roadblock at Ft. Clayton he would have been shot as well.

∾

December 1989. I was sitting in the satellite room watching Pay-per-View. Richard Burton the explorer was well on his way to discover the source of the Nile. He had long before finished translating Nafou Sayed's *Ars Amatoria* and was practicing those learned techniques inside a tent with a Sudanese woman, unschooled in the ways of books. Light from a candle cast shadows on the camel hair walls of the tent; it was almost time to see if there was any vodka left in the kitchen.

The phone rang. "I know you have C-band," my friend Bo Hitchcock said. "I think you might want to watch this." Bo was, in my opinion, one of the best criminal defense attorneys in South Florida. I had met him shortly after I came north. He was convinced that I was a Special Agent with the Drug Enforcement Administration. His partner Jerry Cunningham believes that the DEA targeted defense attorneys and was trying to infiltrate their offices. I told Jerry that I was not working for the DEA.

Telstar 4 had a wild feed from Torrijos Airport on transponder thirteen. The cargo area—generally empty—was full of American troops sitting on their gear.

Bo believed me, but Jerry did not. Even now, years later, he is not sure. I can't say that I blame him. The drug war, like all civil wars, is a war of informers. The target of an informer is concerned that at any moment he will be summoned before a tribunal and asked to explain a catalog of idle comments taken out of context. He is afraid that I will take the stand amidst tape recorders and stacks of eight and a half by eleven black and white surveillance photographs, and permit myself to be led through a story by a prosecutor who only too recently was licensed, and who still believes that civil wars can be won.

But in war all is destroyed.

∾

On the evening of December 19, 1989, US Forces seized Torrijos Airport, the country's main international airport as well as the domestic airport at Punta Paitilla where General Noriega kept a small jet. Fifty-caliber bullet holes fired during the landing made the jet inoperable.

The treaties were pushed to the side and the United

States invaded anyway. In war the laws are silent, the Romans said, *in bellum legis silentio.*

A few years before, an Israeli intelligence colonel had been sent to Panama to organize the Panamanian Defense Forces along the lines of the IDF, the Israeli Defense Forces. His name was Michael Harari; he was part of Israel's "Wrath of God" operation in response to the 1972 Munich bombings and was responsible for organizing the assassination of Black September's "Red Prince," Abu Hassan Salameh, by car bomb in Beirut[12] in 1979.

On the night of the 19th and on the 20th, there were no commercial flights out of Panama. There were no general aviation flights either. The airport at David remained open, but it was hours away and only handled domestic traffic.

Two days later Harari appeared in Jerusalem. Somehow he had flown out of Panama. Spies take care of each other.

Noriega sought asylum in the Vatican Embassy in Panama City. This contingency had not been considered in the invasion plans, so the Army laid siege to the Embassy in violation of international law. Noriega gave himself up.

Soon thereafter, General Noriega was brought to a federal courtroom in Miami. The US Attorney's office never really thought that the trial of the general would take place. There was little likelihood that Noriega would resign his position in Panama. As long as he led the government, extradition was unthinkable. The original prosecutor on the case told me that if the case against Noriega were dismissed for political reasons, the case against my client would be dismissed as well.

With Noriega in custody, there was no longer any possibility of the case being dismissed, so I prepared for trial. Two officials from the Department of Justice—or so they said—came and invited me to apply for a classified clearance so that I could receive classified information that would be released to the defense.

But I was the only one to say "no." "I don't need it," I told them. "I'll get my own classified information."

I was the only defense attorney who declined. The others all rushed to get their clearance, to receive the imprimatur of the prosecuting authorities that they were worthy to join the club and be entrusted with the government's holy secrets.

I did not understand why Noriega's lawyers accepted government constraints and control. My guess is that the lure of being approved for the classified information club was just too strong. Noriega didn't need access to US government classified information for he had been the source of that information for many, many years.

When the prosecutors brought the case against General Noriega, they had not researched Panama's infiltration of the 455th Military Intelligence Brigade, Panama's training of the hemisphere's military police at the School of the Americas, the war in Nicaragua, the war in Honduras or El Salvador. They didn't know what secret deals lay behind the offer of asylum for the Shah of Iran. Noriega himself blamed Bush for the indictment—not so much President Bush, but the former CIA director, his friend, who had betrayed him.

Just as McManus was unaware of Dr. Diaz' national security work, at the beginning of their case, they did not know how deep the intelligence rabbit hole went.

Before he became head of the Panamanian Defense Forces, Noriega was head of G-2, the intelligence section of the chiefs of staff. He held this position since 1968, when General Omar Torrijos led a coup against Arnulfo Arias, the duly elected president of the country. Noriega held the position under Torrijos and continued to hold the intelligence portfolio for the rest of his military career.

In this position he liaised with American intelligence when Central America was burning. The CIA did not sit back and do nothing while the Sandinistas fought Somoza for power in 1979. As is now well known, Panama was a key player in the US-backed contra mission to overthrow them.

In that year the Shah of Iran was overthrown and came to Panama; Panamanian intelligence was privy to discussions among the United States, the Shah and Anwar Sadat.

Noriega knew about intelligence operations on Panamanian territory and elsewhere. He knew about the black C-130's that left Panama in the late afternoons towards Honduras and returned in the morning with the overused barrels melted on the.50 caliber machine guns they carried.

He knew about the Sandinistas' assistance to the Medellín Cartel and he knew that the CIA was looking the other way in order to obtain financing for the new freedom fighters, the contras, the moral equivalent of America's founding fathers, or so they claimed. He knew about Oliver North.

He knew about Mossad's activities in Panama—he had invited them there. The Israeli armament industry sold weapons to the Panamanian military and fragmentation grenades to the Peruvian military.

If he did not know for sure, he probably even had a pretty good idea how Mossad General Michael Harari got out of Panama in order to appear in Jerusalem two days after the invasion when there were no commercial flights in or out of Panama. The soon to be renamed Torrijos Airport was under the control of the United States Air Force.

General Noriega knew all these things and more. Noriega did not need access to US classified information in

Miami; he had all the classified information he needed sitting between his two ears. The only way the government could silence him was to get to his lawyers.

∾

Douglas Vaughn was working for and with me as an investigator on the case. Doug is also a journalist. While copying documents in Panama at my request, he came across a secret inventory of seized Panamanian documents that the government had claimed did not exist.

The press covering the case were almost universal in their condemnation of Vaughn, as if it were somehow being a journalist prevented you from accepting a gig working as an investigator on a case; or that working as an investigator on a case prevented you from writing about it. This was in the day before blogs were common; today Vaughn might have blogged his activities. I might have blogged my own. I did not see any impropriety then and I do not now.

The Florida Bar opened up an investigation whether or not it was ethical under the Code of Professional Ethics to hire a journalist to work on the defense of the case. Florida Bar inquiries may not be ignored; they must be answered. This took away from the time available for the defense of the case. The *Miami Daily Business Review* asked why I didn't go along "with the rest of the defense attorneys."

Vaughn's discovery spooked the government into concluding that I had access to a vast cache of classified material. I tried to subpoena tapes of intercepted conversations and in the process revealed the existence of a secret— well, they claimed it was secret—National Security Agency facility dug out of a mountain in Panama.

Today I am more convinced than ever that the NSA

listened in on air traffic control conversations when there was a reason to do so. The facility, known as "the Tunnel" was inside the Quarry Heights military base, the US Southern Command's headquarters in Panama. I file a motion seeking disclosure of these intercepts and included a diagram of the Tunnel's location as a good faith demonstration that the facility did in fact exist to support my judicial application.

The Justice Department officers who had received my rejection of their offer of a clearance were dismayed by the revelation of what was supposed to be a super-secret NSA facility and went to Judge Hoeveler seeking an order for my arrest. Fortunately, Judge Hoeveler knew me. Moreover, he was a very reasoned, calm judge. He asked his courtroom deputy to get me on the phone instead and see if I could come to the courthouse, immediately.

I did so, and immediately found myself in an impromptu hearing in which I was asked to reveal how I had learned about the Tunnel, why had I leaked the information to the press, was I a traitor or what and how much more classified information did I have?

Federal court questioning of this type can unnerve anyone. Answering the questions was unpleasant but I tried to stay calm. I explained to the judge and the assembled lawyers—all the others in the case had come for the show—that the diagram had come from the Canal Zone phone book and I used to pass the facility every week on my way to the Quarry Heights Officer's Club to meet my friend, the crime novelist Michael Wolfe. "The bartender's name is Gus," I told Judge Hoeveler. "He makes a mean mojito."

The Department of Justice Security Officers were unfamiliar with the Canal Zone phone book and I have to assume that they were unfamiliar with Gus's mojitos as well.

They probably didn't really know that Wolfe wrote crime novels either, since he wrote them under a pen name.[13]

Fortunately Judge Hoeveler chastised the Department of Justice Security Officers and pointed out that classified information is rarely published in the phone book, but that is where Judge Hoeveler was wrong. Classified information is very, very often publicly available material. I would hazard a guess that, except for electronic intercepts, it is more often public than not.

While I escaped any adverse consequences from this episode, CNN was less successful in its interactions with the court security officers. Though few remember it today, one of the few press prior restraint orders in American history was issued stopping CNN from broadcasting classified information. The spies won that battle.

Because Noriega's lawyers had accepted classified clearances, they in effect consented to the government's control. The penalties for violation of the rules relating to classified information are severe, as Edward Snowden found out. The next time wouldn't be a friendly call from a courtroom deputy summoning a hearing at the courthouse at 301 N. Miami Avenue; it would be an arrest order and indictments.

∼

The prosecutors were concerned about the damage General Noriega's testimony would cause to the intelligence community. They sought protective order after protective order. Having accepted CIPA clearances, Noriega's attorneys were already under government control. They had an informant inside the defense team. One of Noriega's attorneys, Raymond Takiff, had pled guilty to tax crimes and was working as a government informant. Takiff's conviction and plea remained secrets while he worked as an informant.

Under the rules of both the Florida Bar and the US District Court for the Southern District of Florida, commission of a felony is grounds for immediate disbarment. But that did not stop Takiff from advising his client, a client who was unaware of Takiff's legal disability, a disability the government kept secret. The government later claimed that they didn't really learn anything from Takiff about the general, and that they had instructed him not to inform on the general. You are free to believe this assertion. I do not. Takiff was part of the defense team during key negotiations with the US Attorney's Office. At the very least, there is a compelling appearance of impropriety.

During the pretrial proceedings, one of General Noriega's lawyers claimed that Noriega had documents which showed that the United States had tried to assassinate both him and General Torrijos. Judge Hoeveler prohibited Noriega's defense team from discussing these documents under CIPA provisions.

Noriega could have been a martyr to the overreach of American interventionism, an interventionism that the new Panama Canal treaties were to put an end to, once and for all. The trial of General Noriega should have been a trial of the United States itself over an illegal intervention. It should have been a trial over the limits of sovereign authority, and whether a weaker sovereign is permitted the same tactics granted the stronger in a hopeless battle against human nature and human biology.

In part because of CIPA, the Noriega trial was none of these things.

If you are ever asked to handle a case involving classified information and are offered a clearance:

Just say "no."

Because if I had accepted a clearance, I wouldn't have been able to write all of this, would I? Last time I checked there is still a copy of the Canal Zone phone book in the Miami Dade County public library, but they left a lot out. Like how to fly out of a country that is under a US invasion.

Criminal defense attorneys should never seek or accept CIPA clearances.

~

The Noriega trial was a notorious trial; the trial of Dr. Diaz took place in obscurity. What both trials have in common is the error of the defense attorneys to apply for and accept a CIPA clearance.

Historically there have been very, very few cases of one sovereign being hauled before the courts of another. There is Vercingetorix, King of the Gauls, brought by Julius Caesar for trial in Rome. Mary, Queen of Scots was executed by Queen Elizabeth following a trial whose result was predetermined. Atahualpa, the Inca, was tried before a court established by the invading Spanish army.

And then there is the case of General Noriega. The Noriega trial was historic as much for what went on outside the courtroom as inside, starting with the illegal invasion of Panama, an invasion that clearly was in violation of the multinational Panama Canal Neutrality Treaty.

The trial of General Noriega might have been a historic trial; it is really too early for history to give its final judgment. The trial of General Noriega will not be judged historic because of forensic examinations of the witness or any fireworks heard by the gallery. The trial will be judged, historic, if at all, because of the strange precedents it spawned:

CIPA orders. An illegal money deal to finance some of the defense team, agreed to by the prosecution. One of the first prior restraint orders issued against the press, in this case against CNN. The arrest of the general's wife for shoplifting in Miami. The Swiss Red Cross' demand and subsequent declaration of prisoner of war status, a status objected to by the Bureau of Prisons but insisted upon by the Pentagon. A plea bargain for Carlos Lehder, the previous drug lord crowned by the press, so he could testify against the general. The travels of a Mossad general from Panama to Jerusalem. A secret inventory of documents that officially did not exist.

It is fair to forgive the Miami criminal defense attorneys for this lack of historical perspective. They shared this deficiency not only with the prosecution, but with the press. I cannot remember a single instance where this point was ever raised. Make no mistake—the new president of Panama, Guillermo Endara, was sworn in at Howard Air Force Base during the invasion, a fact glossed over by the 11th Circuit in their decision affirming General Noriega's conviction.

It is interesting to hypothesize what would have happened if Noriega had refused to participate in the trial, had pointed out the illegality of the proceedings, and claimed that his actions were just as authorized by law and the DEA's daily actions in buying and selling cocaine. In fact, General Noriega's acts, considered in the context of drug trafficking, were insignificant. He did not buy or sell cocaine. Ever. Not once. McManus cannot make the same claim. On what basis is McManus permitted to buy and sell but Noriega is prevented from taking desperate action to protect his country?

Non-cooperation was the only real strategy in the Noriega case. But by accepting CIPA clearances early on, his attorneys showed that there would be cooperation with the government in the effort to convict the general. It wasn't even a defense lawyer who won General Noriega prisoner of war status. The Swiss Red Cross demanded visitation rights under the Vienna Convention after receiving an inquiry from a journalist.

∾

A show trial with a political defense would have served Noriega better in the long run.

His attorneys could have objected at every station along the road towards conviction. They could have objected to the jury: in what way are a group of American citizens the "peers" of a foreign sovereign? They don't even speak his language or understand his laws, the laws of his country. If General Noriega had taken the stand, the judge could not have permitted him to speak freely. The court security officers would have egged the prosecutors on to obtain a protective order. Silencing the general would have served his cause well. The spectacle of the silencing would have flashed around the world. After the revelation that Noriega was a CIA asset—or was the CIA a G-2 asset?—*New York Newsday* headlined, "He was our Guy." American duplicity would show that far from being a drug trafficker, Noriega was indeed, America's Prisoner.

Of course, the General would have been convicted—that result was foreordained the minute the C-130's headed south from Homestead Air Force Base in Florida. He would go to his prison cell, anomalously permitted to wear his general's uniform. Checked on monthly by a US Army general. Even paid a salary. He was, after all, a prisoner of war and entitled to such courtesies under the Vienna Convention. The Swiss Red Cross, arbiters of the Convention, had insisted.

The real question would be, who did General Noriega answer to? If he answered only to himself, he would be lost. But if he answered to history, the prison cell would soon become irrelevant. Calls for his release would come from quarters around the world. The illegal invasion would be exhibit #1, the show trial exhibit #2 in the world's petition for release. Washington would get sick and tired of hearing about Panama.

Believers in Latin American independence and non-interventionism would make the pilgrimage to Kendall to visit the general. Soon his prison cell would mean nothing. The last time Washington got sick and tired of hearing about Panama, a new treaty was written. On January 1, 2000, when the treaty finally expired, as a goodwill gesture Noriega would be returned to his country.

There is a tradition in Panama for such dramatic gestures. At the signing of the 1955 treaties, a long-serving inmate of the Canal Zone's prison in Gamboa was pardoned and invited to the ceremonies. Nelson Mandela went from a prison cell that had become a vital political symbol to the presidency of South Africa. In an alternate history, General Noriega might have done the same.

But Noriega was not a sympathetic character. His attorneys represented him as if he were only a narcotics defendant. A special drug defendant, but a drug defendant nonetheless. Instead of answering to history, he answered to himself. Or at least, it seemed that way.

∽

The rules for notorious trials are different from trials held in obscurity. At the beginning, the whole world was watching. A slumbering History raised an eyebrow and stirred; something was happening in Miami. There was a world audience. Imagine if the defense had let their client spoon-feed the press with occasional interviews. "Oh no," they would say, "a good attorney never lets his client speak to anyone, never mind the press."

Look what happened to "Pharma Bro" Martin Shkreli. He raised prices in order to pay for research and was condemned; convicted because of impolitic tweets and like Noriega, massive unpopularity. The Shkreli trial was almost a notorious trial, but not quite. Nothing was really at stake. The public wanted revenge.

In the case against Noriega, this rule should have been abandoned. Federal rules prohibit defense attorneys from talking to the press, though the prosecution is permitted a perp walk and a press conference at the beginning of the case, not to influence public opinion, of course, but to influence public opinion. The prosecutors claim that they act with good intentions and that only defense counsel could have bad intentions. Shkreli was a pioneer in using social media in his defense. He failed, but that does not mean a more sympathetic defendant cannot use social media more skillfully. Either keep both sides from the press or permit both sides access.

Such a rule would not have applied to the Noriega case had his attorneys—and the General himself—answered to history. Journalists would have been tripping over each other to get an interview. Imagine a prison television interview in which Noriega addressed the issue of the Panamanian dead due to the invasion. The prosecution would have moved heaven and earth to prevent him from talking, and that would only lead to more censorship, still more efforts to reach out, and accusations of a scripted show trial.

∼

The fact that the rules are different for notorious trials means that the defense attorneys' courtroom skills will not be enough to win the case. The prosecution will assign dozens of agents and attorneys to a case, extending the range of the prosecutorial team.

The lone defense attorney must do legal research on his own. Once this meant late-night visit to the local university law library or an expensive subscription to legal materials. Today computerized legal research is inexpensive, but at the time of the Noriega and the Diaz cases, it was a costly duopoly. Federal cases are now available for free on Google. In those days, research was conducted the old-fashioned way, by pulling cases from physical volumes on bookshelves in the library, Shepardizing the cases you decided were relevant to make sure that they had not been distinguished or overruled, and of course, making courtesy copies of the cases for the judges. Broward County has a rule requiring counsel to highlight in yellow the relevant portion of the case with a highlighted copy for opposing counsel. A secretary could help with the highlighting, but if you had no secretary you had to do this yourself.

Few defense attorneys had the luxury of devoting their entire attentions to the case at hand, especially if those cases went on for weeks. Law, the Supreme Court tells us, is a business, so what happens to your other clients while you are in trial? They wait. In business school one of the first things you learn is that if you don't take care of your customers they will go somewhere else. Lawyers don't go to business school, and any problems that you have with other clients' scheduling conflicts with other judges who have set crucial hearings during your trial? That's your problem. To say that these are bad for business is an understatement. These inevitable events destroy the viability of a law practice.

For scheduling purposes, judges will accept—though sometimes begrudgingly, that you are in the middle of a trial and for that reason cannot appear in their courtroom. After that, there is an informal hierarchy of schedules: the local federal court takes precedence. Then a federal district court in another federal district. The State court in the local county comes next. Then a State court in another county. State appellate courts trump State circuit courts, and the federal Circuit Court of Appeals trumps them all, save for the United States Supreme Court. The US Marshals can get you out of a State jail, but the State Police cannot get you out of a federal facility.

Even a motion on a trivial issue, like bringing a television into court, required a good deal of work left to the defense attorney. With a team of federal agents on call, the prosecutor in the Dr. Diaz case did not have to worry about getting audio visual equipment into the courthouse. The US marshals permitted them to walk in, carrying the equipment. That was not the case with defense counsel.

Courtrooms today are designed for a multimedia experience, but in the early 1990's if you wanted to use audiovisual aids, you had to bring them yourself. For security reasons, you needed a court order to bring audiovisual equipment into the courthouse.

This meant another motion, making photocopies, filing

and mailing copies of the motion to the prosecutor and other defense counsel. Making copies sounds trivial, but even a short, three-page motion[14] (double spaced, Courier type at 12 points on letter size paper) and five co-defendants. Add two sets for the clerk's office, and during trial, one for chambers in case the judge asks, as well as one for the prosecutor, one for your own use at trial, one for your client and one for the file means twelve sets of three pages—thirty-six pages in all, all which must be collated and stamped, addressed envelopes prepared—otherwise the clerk will not accept the filing. And all this just to get a television into court. And keep in mind that usually, the defense attorney has no help. He has to figure out some way to get the television from the trunk of his car into the courthouse.

Do not think necessarily that you will get a recess to go out to the car to get the television either. And do not think that all of these "for want of a nail" problems are merely a result of poor planning. District judges are under no obligation to answer your routine motions before trial. They might want to wait and see if you really need that television. Maybe there's a television that's available—sometimes the case—or that the prosecution or even the DEA will provide an assist. But don't count on it. On at least one occasion I had to return a permitted television set to the car because the order permitting its entry had not made it to the Marshal's Service and the photocopy in my hand was not adjudged to be "good enough."

"Anybody can make a photocopy," a marshal once told me. Indeed. But in those days it was usually a defense attorney standing by the machine at 10:00pm in the local university law library hoping not to run out of quarters.

Modern electronic filing has done away with some of these tasks, but not all. In the US Supreme Court, paper filing remains the official method of service. Electronic filing is required in addition to filing paper copies. In the lower courts, parties may consent to receiving copies of documents by electronic service.

Perhaps there are courts where attorneys collegially agree to electronic service. The spirit of cooperation is rarely encountered in the beginning stages of litigation. A wise attorney cannot necessarily expect that an opponent will consent in writing. The only safe course is the conservative one; that is, to continue service with physical pieces of paper. Rather than eliminating work the new rules have only created more. *See*, FED.R.CIV.P.RULE 5(a); FED.R.CRIM.P. RULE 49(d).

If a witness surprises the prosecution with his testimony, the prosecutor's team has at least a chance of tracking down the facts. During the testimony at issue, all the prosecutor need do is pass a note to one of the agents who can then immediately start working on the problem. If the defense lawyer is surprised, too bad. He has no one to conduct surprise research and can't leave the courtroom himself because he is preparing for cross-examination or the next witness.

With government funds, a prosecutor can obtain daily transcripts of witness testimony. These are not cheap—the going rate is in the area of $2/page. A transcript can cost several hundred dollars and the defense attorney must pay in cash, up-front. The court reporters know not to trust a defense attorney's promise to pay: because the government is a "slow-pay" customer, the court reporters know they will not be paid unless and until a defense attorney's bill is paid. And it may not be: the judge may not reimburse the cost of the transcript, saying that it was not necessary.

This decision is easy to make after the fact, but before

the trial these matters are rarely clear. Failure to order a transcript may constitute malpractice. After the trial, after the defendant was found guilty, it is easy to say that the outcome was inevitable and extraordinary measures unnecessary.

Meanwhile, in those two or three or four months the attorney waits to find out if he is going to be reimbursed trial preparation costs, he is trying to keep the lights on, the phone working, the envelopes stamped with proper postage. In a major trial, these costs can easily run tens of thousands of dollars.[15]

The American federal criminal justice system presumes that those who take appointed cases are independently wealthy, or that they are donating their time and paying the costs as a matter of charity.

Law is now specialized. You cannot handle wills and divorces alongside sophisticate narcotics trafficking cases. Imagine the scene in your waiting room as Ma and Pa Kettle wait for you to come and help them execute their wills while sitting across from an associate of El Chapo, who is looking menacingly at a group of MS-31 gang members, who are returning his menacing gaze. You've got to get all of them out fast because you've got to beat traffic to get to MCC before count time. Inevitably, in a short time your civil clients will disappear. The techniques taught for developing a civil practice do not translate to building a criminal practice, unless you want to be indicted yourself.

$\sim$

There are always unexpected consequences to political trials. This is the case even though there is absolutely no reason for them. You defend your client, the trial ends; you

would think that would be it. You are wrong. The consequences will come and they are not reserved for the end of
the trial. Soon you may find yourself defending not only the
case against your client, but other cases, your education and
your experience and your political views.

Such was the case with José Baez. Casey Anthony, a
young mother from Broward County, Florida, was charged
with first-degree murder in the case of her missing daughter.
She had told a story about leaving the child with a babysit-
ter. The story was quickly proven to be a lie. The child could
not be found; there was no body. She was the last one to
have seen her daughter alive.

Eventually what was left of the body was found in the
forest near her home. Casey Anthony was not a sympathetic
defendant. Rather than mourning her daughter, she had
gone out to nightclubs. The excuses she gave the child's
grandparents were contradictory. The State decided to seek
the death penalty. The American public wanted an
execution.

When José Baez was named to the case, the newspapers
questioned his death penalty experience; they brought up
the fact that once he had trouble with the Florida Bar
because of unpaid debts; they dredged up the fact that he
had once filed bankruptcy as proof of his incompetence. In
the echo chamber of the press all that was heard was that
José Baez was not expert enough for the job. Court TV
covered the case in depth as did CNN. The general
consensus was that conviction was a formality.

Baez had to spend time not only organizing the defense
of his client—clearly, no simple task—but also to defend his
own reputation.

Listen to the pundits and you will be led astray. Baez'

defense and closing arguments were masterful. The jury came back with a verdict of "not guilty."

Baez' subsequent defense of ex-NFL tailback Aaron Hernandez proved that this result was no fluke; Baez is not just a competent attorney, he is a masterful one.

The threat of violence is a very real collateral consequence as well. After the Mumbai terrorist attacks in 2008, the Mumbai bar association passed a resolution condemning anyone who might defend the perpetrators and all but invited the public to murder those responsible. Why waste money on a trial?

Attacking defense counsel is not just an exotic, irregular practice seen in faraway countries. It happens in America too. The public is unable to distinguish between the defense attorney, the spokesman for his client, and the client's alleged crimes. When Professor Ronald S. Sullivan, Jr. joined Harvey Weinstein's defense team, there was an outcry at Harvard by students who conflate defense with approval.

The conviction in Nevada on federal charges of the Wyoming ranchers arising out of the stand-off between the federal government and Ammon Bundy was, as television journalists like to say, "expected." Unfortunately for the government, these expectations were kept from the jury who went off-script and freed most of the defendants. They could not reach a decision as to Bundy himself.

Judge Anna Brown declared a mistrial, which is provided for in the Rules of Criminal Procedure when a jury is unable to reach a decision.[16] The defendants had all been denied bond since the government believed them to be dangers to the community: after all, they had taken up arms against the American government. The judge, who, I think it is fair to say, was starting to contemplate what sentences she might impose, was just as shocked as the prosecutors by the verdicts. The acquitted defendants had to be freed.

Ammon Bundy, the chief defendant, was not entitled to be released because a mistrial means that the government can try to prosecute him again. Double jeopardy does not prevent a subsequent trial in case of a mistrial. The government, licking its wounds, wanted Ammon Bundy kept in jail.

Marcus Mumford, Bundy's attorney, asked Judge Brown to release Bundy. The other defendants had been acquitted. It was a very emotional time for all in the courtroom. The prosecution had lost what they thought was an obviously winnable case. The several defense lawyers perhaps had the greatest victory of their careers. Bundy, who had spent more than a year in jail, could sense a restoration to freedom.

With emotions running high, Judge Brown denied Mumford's motion to release Bundy on jail. The denial only caused Mumford to argue even more vigorously, protesting the injustice. You can watch what happened next on YouTube. Court bailiffs are seen throwing Mumford to the ground, telling him all the while to "stop resisting." If a person is truly resisting arrest, then the officers should indeed forcefully command compliance, both orally and physically. But that was not the case in Judge Brown's courtroom.

I should point out that it is now standard police practice to say, "stop resisting" whether an individual is resisting or not. This is akin to prosecutor's advising their witnesses to turn to the jury during cross-examination and not face the defense attorney, or in little league, the coach will tell the catcher to quickly move his glove back into the strike zone in case the umpire wasn't paying attention. Thus children are taught at an early age to game the rules. A courtroom, if nothing else, is a place of rules.

Unfortunately, there really is no trick to counter this police practice. Usually the victim will say, "I'm not resisting." It is humorous to watch a non-resisting victim lie on the ground all the while why hearing the officer repeat, "stop resisting." The officers must hate the practice because it is, at its heart, untruthful. Eventually this gaming the system practice will end. All it takes is a few cross-examinations inquiring why the office kept repeating something that objectively was untrue.

As a result of the fracas, Mumford was arrested and charged with resisting arrest. Those charges were quickly dropped, but Judge Brown was not satisfied. She filed a bar complaint against Mumford with the district court's own disciplinary committee. That complaint was eventually resolved with Mumford agreeing not to handle any more cases in Utah.[17]

Ammon Bundy was acquitted of all charges in a subsequent trial in Portland. He lost several years of his life to the criminal justice system. So much for the right to bail in the United States.[18] Judge Brown might well have paid more attention to the acquittals and the defense attorney's bail application.

∾

Remember that all of these attacks are defended alone. There is no assistance from bench, bar or anyone else. The US Attorney can call on security to protect him in his home. The lone defense attorney has no such support system, no back-up.

Jacques Vergès was a French-Vietnamese lawyer who

came to world attention because of his defense of Algerian freedom fighters seeking independence. He too was marked for assassination because of this work. Later, he became close to the Palestine Liberation Organization; he defended SS officer Klaus Barbie, the Butcher of Lyon, after the Nazi's deportation from Bolivia and ended his career defending Brother Number 2, Pol Pot's second in command in the genocidal Khmer Rouge hierarchy. It is hard to imagine less sympathetic clients.

Vergès was an astute observer of trials and trial practice and wrote extensively on the proper tactics to be employed in political trials. Political trials—for all high profile or notorious trials are political—are subject to different rules. A defense attorney who tries to defend such a case as if it was a conventional one is doomed to failure, as the Noriega case shows. Instead, there is but one defense that will triumph, though a positive result is never guaranteed.

That defense is what he called the disruption defense, or the *defense de rupture*. A conventional defense, Vergès believed, will only lead to the client's conviction. Vergès knew, of course, that victory at trial is always unlikely in a political case and so victory must often come from outside the courtroom. A defense that leads to a prisoner exchange or a pardon is always better than a defense that ends with the client's end in jail or worse, by execution.

Vergès, who fought in the French Resistance in World War II, taught that the attorney who defends the political case conventionally is a collaborator while the attorney who practices the disruption case will be condemned. Neither fate is neutral.

Vergès understood that justice is nothing but tawdry deal making. There is no morality. There is no real fairness.

Anyone who thinks otherwise is delusional and lacks experience.

How is it possible, if there is any kind of absolute impartiality, that a drug kingpin can give up his underlings in order to go free? How is it possible that in an armed robbery, the triggerman receives a lighter sentence than the getaway car driver who had protested his innocence? Why are some murderers, like Carlos Stier, able to charm their DEA control agents and have their criminal records wiped clean, while others rot in jail?

The essence of the disruption defense is to try to block every step of the proceeding. The disruption defense puts the government on trial. What the defendant did was objectively wrong, perhaps, but required in order to respond to a government that had done worse. Or that the defendant's acts were no worse than the acts of the government. Or that the government was complicit in the defendant's acts.

To borrow a phrase from James Joyce, the essence of the disruption defense is the Latin phrase, *non serviam*. I will not cooperate. I will not mount the conviction train with you. I will not facilitate your injustice, your illegal invasion, your beatification of a murderer: I will not serve.

Except for Vergès, writings about political trials are merely guides to collaboration. How to manage the press (i.e., reward the few so they all clamor for inclusion). How to pressure counsel: through their bar associations, the threat of discipline, or induce them to ask for clearances. And how to manage the public: keep cameras out of the courtroom.

For Vergès, conventional trial manuals are also a guide to the disruption defense. Where the guide advises a certain action, do the opposite. But to do so, you must be fearless, absolutely fearless. Any personal weaknesses you might have will come to light, as José Baez found out.

Gabriel Garcia Marquez, the Colombian Nobel Prize winner, said that everyone has three lives: a public life, a private life and a secret life. Do not accept the defense of a political case unless you are ready to have your secret life revealed because it will be revealed. Nothing is off-limits, and everything is somewhere.

There are limits to the disruption defense; it is not about breaking the rules for the mere sake of breaking them in order to be held in contempt. The English legal historian John Maitland observed that a lawyer must be conventional to even be a lawyer.

Instead, the defense seeks to bring the reality outside the courtroom into the limited theater-space of trial. Vergès did not merely advocate breaking the rules. Vergès advocated using the rules to turn the system against itself.

In small ways, these disruptions will lead to a positive result. When magistrate's court fills with the press, do not waive reading of the indictment, as attorneys always do. Better to insist that the prosecutor read the indictment. This will infuriate the magistrate. So be it. He is not on your client's side. Even better: if the magistrate says "read it yourself" you have just been given dramatic license to read before the press who you now have an opportunity to play to.

Moreover, this sends a clear message: this trial will not be like other trials. In 99.9% of federal trials, the defendant is convicted. A trial is just due process theater. But I will not serve. My client is innocent. You have never seen an attorney forced to read such a document. Indeed, there is nothing in the rules which require me to read out loud. But if you give me license to do so, I will take every single opportunity to make the case of my client's innocence, and if the reading comes to resemble the Theater of the Absurd, Andy

Kaufman reading a novel to an unbelieving college audience till late in the night, so be it. My client is innocent. This trial will not be like the other 99.9%.

~

On appeal, Dr. Diaz was granted a reversal of fortune.

The judges who heard the appeal were uncomfortable with having the dark blanket of secrecy thrown over the proceedings. The trial of Dr. Diaz was not a notorious trial; thus, the standard Rules of Criminal Procedure could be more easily applied. Defendants must be allowed to confront the testimony of witnesses against them by cross-examination. No rights in criminal trials are absolute, but the right of confrontation guaranteed by the Sixth Amendment comes close.

Among other points, the Eleventh Circuit noted that three FBI agents testified in a closed session to the effect that Dr. Diaz was not authorized to buy and sell drugs like other government agents. Dr. Diaz may not have been a paid civil service, general schedule federal government employee. But that does not mean that Dr. Diaz was not an agent of the government. This is the deniability distinction. This is a subtle point, but its use permits the FBI and the CIA to deny that all sorts of people who work with and at their direction are not employees. But an informant, while not an employee, may nevertheless still be an agent. The jury was entitled to hear the evidence and decide.

In the same way that Carlos Stier was a government agent, that is, acting at the behest of the government, so too was Dr. Diaz. The FBI claimed that Dr. Diaz was only authorized to act as a spy and was authorized to buy and sell drugs. But the government was willing to review the cases brought to them by Dr. Diaz.

To make those cases, he had to offer to buy and sell drugs—remember that in neither of the two transactions between Carlos Stier and Dr. Diaz, there were no drugs. It was all a fantasy, play-acting. Carlos Stier was a drug dealer now acting with government authority. Michael McManus was a DEA special agent play-acting at being a drug trafficker. And in reversing Judge Moreno's decision, the Eleventh Circuit accepted that Dr. Diaz may have been play-acting at being a drug trafficker as well.

The judges felt that the trial judge's restriction of cross-examination was too prohibitive and ordered a new trial for Dr. Diaz. But there would be no retrial. Three sets of lawyers would be expensive and the case had destroyed his medical practice. Even though he had beaten the government once, he had already lost once and could lose again. His resources, unlike those of the government, were limited. This time, he accepted a more favorable plea bargain.

Unfortunately, Robby Clavo lost his appeal. The prosecutors found $40,000 in cash in Clavo's apartment and claimed that this was proof he was involved in the drug trade. Clavo presented a cashed Florida Lottery ticket in the amount of $40,000 to show that he was not. The murderer Stier only testified against Clavo through hearsay. The prosecutor was justifiably afraid of putting a murderer on the stand so McManus testified as to what Stier and the defendants said in his presence, statements in furtherance of a playacted conspiracy.

Stier never got near the courtroom, never mind the witness stand. The defense attorneys were prepared to cross-examine Stier but never got the chance. McManus testified truthfully as to what he believed were the facts.

During the playlet, no one from the FBI had bothered to tell them that Dr. Diaz worked for the FBI. Clavo was merely caught between the two government informants playing their roles: Dr. Diaz the physician and a part-time casual, informal government informant and Carlos Stier the murderer, whose relationship with the DEA was better documented. If neither buyer nor seller is real, can the transaction itself be real?

When there are undercover actors on both sides of a transaction, can a crime be committed? If your answer is yes, then Hollywood movies that show drug transaction necessarily show real crimes. But if such Hollywood films are make-believe, are acting, are not real, then so was the Dr. Diaz show.

෴

From my first days as a criminal defense lawyer I tried to figure out why some defendants were given a pass; some were allowed to cooperate, while others went to jail for unconscionably sever punishment. I examined those who cooperated in different cases, in different classes of crime to see if there was a common thread. I looked at the criminal histories of informants to see if there was something special about them, to see if there were any limits that might preclude them from working as an informant.

I have always wondered what standards were used to make the decision to grant or withhold such significant benefits. What is the secret sauce? Why are some so blessed and others ignored? I have a theory, but that theory has absolutely nothing to do with justice or law.

The Stier case proved that murder is no obstacle to working as government informant. So if murder is no obstacle, is there any crime, any heinous act, that would disqualify a person from working as a government informant? The answer is no.

What is the worst crime imaginable? One might think that committing serial murders must be disqualifying, but contract assassins are anointed with the oil of government forgiveness all the time. The Department of Justice made a plea agreement with Sammy "The Bull" Gravano to obtain his testimony against mob boss John Gotti, overlooking the fact that Gravano had committed at least thirteen murders.

A low level employee may be granted forgiveness in order to pursue the boss of an organization, but pursuing crime lords is not a universal goal. Sometimes the crime lord is granted forgiveness in order to pursue the underlings, as in the case with Joseph Massino, the former boss of the New York Bonanno crime family.

I could see no logic to any of it. If there is a logic, a universal principle, it is well hidden and only a few know, contained perhaps in a tape that Mission Impossible style will self-destruct after listening, or a volume of the US Attorney's Manual that contains a page that may be read only once and is then destroyed.

If there is no logic to these pardons, what force is then at work? We must assume that human beings act rationally—what is the rational explanation then, for these pardons? In my years of criminal defense practice, I never really could come up with a provable hypothesis that could be corroborated empirically. It is wrong to say that prosecutors will do anything to win. The fact that some do so proves nothing. The fact that extraordinary amnesty is common proves nothing.

What remains is the idea that what qualifies an informant is his attitude. A gregarious, friendly person will be more successful than a loner. A person who can win friends and influence people is a perfect candidate. Charisma counts. So if the informant can make friends with the agent, the very same agent that has been pursuing him, who yelled obscenities when he was arrested and thrown to the ground; if under such circumstances the informant can get the agent to *like* him, then he will get an opportunity to repent, find forgiveness and obtain redemption. If a potential informant cannot make friends with the agents, then he is doomed.

What kind of skill set must a person possess to accomplish this goal which, on the face of it, appears impossible, fantastical, almost bizarre? The answer is sales skills. An informant must be a master salesman, a con artist. He must charm the agent, charm the prosecutor. He must make friends with everyone, even his targets. His own personality, his own identity is secondary to what he must become to make the sale. The sale is all important. Nothing else matters.

Some people are naturally gifted. Others learn, reading Napoleon Hill,[19] or on the job, watching others, making everyone believe. Selling is about faith. An informant must convince a real government agent to believe, and once that agent believes, he will pray next to the informant with all the fervor of the converted.

The informants become as saints for they are converted themselves: they were the persecutors before the light struck them down on the way to Damascus and now they follow in the steps of enlightenment. There is no real word in English for this, but there is a Spanish word coined specifically for these drug informants: *narcoarrepentidos.*[20]

The idea that those we hire to protect us from evil must make common cause with murderers is a disturbing one. Judgment is altered. The moral compass loses direction when murderers become friends and acquaintances. What happens to your moral compass when you count murderers among your friends, or even just your acquaintances?

To be a successful informant, learn how to sell. Criminal defense attorneys should know that if their clients wish to become informants, they must be likable, friendly and excel at salesmanship. Nothing else matters.

Not even murder.

~

The DEA is very good at its job. The agency is very successful at putting powder on the table. They have analyzed drug transactions and found that they contain three, but only three elements. All illegal narcotics sales can be distilled to these three components, namely price, quality and terms of delivery. The one missing element is need. This is never questioned; it is assumed. Richard Price wrote "if God made something better than cocaine, he kept it for himself." The product sells itself.

Historically, the DEA recruited its agents from the ranks of police officers while the FBI preferred lawyers and accountants. The DEA then, is closer to the street where street drugs live. The FBI is a politicized, national police agency. J. Edgar Hoover did not want his agents interdicting drugs because there was so much money in it, too much money, and so much money, he was sure, would surely corrupt his agents. But drugs were the next big thing. The Vietnam war was over and America lost, we needed a war we could win.

Even though the FBI did not join the federal drug interdiction effort till fairly late in the game, the DEA was never alone in its efforts. All fifty States formed anti-narcotics squads and State legal codes matched the federal prohibitions. Despite all of these heroic efforts, despite all of the hard work of these dedicated agents, nothing was accomplished. Americans turned to drugs because they are pleasurable. There are consequences to their use, to be sure, but the preference for pleasure usually triumphs. Human nature is unchanging; human biology is not altered by legislation drafted in Washington.

We didn't win the War on Drugs either, but it was a useful diversion until there was a real war again. In 2001 the Defense Department wondered if it would be the Russians again, the Chinese, perhaps maybe even the Mexicans would turn against us.

No one was expecting calm, religious Saudi Arabia to cross an ocean in an audacious act of asymmetrical warfare. That attack led to the invasion of Iraq. Once the invasion of Iraq was underway, the drug war was no longer needed. It was allowed to quietly fade away.

The Drug Czar in Washington, the five star Eisenhower ready to lead an assault on Fortress Colombia became just another civil servant mouthing Smoky the Bear platitudes. Worse for the DEA, one State after another legalized marijuana. The Boomers were full of aches and pains and had the power of the ballot to get the weed that had soothed those pains in their youth. With eyes focused on the wars in the Middle East, there was little political will to argue against them.

There was little political will because for all the money spent, all the lives lost and wasted, courthouses and prisons built, boats interdicted, fast boats built, cocaine containers seized, for all of that we had little to show for it.

It would have been more effective to send government buyers to the Upper Huallaga Valley in Peru to simply buy up the whole annual harvest. The coca plant couldn't be wiped out—apart from the possibility of ecological disaster, the plant was needed to flavor Coca-Cola.[21]

If the government really wanted to stop the importation of cocaine, all they had to do was buy it. The DEA bought it on a street level scale; if they started buying by the ton scarcity would follow.

Introducing a customer who did not obey the laws of supply and demand would destabilize the market and lead to the cultivation of new areas, but even with these collateral consequences it would still be cheaper than building yet another federal battle courthouse in South Florida—they are now up to four in Miami alone, not counting the one on Broward Boulevard near the State courthouse where Stier pled guilty, the courthouse on Clematis Street in West Palm Beach or the friendly, New Deal-era building on Simonton Street in Key West.

We cannot win the drug war because it is a war against ourselves. As long as people want drugs, there will be someone to supply them. The military solution to the problem is deprecated—it never really worked in the first place. Many battles were won, but like in Vietnam, ultimately the war was lost.

Sandra Suarez died and her murderer, Carlos Stier, went to jail until he was freed by the DEA. Stier helped put Carlos Lehder in jail, but Lehder was just another kingpin, another drug lord whose fall would birth another. George Orwell's *1984* hypothesized an enemy, called Goldstein, against whom the people could spew their collective hate. First, there was Roberto Suarez, the Bolivian King of Cocaine. He was replaced by Carlos Lehder. Lehder in turn was supplanted by his colleagues in the Medellín Cartel, the Cartel by General Noriega, General Noriega by Pablo Escobar, Pablo Escobar by El Chapo Guzmán. The line stretches back to Al Capone. And how did Al Capone become the Big Fella? Because we tried to legislate desire. It did not work then; it does not work now.

After the Diaz trial, Stier continued to work, under DEA supervision, as a drug trafficker. The key difference, this time was that he was working with government authorization.

After a long and successful career, Stier was forced to retire from his career as an operative. Homeland Security moved then to deport him to his home country, Colombia. Carlos was destitute and without money for expensive, but needed medical care. At the request of the DEA office in Paraguay, the agents who had worked with him for years put in a request for a special award to compensate Stier. Though South Florida had been the scene of most of Stier's crimes, the request for a government bonus came through the DEA office in Paraguay. Ultimately the DEA decided to grant him $80,000, a substantial sum though not as much as Stier wanted. He wanted the government to pay him half a million dollars to fund a comfortable retirement.

No one else has ever been prosecuted for the murder of Sandra Suarez. The murder of Sandra Suarez remains an open cold case. Perhaps modern DNA analysis can solve the case; perhaps modern science can provide an answer that, unlike Stier's responses to the polygraph examiner, does not show deception.

In a hundred years or so next to Disney's *Pirates of the Caribbean* ride there will be a show called, *Smuggler's Blues* where the good guys haul the smugglers off to jail to the delight of the applauding tourists, all in good fun.

But it wasn't fun for Sandra Suarez. As A.E. Housman

pointed out, young boys throw stones at frogs in fun but the frogs die in earnest.

∾

It was only with the rise and subsequent analysis of the sharing or gig economy that one of the great mysteries of drug prosecutions was explained.

The rise of the Internet did not give rise to the creation of the gig economy, it just expanded the gig economy to other areas like taxicabs and hotels, what the Harvard Business Review called, "spontaneous deregulation." Regulators struggle to keep up with the gig economy.

The law hasn't kept up the pace with the gig economy either. Even well-intentioned laws like worker's compensation are essentially useless when you let the employer define the terms of the relationship with his workers in such a way that he is not responsible for them.

The Internal Revenue Service is facing a growing gap in collections with respect to gig economy workers because they never save enough to cover their annual tax bill. Accustomed to receiving a refund once each year in April, they are surprised that they do not have the cash to spare for the taxman.

This is not surprising—the reason why tax collections used to be high in the United States is because the job of collecting taxes was subcontracted to the employer, who did so on at least a monthly basis. Each month, the employer put a little aside for the employee's tax bill. But since most people live to the limit of their paychecks, the employee doesn't—no, can't—set money aside this way. The first unbudgeted expense, say, a visit to the doctor not covered by the health insurance you forgot to buy—and the tax savings account is emptied.

I always wondered why, whenever there was a drug arrest, that the overarching drug organization the defendant was alleged to be a part of, never or almost never, came to his aid. This behavior made no economic sense. Arrest, pilferage and the loss of consignments is a risk of any commodity business and narcotics were no exception. If anything there was a greater risk because the drug business is carried out clandestinely. It is dangerous to maintain records and there are no audits. Occasional arrests and seizure of shipments are a fact of life and a routine business expense.

What was also routine was the abandonment of the person arrested. It is true that at a very high level the organization, to the extent that term could be used, would send a lawyer, a message or money, normally they would send nothing. The defendant was on his own. This lack of institutional support guaranteed that indictments would be superseded, defendants would become government witnesses and historical conspiracies investigated. Considering the low level of support needed to keep a defendant's loyalty, I could never understand why an organization would not supply it.

The received wisdom was that the organization would attack the family of the defendant if he decided to cooperate. The fact is this almost never happened, and if it was going to happen it happened in the context of street-level sales. The families of the defendants were left alone due to the simple fact that for the most part, the organization had no idea who they were.

Defendants left to their own devices would soon see that the only way out was to become a government witness. And government witnesses had to give up people who were involved. When an arrest was made, the DEA often did not know how extensive was the narcotics operation. In South Florida, an arrested person might represent the tip of an enormous historical conspiracy iceberg, or he could simply be someone who sold joints to his friends.

In legacy companies, employees enjoy benefits derived from their employment, but in the gig economy you're on your own. You can't expect your employer to do anything for you. You don't get health care benefits, if you are injured while working you have to prove it's somebody's fault before you can recover or get your hospital bills paid. There is no employer so no one pays worker's comp insurance. The company that pays you doesn't even deduct taxes from your salary. Taxes are your responsibility. Pension? Don't make me laugh.

Keeping employees is expensive. There are so many benefits and taxes to pay. Federal income tax. State tax. Unemployment insurance. Worker's compensation insurance. Health insurance. Add the services of an accountant or a contract with a company like Paychex to keep track of it all. In the past thirty years the entire American economy has seen a transition to the gig economy. The only difference with the drug business is that it always was based on the gig economy.

Gig workers don't expect any corporate support. They understand that if there is a problem, they can't look to corporate headquarters. They're not even on the payroll. They know they're on their own. The noise a large corporation can make is greater than that of a single voice. Gig workers know that they only have their own voices. If there's a problem, they usually can call on no one for help.

The drug business is no different. Just as in the gig economy, everyone is on his own. Even though it would be good business to provide lawyers and a pension or funds to take care of a family, this is almost never done. After an arrest, there is no organization to turn to, no headquarters to help. The organization the DEA and the prosecutors talk about simply doesn't exist. The drug business is the gig economy at its purest.

That is why those who get arrested are treated as if they were abandoned. It's not that at all. They aren't abandoned. They were never part of anything in the first place. They did their job, got their money and went home. To suggest that they were part of a bigger whole is legacy economics not catching up with the gig economy.

The fact that the drug economy is the gig economy means that everyone is a principal and everyone is an accessory. Anyone can be a major player entitled to a Sentencing Guideline enhancement and the same person, for the same conduct, might be entitled to a Sentencing Guideline reduction.

Whether you are a principal or an accessory depends on criteria which are nowhere stated in the drug laws. That is to say, they are arbitrary and capricious. The federal Sentencing Guidelines "role in the offense" can be so easily gamed. There is no logic or rule for where you draw the line on a faux organizational chart, a chart that has no relationship to economic reality in the first place.

Like any legacy corporation, there will be distributors—employees or Mary Kay-like independent contractors—making sales. But unlike legacy corporations, there is no Board of Directors at the top. Instead there are dozens, hundreds, perhaps thousands who enter the business and fight for product, territory. Few ever think they will get caught. There is no corporate ladder to climb up.

The risk of becoming Public Enemy #1 is extremely slim. There will always be such an individual *du jour*, but the fact that this is a public relations construct is shown in the difference between the take down of an organized legal corporation—let's choose Enron or Arthur Andersen—and the take down of a drug organization.

When the government took down Enron, that was the end of the company. All the employees found themselves without employment. When Arthur Andersen plead guilty to criminal charges, they were disbanded. When a drug organization goes out of business, there is no consequence, except for the few who are put in jail themselves.

Because the "organization" consists of gig workers, they do not find themselves without employment—they were never employed in the first place. Instead they take their services somewhere else and work no gigs. The proof of this is that despite the DEA professionalism and fifty-plus years of effort, they have proven wholly incapable of stopping the traffic in narcotics.

～

The plea bargain system in the United States has frequently been the subject of criticism. The idea is that an individual, even if innocent, will pretend to be guilty in order to obtain a lesser sentence. Abandoned by the FBI, Dr. Diaz did not have many choices. His co-defendants were not so lucky and remained in jail to serve the sentences previously imposed by Judge Moreno. Even though the defendants were tried together as if they were a single wrongdoer, and even though the government's witnesses were cross-examined by each of their lawyers, the appellate court only granted the benefits of the defect to Dr. Diaz.

Robby Clavo did not see his sentence reversed. This also, is arguably unfair. The excuse given for not conducting separate trials is a common one: time and money. The conviction is a consequence of the arrest. As in a play, the outcome is predetermined, the script the same. The Dr. Diaz show was a little bit different because Dr. Diaz was given a second chance—that is, a second chance to go to jail. But Robby Clavo did not win his appeal.

In the same way that we do not really know if Dr. Diaz was guilty, we do not know if Robby Clavo was guilty. We do not know if Dr. Diaz, pretending to be a drug trafficker, enticed Clavo with pleas to his Cuban patriotism to join a venture that would make money that would be used for the eventual liberation of Cuba. We do know that Dr. Diaz was a revolutionary, a Cuban patriot who sought to free his country. These days, though, he would be considered a terrorist. Even after the Bay of Pigs Cubans who sought the liberation of their country were in turn supported by the FBI.

Seeing Dr. Diaz on the stand, it was obvious that the liberation of Cuba was his life's work. It is not much of a leap that he maintained a relationship with the FBI, a relationship whose existence the FBI conceded, to further those efforts. Maybe in furtherance of those efforts he recruited Clavo. Maybe Clavo wanted to do his part to liberate Cuba as well. Both men knew that the US government could bend the rules. They had sold cocaine to get arms to Iran in a complex deal to fund anti-Communist guerrillas in Nicaragua. That they would do the same for Cuba was not a stretch at all.

But for the second act of the government's play, Clavo did not get a ticket.

We will never know if Clavo was play-acting like Dr. Diaz claimed to be. We will never know if Dr. Diaz was play-acting like Carlos Stier was play-acting. In their playlet no drugs were bought or sold. The drugs did not exist. The only one with real, provable access to drugs was Carlos Stier. And while we know that Carlos Stier was acting under the authority of the DEA, we can also be certain that not only was he once a vital clog in a drug operation and a clever actor, he was also a murderer.

Just ask the family of Sandra Suarez.

PART I

PREFACE

THIS IS A TRUE STORY. It is the story of a number of men and women involved in a nightmare of greed. I, Carlos Stier, was one of them. Working very closely with Carlos Lehder, chief[1] of the Colombian cartel, I became the man whose planning and coordination made it possible for the cocaine producers to import vast quantities of the illegal drug into the United States between 1983 and 1985.

Eventually I cut off my involvement with the drug empire and tried to start a new life far from the scenes of my previous occupation. I could not escape the consequences of my former illegal activity, however, and I was arrested and jailed.[2] To atone partly for my crimes I posed as a transportation broker with assistance of the Federal Government through the Drug Enforcement Administration.[3] Under the close supervision of Michael McManus of the Fort Lauderdale office I helped carry out undercover operations. For years I lived a day-to-day adventure exposed to the dangers related to drug trafficking and money laundering, experiencing these activities from both sides of the law.

I am now[4] under the United States government protection program, as a key witness in the notorious trial of the United States vs. Carlos Lehder. Although my fellow Colombians may call me a coward or a traitor for testifying against these citizens of my own country, I view them as the traitors for bringing corruption, violence and death to proud Colombia.[5]

I am at greater risk now than in my drug dealing days, for the Colombian Mafioso is unrelenting. Nevertheless I am anxious to tell my story, the story of a ruthless and far-reaching Cartel, whose secrets I am uniquely qualified to expose.[6]

1

FEBRUARY 14, 1987

"I've got some good news and I've got some bad news," were Michael's words on the phone.

I hadn't expected the call; even the news media had not yet learned that drug king Carlos Lehder had been turned over by the Colombian Government and arrested moments before.

"The bad news is that we lost Lehder to someone else," Michael continued. "The good news is that right now he is being transported in a Colombian Air Force plane to Bogota, where one of DEA's planes will fly him to the United States."

My whole world seemed to come to a halt and there was a time of hush[1] on the phone. I slowly put down the receiver without comment and ran both my hands over my face in unbelief and shock.

How could a man of Carlos Lehder's caliber, influence and intelligence...the undisputed lord and ruler inside his own country...allow himself to be arrested?[2]

How could Lehder, with access to huge sums of money

to bribe the underpaid Colombian Army, be caught in this trap?

There had to be an explanation of something gone wrong, very wrong. I dialed my private line to the DEA for an insight into what had just become the most important arrest in the history drug trafficking, and a triumph for Vice President Bush and his task force against drugs.

At that moment the television networks broke in with a bulletin; "Carlos Enrique Lehder, reputed to be by far the biggest drug lord in the world, has been arrested in Medellin, Colombia[3]. Details are very sketchy at this point, but an exchange of gunfire has been reported between his heavily armed men and troops of the Colombian Army cooperating with American Drug Enforcement agents. We will have full coverage on the eleven o'clock news tonight."

Michael McManus' crisp voice on-the other end of the line interrupted my silence. He could give me only a brief account; we would just have to wait with the rest of the country for the eleven o'clock news unless government tele-types came in sooner. All we had was a blurry statement that a Colombian informer had given the Ministry of Defense a clue to the whereabouts of Lehder, who had been running an underground operation somewhere in Colombia with a large number of faithful followers and hired bodyguards.

To Michael McManus and to me this arrest was disquieting, for it meant our months of planning and careful work to make Lehder our own "prize" had gone down the drain. Yet how could we not applaud those who had been working in a parallel direction and had succeeded where we had not?

On that next afternoon on February of 1987, Lehder arrived in the United States. He was not on board his luxurious Turbo Commander which bypassed Customs and

Immigration. Instead, Lehder's last trip out of his own country, from Bogota to Tampa, was on board a DEA plane with chains on his hands and feet.

This was perhaps his last trip anywhere as a free citizen of the world.

Later that week Mr. Lehder was transferred to Jacksonville, Florida, where his lengthy trial has begun. Its shock waves are already reaching thousands of miles. It is the biggest trial yet for his defense attorneys, Mr. {Edward} Shohat and Mr. {José} Quiñon[4], who are specialists in handling major drug offenders. These two lawyers are considered aggressive and skilled advocates in the courtroom. They are summoning all their skills to defend Mr. Lehder, who has been called "the embodiment of narco-terrorism" by United States Attorney "Mad Dog" Robert Merkle, the prosecutor in charge of the case. Mr. Lehder, now heavily guarded in Jacksonville's courthouse building, is charged with running a smuggling ring from his own private island in the Bahamas, and bringing approximately four tons of cocaine to the United States.

Carlos Lehder (alias Joe Leather or Joe Lemon) is allegedly the biggest of the drug kings. He started small.

His father was a German civil engineer who moved to Colombia at the beginning of World War II. The family settled in Armenia, a small city some five hour's drive over the mountains from Bogotá. My friend Carlos Lehder left for the United States at the age of fifteen. It wasn't long before he was arrested in Detroit for exporting stolen cars to South America, and again in Miami for possession of 200 pounds of marijuana. After serving nearly two years at Danbury Correctional Institution he was deported to Bogota, Colombia in 1975. His criminal activities flourished in his own country.

In 1979 the Drug Enforcement Administration learned that Lehder had purchased an island in the Bahamas called Norman's Cay. Although he was listed as president of Air Montes, a Bahamian corporation, his real business was transporting cocaine and marijuana between Colombia and the United States. Lehder's island was used as a stopover for refueling drug-laden airplanes; he built a 3,300-foot radar-protected runway for this purpose.

Security was tight, and the grounds were policed twenty-four hours a day by Dobermans trained for attack. Some of the aircraft in his fleet, according to a DEA informant[5], were bought through an associate of Bahama's Prime Minister Lynden Pindling.

A sprawling villa housed Lehder during his visits to the Bahamas, and nineteen cars serviced his transportation needs. His clubhouse on Norman's Cay was a center for wild parties and orgies with Bahamian officials and the Colombian women who shared his lifestyle. Fugitive financier Robert Vesco was a frequent partner in Lehder's degenerate pursuits, and they also enjoyed shooting automatic weapons and smoking marijuana together.

In 1981 a United States Grand Jury indicted Lehder for cocaine smuggling, and about that time he moved his base of operations to Colombia. His presence there was felt immediately as swirls of activity, financed with drug money, began rolling out in all directions. He bought a coffee plantation and purchased a local newspaper, the *Quindio Libre*, which he used to make strident attacks on US and Colombian officials. He built a huge hotel on the outskirts of Armenia called *La Posada Alemana* (the German hostel), a luxurious cabana style vacation-land replica of Swiss architecture. In that resort he built a discotheque dedicated to John Lennon, and paid a well-known sculptor to carve a bronze statue of the ex-Beatle at the entrance of the building. Young Colombian women flocked to his side, attracted by his charisma and his fortune in American dollars.

Lehder had another bizarre obsession–Adolph Hitler– whom he called "the greatest warrior in history." To forward his views, Lehder founded a fanatically nationalist political party, the *Movimiento Cívico Latino Nacional* (MCLN). Hundreds of followers thronged to Lehder's "patriotic Saturdays" where cash and groceries were given to underprivileged families in exchange for their votes to put his new political party in Parliament. Lehder is also alleged to have founded a right wing paramilitary group called MAS (Muerte a Secuestradores) "Death to Kidnappers." MAS is charged with the killing of dozens of leftists and labor organizers.[6]

Lehder's reputation for violence makes him a suspect in the killing of Rodrigo Lara Bonilla, Colombia's Minister of Justice. Lehder, in conjunction with the M-19 terrorist group, has also been linked to the 1985 attack on the Colombian Supreme Court, in which 97 people, including 11 judges, were killed.[7]

In 1984 when Colombia's president, Belisario Betancourt, vowed to begin enforcing a two-year-old extradition treaty with the United States, Lehder went underground. Later that year the Colombian Army raided a hideout in Los Llanos, Colombia's eastern plains, and found evidence that Lehder had been living there. They also found laboratories capable of processing huge quantities of cocaine. A pilot working undercover for the DEA sighted Lehder and his crew loading more than 2000 kilos of cocaine onto a plane bound for Nicaragua.

In January of 1985 Lehder invited a Colombian freelance reporter to meet him at his hideout in a remote location of the Amazon jungle near the Brazilian border. Looking cool and confident in a sleeveless black shirt, and surrounded by men heavily armed with automatic weapons, Lehder didn't deny that he was Colombia's drug king. Instead he boasted of cocaine as a "Latin American atom bomb" that would force respect from the imperialists. He used the television exposure to portray himself as a revolutionary with a vision, and threatened to unite his army of followers with Colombia's M-19 terrorist organization.[8]

My childhood friendship with Carlos Lehder was renewed at social gatherings now and then when visiting Colombia. The closeness of our family's relationship made it inevitable that we meet on each occasion. Armenia always had a small number of elite families who frequented El Club Campestre, El Club America and the Polo Club. While the wealthy coffee growers played long hours of poker, Carlos and I danced the night away with their spoiled daughters. Parents were most protective of their daughters and their conservative upbringing didn't leave room for any hanky-panky.

But I was an American now, establishing a business and starting a young family. I never suspected our lives would become intertwined again; nor even less the consequences to both of us of such a union.

2

JANUARY 1983

FOUR YEARS EARLIER

~

The minute I entered the lobby of my office at All Nation Property Maintenance, Inc., in Fort Lauderdale, my pager emitted a loud beep. Sarah, my secretary, was in a near panic as she tried to locate me.

"Oh God, I'm so glad you're here; there has been an accident at the main office of Southeast in Miami; some plumbing ruptured and the top six floors are flooded."

I shared her concern. Southeast Properties was the firm responsible for the buildings of the largest full service banking institution in the state of Florida, and our contract with them was worth two million dollars; 70% of all our profits. Any negligence on our part in answering this emergency and our contract with Southeast—as well as our jobs —could end in the trash can!

Immediately I called Mr. Soto, the company's president

and calmly reassured him that the situation was under control.

"We'll have your building dry and operational in a matter of a few hours," I told him over the phone, even before I had looked at the intensity of the damage.

"Call every mobile unit we have in the Miami area, and get me at least three more men willing to work overtime... please, Sarah." Situations like this one were common, especially during the hurricane season, when we hired extra help and set up a task force to deal with emergencies. I was becoming adept at handling crises and hiding my own anxieties behind a smooth line of patter.

I had joined the company in early 1980, and within one year earned a promotion to VP of operations. A company car, liberal expense account and opportunity for growth amounted to good reasons to give All Nation my loyal dedication and total commitment.

Life was good in spite of the minimal amount of hours left to share with my wife and small child, but I was securing their future by putting in extra time and effort. My wife, Cristina, was attending a small college near our apartment in Wilton Manors, where she worked hard to earn a degree as a Medical Assistant. Time passed and we were content with our lifestyles.

We considered ourselves lucky. The year was 1983.

Just about the time I was working beside my men to dry out Southeast Bank, back in Colombia Alvaro Triana paid a visit to my mother's house. Alvaro had been a dear school mate from the early sixties, and his parents had kept a casual friendship with all members of my family. No one, not even his own family, knew that Alvaro was now working with Carlos Lehder in Armenia, and his visit to my mother was assumed to be a social call. But he needed to speak to me; "It is important," he told my mother," that I get Carlito's phone number in the States. I am going to make your son a millionaire by this time next year!" he concluded.

His phone call to me came in loud and clear; the phone call that changed my life and marked the beginning of a journey with "The Crippled Mule[1]."

The time was approximately ten a.m, on a sunny Saturday in South Florida. I stretched lazily and put down my second cup of coffee as I reached to answer the phone.

"Mr. Carlos ?" the voice of Colombia's Telecom's -operator said with barely concealed curtness under an artificially courteous tone.

"This is Carlos ," I answered quickly with surprise and a little flutter of anxiety Somehow I had developed a clinical ear for overseas calls. There was something in the wire that made them sound entirely different from domestic long distance calls.

"Please hold on..."

"Mr. Triana, are you still holding?" she asked someone on the other end.

"Itos?" The nickname took me back to my childhood.

Only one person still called me Itos and of course I knew who it was instantly.

"Alvaro?" I asked, although I needed no confirmation.

"*Como estás, hermano*?" he said, in his characteristic husky tone. Alvaro had nicknamed me Itos (short for Carl ITOS) when we were maybe ten or eleven years old. A few weeks later all members of my family began calling me ITOS until I left home at 14. Only Alvaro had never stopped calling me by that name.

"Where the hell are you, Alvaro?" I couldn't believe my ears. It had been more than a decade since we had last spoken.

"Listen, I am in Colombia, your mom gave me your number.

By the way, she is fine and sends her love. I don't have too much time to waste.; can you pick me up at Miami International tomorrow?"

It was obvious that he didn't want to stay on the phone much longer.

"It can't hurt to hear what he has to say." I reassured myself. "It doesn't need to affect my life at all."

After a traffic-free drive from Fort Lauderdale to Miami on Interstate I-95, I arrived at Miami International Airport just in time for Alvaro's flight. It was a Sunday morning— probably the only time you can drive that distance in forty minutes; normally it would take about an hour each way. The airport terminal had its regular congestion regardless of the day of the week. The International Arrival's gate was crowded with the expectant faces of Colombians awaiting their dear ones from the homeland; I had only a glimpse of the arriving passengers since the couple in front of me blocked my view to the gate. In the faces of many of the arriving Colombians I could see the excitement and anxiety of a first visit to a foreign country. I could almost pinpoint the new immigrants by their expressions.

Memories flooded back of that day in 1966 when I first came to this land; young, alone and scared—yet wanting my share of the American dream. It was during my first cold winter in Elmhurst, New York that I ran into Carlos Lehder.[2] I moved in with him and two other Colombians. Our two bedroom, one bath apartment became a playground for the teen-aged bachelors. Both Lehder and I got jobs at a factory not far from the apartment, where plastic hangers were manufactured. Lehder was too smart and too restless to remain in a factory job, however, so it wasn't long before he quit and moved out of town to start a profitable career as exporter of "hot" automobiles.

Alvaro was easy to recognize in the mass of people.

He wore a flashy Hawaiian short-sleeved shirt and matching Bermudas. Although I identified his face right away, I was startled to see how much weight he had gained since we last met. I remembered his red hair and freckles, but now his short frame looked out of proportion and obese.

I waved to him and he motioned back in an excited gesture of acknowledgment. We mutually opened our arms and with a brief hug shouted "*Hola hermano!*"

As Alvaro raised his arms to embrace me, his passport dropped from under his left arm. I knelt to pick it up, and to my puzzlement I noticed the passport was not a Colombian document but "Venezuelan passport?" I asked him in surprise.

"Shhhhh" he motioned, putting a finger over his lips. "Keep it quiet. There are customs and immigration officers all around us" he whispered in my ear.

I looked around, and without a word followed him to the luggage carrousel.

"How was your flight, Alvaro?" I inquired, forcing myself to be casual.

"Shhhhh..." he motioned again. "My name is not Alvaro, it's Antonio," he whispered again.

I scratched my head and decided not to -say another word until we were inside my car.

Alvaro or Antonio did not have much luggage, only a midsize leather case, and we were soon out on the Florida highway.

For the first ten minutes of our ride there was not a word spoken by either of us. I believed he owed me an explanation, and as curious as I was to know about his charade, I proudly refused to talk first. Suddenly he said: "So Itos, why are you so quiet?"

"Well....ahh...what should I call you...Alvaro? or Antonio?... or maybe I am not supposed to talk until you say so."

"I am sorry. There is a long story behind all this, and it'll be all straightened out as soon as we get a chance to sit down comfortably," he said calmly.

"Bull Shit!" I exclaimed, "do you think I'm gonna take you home to my wife not knowing who you are and what to say to her?"

"OK, don't tell her what happened at the airport.

Call me Alvaro just like you always have, and you and I will discuss the rest later. All right?" At least he would not make me look foolish in front of Cristina. I agreed and we filled the rest of the drive north on Interstate 95 to Fort Lauderdale by talking about my family and receiving all the messages they had sent me by way of Alvaro.

Upon arrival at our apartment, I made Alvaro promise not to discuss any business that was out of the ordinary. We left the elevator and were greeted by my wife, who very politely introduced herself to Alvaro. I knew she would make him feel at home no matter how unpleasant his visit might become, in deference to my wishes.

We sat in the living room sharing a cocktail while Alvaro told Cristina endless anecdotes of our early childhood.

We laughed and chatted, later on enjoying our paella and a couple of bottles of wine to complement the occasion. I was happy to see that Alvaro refrained from discussing his so-called business trip, and also happy that Cristina did not ask questions that could open a can of worms.

It was obvious to me that Alvaro's travels under a faked identity and a faked passport had to have a good explanation, and I just could not wait to have a moment of privacy with him to get to the bottom of it.[3] To my surprise, right after dinner Alvaro asked me if I could drive him to Boca Raton. It was late and both my wife and I had set up the guest room for the duration of his stay.

"Can't Boca Raton wait until tomorrow?" I asked him firmly.

"I have a house waiting for me, already furnished, all I have to do is pick up the keys at this address." He then pulled a piece of paper from his shirt pocket. A hispanic sounding name and address were typed on it. He handed the note to me.

Cesar Londoño
2659 East Palmetto Park Road
Boca Raton, Fla.

"Do you know how to get there?" he asked me.

"Wait a minute. We thought you were going to stay with us," I protested.

"No, Itos and Cristina, I thank you very much. I came to the United States to stay. I have started a corporation with some very important people from France, and things are going so well that I decided to move to this country and run my operations from here." He kept on talking while I began to hope that his recital would allay my suspicions.

"Well that sounds wonderful; tell us more about it, Alvaro" said Cristina with admiration.

"OK, and I'll have another scotch and soda, but only if you promise me .you'll drive me to Boca tonight."

"I will," I offered, "but if you really have to pick up those keys let's not make it too late." I wanted to be alone with him to do my own fact finding, away from Cristina's shrewd intuition. Alvaro then proceeded with an account of how he was buying French perfumes on the black market in Paris and then importing them into Colombia as contraband without paying duty fees to customs. He went on relating how he worked very closely with members of the board of directors of a number of Colombian banks who made it possible for him to obtain import licenses through the Bank of the Republic in Bogota. He opened his leather case and pulled out a couple of attractive one ounce bottles of perfume.

"These are for you, Cristina," he smiled as he handed my wife the expensive French perfumes.

"Well, these certainly are the best," responded Cristina who has an uncanny taste for French perfumes. She glanced at me quizzically and I smiled in approval.

"Thank you very much, Alvaro," said Cristina with genuine gratitude.

"Call me Archie; that's what my friends call me nowadays."

"Holy shit!" I whispered to myself. "Now he's come up with a third name!"

We left my apartment and headed towards Boca Raton. Now it was just the two of us, and I was hungry for answers French perfume. It sounded harmless enough, despite the illegality involved. Colombians are used to by-passing the laws with bribes, especially when they think the laws are restrictive or silly.

And upper class Colombians soon became knowledgeable of whom and how to bribe; there is usually an eager hand ready to receive one's offerings.

But it was obvious that French perfume didn't require quite so much secrecy and intrigue. A slap on the wrist by way of a fine would probably be the only consequence of being caught. Even as I prepared to ask skeptical questions, however, deep inside I didn't want to hear honest answers. Something in me began to hope Alvaro's perfume story would hold up and I could ignore my conscience's whisperings.

"OK Alvaro, let's lay the cards on the table. What is all that bullshit about perfumes, and what is the truth behind your trip here? And what about that house in Boca?"

"Itos," he grasped my hand trying to convey more reassurance, "What I said in your house is true, and to prove it I am offering you a job; I want you to become my public relations manager. I'll pay you a salary as high as that of any corporate head in America, and as an extra bonus you'll have a house in Boca Raton, plus cars for both you and your wife."

"Alvaro" I started to say.

"Don't interrupt me," he cut in. "I am going to give you a chance to think about it and to check my credentials.

In two days I am going to France. Here is two thousand dollars." He pulled a roll of hundred dollar bills out of his bag and rapidly counted twenty crisp notes. "This will cover your expenses to take a whole week off from work; then when I return next week, I want your answer."

He moved closer and tucked the cash inside my shirt pocket as I kept driving. I was speechless.

For the next few minutes I didn't even look at his face. I was trying to digest his offer. Impulsiveness and risk-taking were characteristics of my family background, and the reward Alvaro was offering surely outweighed any slight danger, didn't it? A short cut to the good life, with no real harm done, was beginning to sound very attractive.

The house right off East Palmetto Park Road was a one

story luxury home with beautiful landscaping and a double car garage. It was too dark to discern the color of its facade, but its silhouette loomed impressively.

Alvaro got out of the car and asked me to wait while he went to get the keys. I watched him walk towards the front door until finally the driveway lights came to life and a young man appeared at the entrance to shake Alvaro's hand.

From the car I could not make out what they were saying-to each other at first, but it was clear to me that an argument had started, soon their voices rose to a point that made it possible for me to understand their words.

"Thirty fucking thousand dollars?" shouted Alvaro, gesturing angrily.

"Well, I had to give the rest of the money to the pilots; I had no choice!"

"OK..." said Alvaro, "but I want a complete account of all those monies by tomorrow... and by the way...YOU'RE FIRED!" he bellowed as he walked back to my car.

I was puzzling over the scene I had just witnessed.

I could not think why Alvaro's opponent looked and sounded so familiar..

We drove to Interstate 95 heading north to Glades Road.

I just drove quietly while Alvaro guided me to what was to become his new residence. It must have been near midnight and the moment was most improper to ask him more questions. When we pulled in front of the house, Alvaro invited me to come in.

"Let's have a drink" he offered, "this house is supposed to be fully equipped with a complete bar and plenty of food."

"No, Alvaro, it's late and I must get back to Fort Lauderdale. I will call you in the morning if you give me your phone number."

"I don't have a phone, and I don't intend to have one installed, so come by tomorrow as early as you can...all right?"

"OK, friend, you've got my number, so get in touch with me if you need anything." - There was no genuine warmth in my words. It was hard to conceal my distaste for the events of the day.

"Good night, then" he said as he walked away from the car.

Oh, by the way, you have no idea where I live...and when you come here it's just you, OK?...no friends, nothing!"

"OK," I agreed—I just wanted to get out of there. Tomorrow will be another day, I thought.

As I drove back home, my mind reeled with his offer and with all the mysteries of both houses and words I had over-heard. Where had I known that other man? What was I opening myself to?

Cristina was half asleep watching a late show and I gently kissed her goodnight. It was not a good night for me. This was the beginning of many sleepless nights.

The routine of a normal working day started with an early breakfast, but the next morning nothing seemed normal to me. This was the day I planned to call my boss in New York and ask him for a six months leave of absence. Last night I had spent hours pacing the apartment trying to find the answer to my dilemma. I finally decided that I would give Alvaro a shot, providing All Nation Property would give me the license I intended to request. The money Alvaro offered was very tempting, and I thought and dreamed of having a lavish new home—perhaps a boat—luxuries I might not obtain in a lifetime at All Nation. A six months trial period would give us a wonderful financial boost, and I could always return to my stable job at the end of that time. If I had any premonitions that I was walking into an indissoluble net, I put them out of my mind.

I had no intentions of telling my wife about my decision until I had an approval from my boss in New York.

I entered my office early that Monday and asked Sarah to hold my calls while I dialed headquarters in the Bronx.

I had a direct line to Mr. Nieto, the company's President; a number we only used in case of emergencies.

"Ray?...Good morning."

"Good morning, what is happening in sunny Florida?" he had recognized my voice.

"Well Ray, this call is personal but it affects things here." I had prepared my speech to make sure he'd buy my story.

"I just had a call from my home in Colombia last night, and it is mandatory that I travel there immediately to handle matters related to our family's holdings. It sounds as if I might be away for a couple of months, so just to play it safe I'd like to ask for an immediate leave of absence, without pay of course, for six months." - There was silence on both ends for a moment.

"That serious?" asked Ray.

"I know, sir, that it seems unethical not to give you notice so you can make the necessary adjustments; however, my trip is not scheduled until next week and I will be on call until you send one of your men from New York. "

"Carlos, you caught me off guard; I need to think about it...call me back in a couple of hours." He hung up the phone without another word.

I got my coat, put it on, and walked out of my office.

"Sarah, if you need me just call my pager, I've got things to do up in Palm Beach county." I left the building and started driving north to Alvaro's house in Boca Raton.

Somehow I felt different. The responsibility of being in

charge of All Nation was being lifted off my shoulders and it made me feel young and adventurous . I was sure the New York office would grant me the leave. It was Carlos who negotiated two of their biggest contracts, and although I knew that no one is indispensable, I had faith I could return to All Nation if things didn't work out with Alvaro six months down the road. I pulled into Alvaro's driveway and blew the horn gaily.

The house was typical Florida stucco, but its sprawling exterior and manicured grounds were far from average. I had been too tired and it had been too dark to observe details the night before.

The garage door opened vertically and at the end of the garage stood Alvaro in a bathrobe, pressing the button that activated the closing of the door once my car was inside. I could not help noticing the license plate on the pick up truck parked next to my car inside the garage; a late model GMC registered in the state of Oklahoma.

We walked from the garage through the laundry room into the kitchen, a spacious room with state-of-the-art appliances and furnishings. Next to the kitchen was a circular room containing a round dinette table with four chairs, surrender by sliding glass panels leading to a swimming pool, jacuzzi and gym.

Alvaro's room was at the opposite end from the kitchen. It was a large bedroom with a king size bed set, dresser, ornate mirror and matching night stands. The furniture was a replica of Louis XV's style, and a thick plush peach carpet added subtle elegance. Connected to the master bedroom there were two adjacent white doors; one leading to a huge walk-in closet and -the other to a Roman marble bathtub and shower with another small door leading to the pool area .

The other three bedrooms were tastefully decorated and furnished. One was a studio or small office with desks and credenza, and the remaining two were set up with twin beds with plump sculptured bedspreads and damask draperies. Next to the kitchen was a sunken living room with full size sliding doors, again leading to the swimming pool, and opposite it a wood-burning fire place served as a divider between the lounge area and the dining room. The house itself was perhaps fourteen years old, but maintained in excellent condition.

"You want some coffee?" offered Alvaro, seated at the circular table.

"Sure...black and one sugar" I requested.

"Well, I don't even know how to use the percolator, so go ahead and make some for both of us" ordered Alvaro, laughing.

"How do you expect to live in this house by yourself when you can't even cook an egg?" I was being honest.

"Oh Itos, I have it all planned. In a couple of weeks I am bringing one of the girls who work in our organization to cook and take care of the house. She is someone you might remember. Of course she won't be treated as we treat the maids in Colombia; she will do secretarial work as well as domestic...believe me, she'll be well remunerated."

"Oh sure, I believe you; which brings us to the issue of our discussion last night. You never told me how much my salary would be if I accept your offer, nor have you mentioned a job description."

I was in the kitchen making coffee and talking to Alvaro, who sat about twelve feet- away glancing at a Colombian newspaper. "Your salary will be ten thousand dollars per month.

That does not include your rent, or transportation for you and your wife."

I almost dropped the coffee pot when I heard those figures. I was actually being offered a salary of $120,000.00 per year tax free, plus all living expenses. Never had I dreamed of making so much money. I was beginning to be very glad I already had asked for my leave of absence.

"Let me warn you," Alvaro continued, "that no one in the organization should, know how much money you make. You will be my right hand and consultant on every move. You will have to travel often, and an airplane will be provided for your use." It was too much for me to handle in one day, and besides, I had not received confirmation from New York about my leave of absence. I explained to Alvaro what I had done, and that as much as I might want to work with him, I was waiting for my boss to give me his word before making it official. He agreed and told me to go ahead and take care of my obligations with All Nation, but to meet him for dinner later to discuss my first assignment. I left his house with a firm handshake and with my pledge to be loyal and to keep all these matters very confidential. I was flattered that Alvaro was offering me such responsibility, even after a ten year interruption of our friendship. Close Colombian ties always remain close, but he also must have checked into my flourishing career at All Nation.

The remainder of the day I spent at my office trying to locate Ray Nieto in New York for his decision. I cleared my desk of any unnecessary paper load and worked hard on schedules for the next few weeks to make it easier for my replacement from New York to manage the interim operations. Just before five p.m. the call from New York came in.

"Well, Carlos, you left me with little choice. Go ahead

and leave as soon as you need, and bring me some good Colombian coffee."

"Thank you, Ray." I meant that from the bottom of my heart.

"We'll miss you," he said. "Good luck."

I telephoned Yesterday's, a five star restaurant in Fort Lauderdale, and made reservations for three for dinner. I was taking Alvaro Triana and my wife to celebrate our new working relationship. Just before Alvaro came to our apartment I had revealed my plans to Cristina. She was slightly disturbed, but trusted my decision.

Archie arrived at our apartment just before eight thirty, driving the GMC pick up truck that I had seen in his garage earlier. We had a drink, then left for Yesterday's, only a few minutes drive away. The restaurant sat by the Intracoastal Waterway and offered a spectacular view of the boats passing by. The decor was elegant, and the food and service outstanding.

We dined and toasted with champagne what I believed was a short cut to riches. After a four—course meal on the first floor, we moved to the top floor where a packed discotheque entertained us to the early hours of the morning. Finally we agreed to snatch a few hours sleep and then meet at Alvaro's house around 10:00 that same morning. Archie collected his truck from our building's parking lot and drove off rubbing his heavy lidded eyes.

I knocked on his door around quarter after ten. I noticed several vehicles parked outside the house, and a voice from inside asked me to identify myself. I knew it was not Alvaro's voice and I hesitated for a second.

"Is Archie home?" Just in time I had remembered that he wanted me to call him Archie or Tony in public. I did not volunteer.my own name.

"Wait just a second," was the response from the invisible man behind the door.

The door opened after a few seconds of suspense, and a thin red-haired man, maybe in his early twenties, invited me to come in. I walked past the red-haired man right into the kitchen where Alvaro, or rather Archie, was holding a meeting with four Latin men and two Americans. I recognized one of the Latin men as the fellow Archie had fired a couple of days ago, when we went to collect the keys for his house. Now I remembered why his face was familiar—Julio and I had met in Colombia years back. Upon my entrance all conversation came to a halt, and everybody fixed their eyes on me. The atmosphere crackled with tension.

"Come right in," said Archie, pointing to the seat next to him. "Gentlemen; this is Richard. Maybe some of you have met him in Colombia in years past and know him by his real name, but from now on his name is Richard." Apparently I had no choice over the matter; I was being baptized unceremoniously with a new name.

One at a time the men came over to shake my hand.

We exchanged names solemnly, but I assumed their names were as phony as mine. Archie called us back to the business at hand. On top of the kitchen counter there were maps and flight plans for routes into the Caribbean. They all looked very foreign to me, and I could only identify those countries whose names were clearly printed.

"Richard is my number one man, and from now on you must see him about anything before coming to me. He is the official interpreter for the C.C.Q.'s operations in this country, and only he will deal with the American employees...I mean the pilots!"

Archie spoke very slowly to make his order completely clear to all present. There was the inevitable whisper from a couple of the guys, and already I could smell the jealousy of most of the Colombians as Archie made the introduction.

Finally one of the Americans, a boney man in his mid forties, approached me and grasped my hand.

"This man looks American," he said to the group, "and if he speaks English better than this bunch of assholes here, we are in business."

Archie requested a translation so I repeated his message in Spanish, leaving out the insult.

"Richard, tell him that from now on under my administration things will be done right, and that he need not worry about communication. Please tell him that you are in charge of the pilots, starting now.

I conveyed Archie's words to the American, whose code name in the organization was Red. The Colombians were silent and made no overtures of friendship so I decided to address the whole group in Spanish to break the ice.

"Señores, I have no idea how many of you will work under me, and I don't even know the extent of my duties. All I can say is that so long as we keep our channels of communication open, we have a chance of building a dynamic working relationship. You will find me a very nice guy to get along with, but on the other hand I can be the worst asshole if I don't get the cooperation that our goals require." They listened attentively.

. "Who is getting fired or transferred to Colombia, Richard?" asked Julio, the clean-cut young Colombian anxious to know his fate.

"I cannot answer any questions. I just got here myself." Everybody laughed. Taking advantage of the good sense of humor, I moved around the room, shaking hands again and giving each individual a more personal salute. I was safe now. They liked me, and I could feel the jealousy fading away and a healthy relationship beginning. I could see Archie was impressed with my PR show, and I was proud that I had justified his confidence in me.

Archie dismissed the Colombians with a request that they meet us again that evening at 8:30 sharp.

Just the pilots, Archie and myself were left in the house. Archie asked us to move to the studio so I could translate for him there. I was-playing all my moves by ear and hoping to look good, but it was a strain to carry on the bluff without complete understanding of the real issues behind these meetings.

"Richard, please tell these gentlemen that their money will be ready in full within two weeks."

They listened carefully as I translated Archie's words.

"I am willing to wait," said Red "but no more than two weeks."

He got up from his chair. "I need at least $40,000.00 now," said the one whom we addressed as Colorado. When Archie learned of Colorado's demand, he started to perspire. "Talk him into waiting at least another week for the $40,000.00 and a second week for the remaining $100,000.00." he ordered me. I could not believe my ears, but I just repeated the messages as they came from Archie's mouth. Colorado reluctantly agreed to the delay, and then told me to expect his visit in seven days.

"I'll be here," I assented. They both walked to the front door, and I decided to walk along with them to their vehicles. Red opened the driver side door of his Mercedes Benz and pulled out a portable machine with two dials and a metal rod attached to a wire. Carefully, he ran the rod through the interior of his car, then switched the machine off with a look of relief. "What is that for?" I asked him, very impressed. "It's a microphone detector." he said. "You never know what happened out here while we were in there," pointing to the house. "You can have it if you like; I have another one at home." "Thanks," I told him, "it may be very handy."

Colorado had already driven off so I went back inside the house. It was time Alvaro Triana and I had our private meeting.

"OK, let's cut the crap and get to some straight answers for a change...who the hell do you think you are, putting me through all this shit of calling me Richard and forcing me into situations I don't know or can't even begin to understand?... take your fucking mask off and be honest for a minute for heaven's sake!" I was fuming, absolutely furious.

"Listen Itos ..."

"Shut up and answer me this. For starters, why are you here under a Venezuelan passport; next, what about pilots, thousands of dollars, deadlines, all this luxury. Do you think I was born yesterday?" I kept throwing questions at him as I paced up and down the room without giving him a chance to respond. "You are dealing drugs, my dear friend, and I'm going to have nothing more to do with you. But you'd better tell me what in the world is going on. In return I promise you I've never seen this house... or even better, you are still in Colombia so far as I am concerned, is that fair?" Suddenly an uncontrollable rage possessed me, and I jumped over the desk and grabbed his neck.

"Do you want to get me killed?" I yelled holding tight to his shirt collar.

"Stop it, stop it!" he shouted, putting the palm of his hand over my mouth. We fell to the floor next to the arm chair where he had been sitting. In an effort to catch my breath, I let go of his neck and he responded by removing his pudgy fingers from my face. I got to my feet, turned around and walked towards the kitchen to find my car keys. As I looked back at the studio from a distance, I could see him still sitting on the floor holding his head with both hands. I hesitated, then decided to go back and help him up. I had come to my senses and realized that it wouldn't hurt to leave on better terms.

"Grab my arm" I offered, straining to balance his weight as he labored up from the floor.

"Let me explain something before you go." His tone was conciliatory and I knew he was sincere. "OK, I work for the Carlos Lehder organization; I have been working for him in Colombia for just over a year. I have made a lot of money, because I am very careful, and I study every move I make."

I listened attentively, leaning back in my chair across from his desk.

"I am sorry for not being straight with you, but the truth is that I have orders to recruit you and to keep hidden the identity of the man we both work for."

I was speechless. I could not understand why Carlos Lehder would take such a devious route when we had been close mutual friends. I was in shock! But my respect for Carlos Lehder's determination and shrewdness rose as I kept on listening. Lehder and I had met often since boyhood and since our apartment sharing days; usually at casual social functions. My mind had fresh memories of our meeting in New York one day in 1970.

Carlos Lehder was the center of attention at a party in the Waldorf Astoria. He was twenty years old, rich, and his reputation for being a playboy who would not hesitate to invest in girls kept him always surrounded by pretty women of all races and creeds. He was a very smooth talker, very knowledgable of all present issues and a great host at parties.

"This is living!" he would say "It just can't get any better!." Later it was no secret that he was becoming a world-renowned figure, nor was the source of his wealth and prestige a mystery. At our last meetings he had made overtures to me about joining his organization, but I had turned flatly away before he could offer a definite proposition. I couldn't help but be flattered now by his interest and persistence, and by his obvious belief in my capabilities.

"Listen, Itos," Alvaro came around his desk to lean close to me: "We'll do this for eight months, maybe a year, and we'll be filthy rich." He paused..."I will not, I insist...I will not expose you to drugs or to areas of danger; those are part of my orders. Carlos does not want you to do any of the dirty work. You are regarded as a valuable asset to us and he wants to keep you well protected."

I was fascinated and at the same time anxious to know the total picture. "What exactly did you have in mind for me?"

"Well is that a YES?...are you accepting?"

"NO! but tell me about this operation and about the job if you want me even to consider it."

"Now you have to understand that I have a serious problem."

"What is the problem, Alvaro?"

"You must keep it a secret the fact that we work for Carlos Lehder . You won't report to him, you'd report to me."

"Well if that is-the way he wants it, then I don't foresee any problems so long as you tell me every single detail."

"OK, let's go to the kitchen and make some coffee... this is going to be a long day."

"I'll make the coffee," I offered with a smile.. I prepared myself for an eye-opening account of a drug running scheme, and thought I was ready to turn my back on the affluence it promised. But somewhere I had crossed the line of decision without recognizing it, and the chance for refusal had passed me by. Lehder and Triana had been my most trusted friends. There is no way they would stab me in the back if I were to get myself involved with them.

The fact that I was not to be an actual smuggler or even get close to drugs quieted my greatest fear. Right then I began to disassociate myself from a realization of evil-doing, and become totally absorbed instead with the logistics and challenge of the job. This dichotomy was characteristic of my entire stay in the organization. I also knew I had what it took to face a world of danger and adventure. It was an innate quality.

In fact, in 1953 my father had to gather our family in the middle of the night and leave our home town of Armenia. He owned a radio station, *La Voz de Armenia*, and had declared private war on Rojas Pinilla, a cruel and incompetent dictator. My father's daily nation-wide broadcasts to awaken the people brought instant retaliation. For months we hid him from Rojas Pinillas' troops by pretending he had deserted us.

My adrenaline was already running wild: "Goodbye, Mr. Stier...Hello, Mr. Exciting!"

We sat by the kitchen counter after checking to make sure the doors were locked so we'd have total privacy.

"What have you heard about Carlos Lehder lately?" Archie asked.

"Oh, there are always rumors about his wealth and how he spends money as if it were going out of style. Of course, I am aware of his involvement in drugs. Last time we saw each other, if I remember correctly, was at the Bogota Hilton and he mentioned something about his island in the Bahamas. I declined to work with him then.

Of course I am talking about maybe six years ago or longer."

"Well, he is by now probably the richest man in Colombia, and true, he has an island in the Bahamas, and that is precisely where you come in."

"How?" I asked with astonishment.

"We'll get to that in a minute. Anyway, he is doing very well, but he has lost a lot of money lately because the men he has working here in the United States are not reliable or responsible. It costs about sixty thousand dollars a month just to keep salaries and expenses here, and things are not getting done the way they should be."

"So that's why he sent you here? To fire every one?"

"If I have to, yes!, but I think we still have a few valuable heads in our. group...it's not so much that they don't want to do it...the root of the problem is called 'GUTS.' They are afraid; they just sit all day collecting thousands of dollars per month and giving the same excuses. 'We can't find a place to land or 'it's too dangerous,' while we wait with cocaine piling up to the roof, and the whole Cartel on our backs!"

"Why the Cartel?" It didn't make sense to me..."Isn't Carlos Lehder the owner of the cocaine?"

"Part of it, but 80% belongs to the Ochoas, Escobar, and the other families.[4] Lehder is an expert in transportation. Nobody knows as much or can do it better. He owns the planes, he handles the police, customs, communications...you name it!

The man is the best in the world, and for that he charges dearly.

He has a track record of only 1% failure...so good is he at what he does, that he insures the cocaine."

"What do you mean, insure?" I asked.

"He guarantees delivery at the other end. If the cocaine is seized or stolen he pays the price, and on the other hand if the pilot or one of the men get arrested, the Cartel will try to get them out by contributing to legal fees, bonds or bribes. " Now I think I understand why a kilo of that stuff costs $40,000.00."

"But Itos, the price is dropping because there are too many small operators sending one or two kilos at a time with mules who get lucky and make it through Customs."

"How much does a kilo cost in Colombia right how?"

"Well, again it all depends...Huge operators like Lehder or Ochoas or Escobar grow their own coca leaf in the mountains of Bolivia. They pay the government of La Paz hundreds of thousands of dollars to protect their investments, and in return the Army of Bolivia guards those plantations. From there the leaf comes to Colombia where it is turned into coca paste, and then by means of a chemical process based on acetone is dried into cocaine powder. Now, to answer your question, the bottom cost of a kilo in Medellin is about $800.00 for Carlos Lehder. If you were a gringo trying to get a kilo smuggled in your suitcase, like you see them every day walking past Park Berrio in Medellin; it could cost you anywhere between $1500 to $2000 each kilo."

I listened with undivided interest. It was an education in the making of the infamous powder, and the vivid style in which Alvaro described each step made my mind travel from the mountains of Bolivia to the jungles of southern Meta where most of the laboratories or so called "kitchens" are located.

"I still don't understand why they charge up to 40 or 45 thousand dollars here in the States...you mean to tell me that 97% of that money is all profit?"

"No not quite!...it costs about $9,200.00 per kilo success-
fully delivered at an American destination, so it is-expensive
to transport, and that is the nucleus of the C.C.Q. TRANS-
PORTATION." Alvaro gave special emphasis to that last
word. Both Alvaro and I had already consumed our third
cup of coffee so I got up to make a new pot while he went on
with his fascinating lecture.

"Did I hear you say C. C. Q.?" I paused after each conso-
nant make sure I repeated correctly.

"Cannabis Club Quindio," he said very proudly.."It
started as a name of a club Lehder founded in Armenia
back in 1968. Its members smoked marijuana, had wild
parties and orgies and it began mainly for fun. But as the
time came to get back to work, it became well known that
those working for him belonged to the C.C.Q. even if they
didn't smoke marijuana, and the code name soon became
well know and revered."

"Did you take part in any of the orgies?" My curiosity
had taken a sharp turn.

"You son of a bitch!" said Alvaro laughing, "I knew you
were gonna ask me that!"

"Well, did you?..." I persisted inquisitively.

"A couple," he confessed timidly. "The man really
corrupted most of the young girls there. He had parties at
his chalet next to the country club where well-known
society girls in their teens did everything he wanted in order
to be close to his fame, his money, his coke...and he threw
money away to satisfy whatever their little hearts desired!"

"Then he must have a lot of enemies in Armenia!"

"Oh, yes. Wouldn't you want to kill the man who takes
your fifteen year old girl, persuades her to leave home, buys
her a BMW and makes a bitch out of her? But then again he
drives around in a bullet proof Mercedes-Benz with a half

dozen bodyguards." I was saddened. I could feel the corruption, and the tribulation of those distinguished families.

"He really turned into a bloody bastard without feelings," said Alvaro.

"How can you work for an individual like that?" I inquired.[5]

"What he does under his blankets is not my business. So long as he doesn't fuck around with any member of my family, I just turn my back. Besides, I don't believe I'll be with him forever, although he is becoming a very important figure within the political arena in Colombia."

"You mean the *Movimiento Cívico Latino Nacional*?"

"Yeah! You know about that?" he looked surprised.

"Well, I've spoken to my family and other Colombians and I hear the man is really obsessed with his idea of becoming the new dictator and savior of the country."

"You're right! and his movement is getting stronger by the minute." I was interested in knowing about the political machinery, but I remembered I had more important unanswered questions.

"All this is great but tell me about my job...what do I have to do?" I was no longer phrasing the question hypothetically.

"I have to go to the bathroom" said Alvaro, and kept talking as he walked through the living room. I didn't want to miss anything, so I followed him.

"You are a diplomat, Itos," he didn't stop talking as he urinated, "and we have serious problems dealing with the Bahamian government and our attorneys in Nassau who are working to regain control of Norman's Cay." He paused for a second to zipper up. "We need you to go there and talk to the attorneys, to the members of Parliament, to whomever you see fit in order to get the DEA out of our property and to make it operational again!"

"Is that all?" I asked sarcastically. "Who do you think I am...Superman?"

"It's not going to happen overnight, Itos, but you have the talent, the charisma, and somehow I know you'll come up with a plan."

For the first time during the whole conversation I felt $10,000.00 a month plus expenses was not enough, but I kept to myself any commentaries on that issue.

"Listen. Alvaro, I want to go home, digest all this and see you later. Why don't you come with me and get a bite."

"Good idea...remember we have a full staff meeting at eight thirty tonight, so let's get some food and some rest."

We both left in separate cars and agreed to meet at Wildflower, a lounge and restaurant East on Palmetto Park Road near the ocean. After juicy cheeseburgers with fries and a pitcher of beer, we shook hands until later that evening.

Oust before we left the parking lot, Archie shoved his head out of the window of his pickup truck and shouted: "Itos: welcome to the C.C.Q.!!"

3

MARCH 15, 1983

The house seemed packed with people; six cars were parked in front, bumper-to-bumper and in the driveway there were four more plus the two already in the garage. I wondered what the neighbors thought of all these cars, since it was a week day and an unlikely time for a party. I hesitated, drove around the corner and parked my car away from the house.

I walked almost a block to reach the front door. Someone inside must have seen me through the eye in the door, for just as I reached for the bell the door opened magically. A young woman with long straight hair, Levis and a short sleeved blouse gave me a friendly salute and asked me in.

"You must be Richard."

"Yes I am!" I answered back... and you are..?"

"Mary... I am Pucho's wife." I thought for a second; that name sounded familiar.

"You must be kidding!" I finally told her excitedly.

Pucho was a young man in his mid-twenties whom I remembered from his childhood. His older brothers had been good friends of mine in Colombia, but both had been victims of fatal accidents while working for the C.C.Q. His father once worked for my father's radio station as a journalist before going to law school.

I rushed inside looking for Pucho, and when I found him I just hugged him tight without a word.

"Brother...what are you doing here!" said Pucho in my ear as I held him in a warm embrace.

"I am your new boss...so you'd better behave if you want something for Christmas!!" We both laughed. That kid was special. Later on that evening I learned he had been hired by Lehder in Armenia, and sent to be in charge of one of Lehder's ranches five hours north of Fort Lauderdale near Ocala, Florida.

He had met Mary, an American girl a couple of years older who had a seven year old boy, and married her in New York before he was transferred to Florida with the C.C.Q. Mary was a charming girl and very much in love with Pucho, for all the right reasons.

He was gentle, responsible, a very hard worker and a loving step-parent. Sprawled around the living room were maybe ten other people, among them Pablo, another very dear friend my own age, who attended early school with Lehder, Triana, and me. He now ran Lehder's distribution operations from the West Coast in San Francisco. There were other Colombians from Armenia, and although I could not recall their names, each face brought up a memory of past associations. I was like a big family reunion. These were not swarthy hardened criminals. They were intelligent, educated young men with whom I felt comfortable socially. Nor were they at any time partakers of the drugs they carried. I soon learned that Lehder tolerated not one gram of cocaine or even marijuana for personal use. Any infraction meant immediate dismissal.

The rest were the American pilots whom I had met that morning, plus two other men; one Puerto Rican called Ramon and another Colombian nicknamed *Gaviota* or 'seagull' who claimed to be a close friend of my brother Fernando. Both men were pilots for Lehder, assigned to the Bahamas and to Medellin respectively. We shared conversations on Colombian politics, personal anecdotes and the drug trade, and even before the official meeting took place most of them began to bring up grievances for me to solve. I just offered to do what I could; it was to soon to commit myself with promises? The common denominator was their fear under the administration of Alvaro Triana whom they regarded as a selfish, inhumane exploiter without regard for anything or anyone except his personal accumulation of wealth. I refrained from comment on those accusations, but because of my feeling of kinship with these people I believed in the overwhelming sincerity of their pleas.

"OK, *hermanos,*" said Alvaro addressing the whole group from the kitchen as we all sat by the sunken living room, making it look as if he were on a pedestal. "You all know why we are here, so I'll try to be brief. We have too much 'merchandise' in los Llanos, and unless we move it out at a rate of at least a thousand kilos a month starting now...we're out of a job. Julio is being sent to Colombia tomorrow, but not before Marta gives me an update on the finances and all monies are accounted for." Julio sat near the fireplace next to his wife. His face reflected fear and anger. There was $200,000.00 missing so far and, when asked, he had blamed the bookkeeper Marta.

Marta was a Colombian woman in her mid thirties who lived in Hollywood with her ill mother and younger sister.

"I am ready to present you the books at any time" insisted Marta defensively.

"Anyway," continued Alavaro, "I am here to be in charge. No one goes anywhere or does anything unless I approve it, and in my absence you go to Carlos who is second to me in everything." He paused to swallow some coffee, then went on saying: "Only I can call him by his real name...from now on we all call him Richard, and let's try to make that a habit. Richard's functions are only related to problems dealing with, attorneys, foreign governments, airplane purchases and parts, and any concerns of a transportation nature. I don't want you guys bothering him because your rent is due, or because you need to go to Colombia for Mother's Day...you come to me for that, but again, I repeat, if I am not here, Richard has full authority to take over."

They all looked at me with approval. The message was clear...they did not want Alvaro Triana and their faces indicated their dislike. I knew from that very instant that Alvaro Triana and I were heading towards a fatal collision.

"Any questions?" Alvaro asked the group. Immediately everyone raised their hands, including the Americans who did not even understand a word of his memorable speech.

"What is it, Julio?" said Alvaro, pointing to him.

"You said I am leaving tomorrow, but I have furniture and cars...I cannot just pack my suitcase and go; it'll take me maybe a couple of weeks before I can leave!" he protested.

"Well, I'll give you money for your furniture and for your cars. I want you to take your clothes, your wife and your baby and take the first plane to Colombia. Leave everything in the house behind. I can use your house fully furnished to set up the person coming to replace you. Upon your arrival in Colombia report to Mr. Lehder and he will give you a new assignment."

"FUCK YOU Alvaro," shouted Julio. "Who do you think you are kicking me out of my own house like this! That house is in my name and I am not going to leave it for some mother fucker to store cocaine in it!" He got up and approached Alvaro, pointing his index finger at him as if wanting to poke his eyes.

The crowd kept silence and watched carefully as the two men took defensive positions. Margarita, Julio's wife, kept her frightened eyes fixed on her husband.

"What are you going to do, hit me?" sneered Alvaro forcing a sarcastic laugh.

"You owe me $75,000.00 and I want it right this minute, and I am not leaving my house nor this country...if you give me or my family a hard time, I don't have to kill you...the authorities will!" Julio's threat was serious and everyone's attention was riveted to him.

"Yes, we owe you $75,000.00...but first I have to check my books to find out why there is $200,000.00 not accounted for, so sit down you son of a bitch before I break your face!"

In a sudden, unsuspected move, Julio raised his right arm and put a firm fist between Alvaro's eyes. The heavy man fell slowly, knocking down a porcelain coffee pot that shattered on the marble floor. With his face bleeding, Alvaro tried to get up, but Julio's right foot was pressed against his chest giving Julio total control over the fat body. In an instinctive move we all went to separate the two men but Julio's 38 caliber was in his right hand in a split second.

"Everybody sit down!!" he ordered, pointing the gun on the group. "Let me deal with this asshole in my own way... you'll thank me when I am finished with him."

"You kill him now and we all end up in jail" pleaded Mary in her broken Spanish.

"Julio, please listen to me" I spoke warily, moving closer.

"You will have your $75,000.00 today and we'll give you time to relocate anywhere you want to...is that fair?"

"Tell him to get me the money" demanded Julio, pointing the gun at Alvaro's nose.

"Alvaro where is the fucking money?!" I roared.-

"I'll get it myself...just get this bastard to leave me alone!"

"Let go Julio," I pleaded..."I promise you it'll be all right" Julio withdrew his boot form Alvaro's chest, and the poor man got up, wiping the blood that kept running down his nose with his shirt sleeve.

"Please give me the gun" requested Ramon.

Julio handed him the gun without hesitation and walked to embrace Margarita who was crying in a state of shock. Alvaro crossed the living room to his office, and returned shortly with a plastic bag full of money.

"Itos, please count seventy-five thousand dollars out of here and give it to him." I started counting as everybody waited in suspense. Conscious of all the witnesses, I totaled each hundred dollar bill and handed Julio his money. After returning the rest of the bills to Alvaro, I pulled Julio to a corner and whispered to him: "Please, get out of here, take your wife and meet me tomorrow at the Holiday Inn on Glades Road at 9:00 a.m."

"I am very sorry Richard, but unfortunately that is the only language he understands...I wish you a lot of luck in your new career—I'll see you tomorrow at 9:00 a.m."

His wife left without saying a good bye to anyone.

She was visibly embarrassed and distraught.

"Gentlemen," I addressed the group, "can we finish this meeting tomorrow?"

Everybody agreed and left quietly without a glance back.

At exactly 9:00 the next morning, Julio Gonzales walked into the Holiday Inn holding his wife's hand. I waited by the reception area reading a Wall Street Journal column on the war against drugs; a concise update of the proliferation of drugs coming from Colombia to this country...nothing worth making a native Colombian proud of his land.

"Good morning, Carlos...I guess we don't have to call you Richard anymore?" was Margarita's greeting.

"Good morning guys...have you had any breakfast?" I invited.

"We'll just have coffee," replied Julio.

The three of us walked outside to the patio next to the swimming pool, and shared a few biscuits, soft margarine, fresh papaya slices and a hot pot of coffee.

"What are your plans, Julio?" I decided to open the conversation since ten minutes of silence were becoming intolerable.

"I plan to go to New York, maybe open a small restaurant in Queens or even a hot-dog stand if the Greeks allow me."

He was right; he knew the kind of monopoly the Greek community had over the hot-dog corner stands throughout the five boroughs.

"What is the status with your house here in Boca?" I asked, pulling a piece of paper out of my pocket to make notes on anything of importance.

"The house was leased for me by the C.C.Q. and the furniture in it was also purchased by the C.C.Q., for us to keep! Our names appear on the lease; that is why I don't want to leave my name to be used and abused by someone using it for illegal activities."

I understood his concern and agreed with him to terminate the lease and put the furniture in storage.

"You go ahead and do what you have to do to break that lease, even if it means paying some penalties for early cancellation. I will take care of Alvaro...but promise me to get out of town as soon as possible."

"How long do I have?" asked Julio.

"How long do you need?" I replied.

"Is four weeks too long?"

"I think it'-s only proper...but please do not go to Alvaro's house again, and refrain from talking to any C.C.Q. member; I'll explain to Alvaro."

"You have been a gentleman, Carlos, we are in debt to you." I felt uncomfortable by Margarita's words, and called for the check to end our meeting. I left them finishing their coffee and walked to the parking lot for a short drive to Alvaro's, alias Archie, alias Antonio's house.

Alvaro, wearing a sweat suit was pumping iron by the pool. I helped myself to a thick cup of awful black coffee obviously made by him earlier.

"I met with Julio and his wife a few minutes ago, and I have taken the liberty to allow them a month in their house before they relocate." I prepared myself for the worst reaction.

"That's wonderful; I was hoping you'd keep them here at least a month, that'll give us sufficient time to investigate where the missing money is." I had forgotten all about that, but felt relieved that he was pleased with my decision. I dropped my guard.

"Who do you think is responsible for all that money?"

"Only two people had access to that large amount, Martha or Julio, Martha is very good at the books, according to Lehder, but I just don't trust her. He paused to get out from under the heavy exercise bars. "As soon as we get to the bottom of this I want you to fire her even if she is not responsible...I'll have an accountant fly from Medellin to take over the books." All my life I hated to be in positions that required firing people...I found great joy in hiring, but shrank back from getting rid of any employees. At least it wasn't I who had offered her the job in the first place.

"How do we deal with Julio if he is proven guilty?"

I as genuinely concerned about the young family. I liked them. "Simple, we ask him to pay it back...obviously he doesn't have that amount in cash, and even if he did pay it back, he's still a guilty party and will be dealt with according to the rules when he arrives in Colombia." I understood what Alvaro meant by "the rules" but, "what if he decides to stay in the USA...? I asked."

"Then his funeral will be American and not Colombian!"

There was no need for more questions..."God, please help him," I muttered silently.

4

MARCH 1983

T he rest of the day Alvaro spent in briefing me on the status of salaries, everybody's job description and future plans.

"Tomorrow," he said, "you'll meet a man by the name of Burt Gordon. Burt is a veteran pilot who joined Lehder back in 1968, and flew the first loads in to Norman's Cay with Ramon and Gaviota. He seldom flies loads, but he will fly you anywhere at any time. His residence is in Port-au-Prince in Haiti, but he often comes to Florida to spend time with his mother in North Miami Beach. Here are his phone numbers both in Haiti and in the USA I suggest you make a code from now on for all the names and phone numbers." Alvaro took a wrinkled piece of paper from his wallet and handed it to me. In the middle of the small page appeared the following letters and numbers:

MURCIELAGO

1234567890

The word *murciélago* means 'bat' as in the nocturnal

mammal, and it had no reflection on the meaning of the code. Its letters and numbers were for me to replace those existing in real names and phone numbers. For example, if my phone number was 555-3279, I would record it in my records as III-RULG. I also used the reverse method to code words with numbers. For example; Carlos would be recorded as 483705.

"Burt has a friend in St. Louis, Missouri who owns a ranch on top of a mountain in the middle of nowhere," Alvaro began to explain. "Burt and I believe that we can buy a long range airplane and fly all the way from Colombia to Missouri without having to make a pit stop to refuel; besides, a Titan can accommodate about 600 kilos each trip. Can you imagine all the money we could save by avoiding a landing in the Bahamas?"

I agreed; earlier that day Alvaro had given me an insight into the cost of an operation of that kind, making stops either in the Bahamas, the Cayman Islands, Cuba or Nicaragua. We were talking in the neighborhood of one million dollars in overhead expenses that could be avoided by making one single non-stop flight into the United States. I had no expertise to determine whether the mountain top ranch could be technically suitable; that is why Burt Gordon was vital in making those recommendations.

"Why don't you join me with Burt?" I suggested, "I am sure both of us can contribute our different views once we check the place out."

"I guess you're right...can you take care of commercial flights?" Alvaro asked me.

"I thought we were going to fly our own plane" I protested.

"It would be faster to go there by commercial flights than by means of a much slower private turbo-prop." He made a good point, and, besides, it would not be smart to give exposure to our airplanes if we were to become 'regulars' on the Missouri mountains.

I left the house and went to a travel agency on Glades Road to purchase return tickets to St. Louis Missouri, via Atlanta, for three men by the names of Bruce Harrison, Steve McMallon, and Joseph Marciano.

Early the next morning, I packed my weekender with the few warm clothes I possessed, in preparation for a Missouri ranch. After picking up Alvaro, we drove to a parking lot of Southeast Bank on Commercial Boulevard where Burt Gordon had previously agreed to meet with us.

Burt Gordon, a six-foot plus thin man in his late forties or early fifties, waited by the parking lot inside his late model Cadillac. He left the vehicle when he recognized us as we drove in. Burt had one of those faces most people like at first sight. He was distinguished looking yet warmly courteous and I immediately felt very comfortable in his company.

He was dressed smartly in a light two piece cotton suit with a coordinated polka dot tie over a very white custom made shirt.

"Mr. Gordon?" I asked him as I got out of my car.

"Good morning, you must be Richard," said Gordon offering his hand.

"Yes, I am, and Archie will be coming with us too,...how do you do Mr. Gordon?" I accepted his hand with a brief shake.

"Call me Burt, please."

"Of course Burt!" I said with appreciation.

"Well, although we are here in Fort Lauderdale, we're going to drive to Miami for our flight." I advised Burt who already had a flight plan traced to Missouri in our company's plane.

"Hi Burt," were the only two words Archie knew in English, so he couldn't enter into our conversation. Unless he wanted me to convey something to Burt, Alvaro just listened to us without comment. We decided to leave Archie's Cressida and my station wagon behind and have Burt drive us in his Cadillac. I remembered I had to return the station wagon to All Nation upon return from this trip, so I made a mental note to ask Alvaro for money to buy my own wheels the first chance I had.

During the drive to Dade County, Burt and I talked casually.

He shared with me how he and Lehder met some fifteen years back in the Bahamas at time; when Robert Vesco had left the United States running from criminal indictments.

'How long have you known Carlos Lehder?' asked Burt.

"Oh, all my life. We became especially close about the time his parents separated and divorced, when Carlos was only eleven."[1]

"You must really know what makes him tick," implied Burt with curiosity.

"Well, let me tell you."

Burt listened avidly as I unfolded the story about the young Carlos Lehder nobody knew.

"He must have been about twelve or thirteen. Carlos, Federico, Guillermo and Elizabeth knew that their parents were having serious problems. I remember them sitting in our living room sobbing, and asking my father for answers he couldn't give them. When the family split up, Federico and Guillermo decided to remain with their father in Armenia. Carlos also agreed to stay in Armenia temporarily while Elena, his mother, looked for a place to live in Honduras.

She had been invited by that country's ambassador to present her works of art in a local museum there. My mother welcomed all the Lehder children as her own, and soon after Elena's departure the other children felt at home with us. But not Carlos. He was always a rebel. He refused to abide by the basic disciplines of my parents, and although he was only a twelve-year-old child he could disappear for days. My mother couldn't cope with his behavior and finally told Mr. Lehder he'd have to make other arrangements.

I would keep running into Carlos every three or four weeks and we'd pick up where we left off. Since our Jesuit school could no longer tolerate his restless and independent ways he seemed to be left entirely to his own devices. Of course I admired this free spirit—this survivor—and was too young to realize the trauma which might be at the root of his personality.

By the time Carlos was fourteen he showed me his passport, a visa to the United States and the few dollars he was taking with him to make his way in New York. I could not believe he would actually carry out such a brash scheme.

Six months later I received a letter from New York persuading me to join him in Queens."

"What are you saying ?" Alvaro would ask every now and then wanting to-be part of our absorbing discussion.

Burt drove inside the short term parking lot since he expected to be back within the next twenty-four hours.

I told him I didn't foresee a reason why we shouldn't be returning the following day. We walked to the Eastern terminal and with the convenience of having no luggage at all to be checked, we went straight to the gate for the first portion of our trip to Atlanta. I handed Burt the ticket with the name Steve Me Mallon, gave Alvaro the one with Joseph Marciano and kept the one with Bruce Harrison for myself.

There was no need to explain to Burt, who seemed to expect to fly under a fake name.

"We have almost two hours in Atlanta before we take the Ozark flight to St. Louis. When we get there let's do a little shopping for winter clothes," said Archie wanting me to translate to Burt.

"How cold is it in Missouri this time of the year Burt?" I asked. "It's pretty cold, and more so where we are heading."

"OK," I said, "Archie suggested we buy some clothes to keep us warm while up there."

"I know a shop not far from the airport in Atlanta, where we can get some thick jackets." It was obvious Burt was a knowledgeable world traveler and could smoothly solve many problems. Just a minute before our flight was announced, Alvaro called me to the men's room and summoned me to a toilet cubicle.

"Is that necessary?" I complained, "They're gonna think we're gay!" I pointed towards other men at the urinals, but followed him meekly.

"Here" he handed me a bundle of hundred dollar bills from his briefcase. "Give Burt five thousand, and take five thousand for yourself... expense money!"

I quickly counted the two amounts and put them inside separate envelopes and sealed them.

Luckily when we left the cubicle no on was in the men's room to make jeering comments.

I waited until we were inside the airplane to give Burt his own envelope.

We were the only three passengers in First Class and had all the privacy we wanted.

Burt leaned over to my ear and said, "How much here?"

"Five," I whispered..."It's just for your expenses."

He smiled. "Archie fell asleep!" said Burt pointing to

Alvaro who rested his head against the window one aisle across from us .

The stewardess brought us fresh croissants, a basket of fresh fruits and two Virgin Mary's.

Burt and I enjoyed our conversation and had a wonderful flight to the city of Atlanta. Alvaro slept the duration of the flight — ninety minutes.

In Atlanta, we took a taxi to a boutique located inside one of the luxury hotels not far from the main terminal. "Mr. Gordon, what brings you to Atlanta this time?" asked the good-looking blonde in her mid forties from behind a small lacquer desk in one side of the shop.

"Hi, Joyce, we need some good winter jackets for my two associates here and myself."

"Hi Joyce, I am Bruce Harrison," I volunteered.

Alvaro just smiled. Thank God!

"Well, I just got a shipment of beautiful pure leather 'Members Only' winter wear...would you like to look at it?"

"Please" responded Burt.

We all followed Joyce to an 'L' shaped section of the store where the men's clothing was on display. Expensive Italian tailored suits, Brazilian leather shoes and fancy accessories were part of her men's wear collection.

I ran my hands over the fine soft leather jackets until I found what I wanted. A waist length 'Members Only,' brown sport jacket with a detachable quilt interior. The price tag was $275.00. Burt went for a tweed short coat and Alvaro decided on a jacket just like mine but in black. We all paid separately in cash. Joyce thanked us for our patronage and we went back to the taxi driver, who was taking a short snooze, with a baseball cap over his eyes.

Wearing our new fashions, we approached the gate to Ozark's flight 165 to fly us to our final destination of the day.

None of us had previously flown on Ozark Airlines, and we were impressed by the outstanding service and fine meal they had for the first class passengers.

I had the lucky opportunity to sit next to a very attractive female attorney from Tucson. Arizona, who shared with me her stories about fights against Washington lobbyists for the rights of Indian Tribe settlements in * her state. Her fervent devotion to that cause impressed me so much that to this day I follow the topic with interest and sympathy.

Alvaro and Burt sat across the aisle, their only means of communication was a very loud and frequent 'Cheers' every time they raised their glasses to what they called..."Our last one before landing."

Jan, the attorney, gave me her card..."In case you're in Tucson, give me a call." I told her my name was Bruce and I was going to St. Louis to visit a friend who was very ill.

Once inside the terminal in St. Louis, Jan and I went our opposite ways. I knew I'd never see her again.

Burt and Alvaro looked very merry, so I decided to ask them to wait for me right next to a lounge where The Spirit of St. Louis hung suspended in the air while I went to take care of the car rental.

Since Burt was a very tall man, and the only one who knew, where we were going, I rented a full size Lincoln Continental for him to drive. He seemed in good enough shape, even though Alvaro insisted, "Let's have the last one" just before we left the airport.

The Sheraton had reservations waiting for us and we had agreed to meet at the hotel's restaurant for dinner at eight later that evening.

The temperature in St. Louis was in the low forties with winds that made it even colder.

In the morning, we were soon out of St. Louis, heading

south towards a small town named Sullivan. From there we kept on driving through mountains of thick wooded areas to a village called Cuba where a couple of 'Red Necks'... the Broiles brothers, waited for us at the local motel.

"How in the world did you meet these people?" I asked Burt.

"They are mountain men. One day I sat on State Road 50 waiting to be rescued by the AAA, for not having a spare tire, and they turned out to be the owners of the only gas station in this remote area." Alvaro and I listened with interest. "The two men were not only helpful getting me a new tire and fixing my car, but asked me to join them for lunch after I told them I hadn't been able to find a restaurant nearby. They took me to their farm and I shared a delicious meal with their families."

Every now and then Burt would stop telling his story to refresh his memory and both Alvaro and I would encourage him to continue his anecdote.

"I spent hours at their house. They told me fascinating stories of the people who live in these mountains. We went on into the night sharing our lives as well as a few bottles of 'moonshine'...the best home brew ever!! To make a long story short, I spent the night at the farm and in the morning just before leaving I discovered a flat solid strip of land a few yards away from the stables. It was weeded but it measured at least 2500 feet. I reversed my car to the house and asked them if they would be interested in leasing me that piece of land. "You can have it...but nothing grows there...only rocks and dirt!"

The rest was history. Burt had left them $1,000.00 to have the strip cleaned and leveled, but Burt never went back to the Broiles brothers because he never had to. Those were the days when Carlos Lehder purchased an island in the

Bahamas and importing cocaine to the States became a piece of cake.

The motel door opened as the Broiles heard the sound of our automobile outside their room. The two men looked like identical twins. The tops of their heads were shiny bald, and from the back of their necks fell greasy curls down to their shoulders. Both men were in their fifties, thin and tall and wearing faded blue jeans and cowboy boots. It was only when they smiled to say hello that we discovered the only thing that made them different...one of them had no teeth whatsoever!

"Burt, tell them to hurry up; we want to be back in Florida tomorrow!" Archie was anxious bo see the mountain top land, and he urged Burt to put pressure on the twins.

"We'll be leaving shortly," replied Burt.

We all squeezed into the rented car and started our long climb into the mountains. Archie fell asleep in the rear seat and Burt kept on talking to the Broiles brothers. It was a conversation only he could understand since their mountain accent was foreign to me. I drove for four and a half hours following the directions I was given. The mountains rose spectacularly around me, but the steep narrow passage kept me from enjoying the scenery. Finally Burt asked me to slow down.

"Watch for an entrance with an iron gate along the side of the road, and just drive in."

The gate was only a few yards away, and I did as I was instructed. The big Lincoln could hardly fit through the iron poles, and the road ahead was not made for that kind of vehicle.

"Don't worry about the car," said Archie as he noticed my concern that it could suffer some damage, "it's a rental " I kept on going over rocks, holes and weeds, at times scratching the sides of the car where branches of trees blocked the way. When I reached the top of the hill the road came to an end. Tall trees were in front and not even a four wheel drive could have continued.

"Well, this where we walk}" We all turned around as one of the Broiles brothers spoke.

Quickly, and hoping to be led in the right direction, we left the car and followed the men through a path of dirt, mud and bushes.

"This is not the way we came a few years ago!" complained Burt.

"Mr. Gordon, this is just a short cut to the landing strip" replied one of the brothers.

We pushed another half mile into the woods until finally we came to an open plateau. It was not as big as I had expected.

"This is it," said one of the twins with a toothless grin.

Burt, Archie and I looked at each other in aghast silence.

Whatever happened to the nice place I paid you to take care of?" Burt broke in harshly...This place looks different!"

I knew very little about landing strips, but any poor estimate could easily see that there was no possible way for an airplane to land there. The ground was overgrown with weeds, and its length was too short. I could feel Archie's anger and disappointment.

"Tell Burt that he must be out of his mind if he expect us to land in this wilderness!" I passed the message to Burt but he just shrugged without comment. It was a silent and crestfallen journey back to the mountain.

I learned a lesson in not taking anything, even the optimistic report of a seasoned pilot, for granted. We all now had to share the responsibility of informing Carlos Lehder that this method of direct access to the United States was not feasible.

Upon our return to Florida I had my hands full moving my family to our beautiful new home in New Floresta, Boca Raton.

Our frustrating mission to Missouri was soon forgotten.

B efore the alarm went off on a beautiful spring morning, I was awakened by the ring of the phone next to our bed. It was Archie. He wanted to see me right away, and from the arrogant tone of his voice I prepared myself for a distasteful encounter. He can wait for me to shave and shower, I decided, though I hurried the procedure along

It was normally a pleasant drive from our house right off San Andrews Road and Glades to Palmetto Park Road, but this morning I was too preoccupied to notice the palm trees and the lush landscaping lining the way. As I approached Archie's entrance I pressed the button on the remote control to the Sears "Genie" that allowed me immediate access to the interior of the house through one of the garages; this avoided delays outside the house, and undue exposure to nosey neighbors.

Inside the house, I crossed the kitchen into a hall that led to Archie's bedroom on the first floor of the house, in the exclusive neighborhood of Captiva, Boca Raton, Florida.

The bulky, half naked, mass of human being was seated

on the king size bed, carefully oiling his .45 caliber pistol, while on his television set an X-rated movie featuring two lesbians played to an invisible audience. As I walked inside, he smiled falsely and raised the pistol towards me as if posing for a "Macho del año" magazine. His attempt to look very masculine and tough succeeded. "I spoke to Joe last night, Carlitos," he said, followed by a "Bang, Bang" noise from his mouth.

"I want you to go and meet a man by the name of Ed Goldberg. Mr. Goldberg has a fine reputation and is recognized as having vast experience in smuggling 'marimba' and Coke." As he entered into the description of Mr. Goldberg, Archie's face twitched nervously. "Goldberg claims to have retired from the business, but Joe managed to convince him to see you and to be our consultant. We want you to bring him back and put him on your payroll, whatever the cost."

Having to meet such a notorious stranger in Florida, USA, the capitol of drug smuggling, was not something I had dreamed of in my childhood. Yet here I was: so deeply involved there was no way to refuse this piggish man's bidding. And I needed a successful mission to build my reputation after the Missouri fiasco.

In many cases, individuals who have been arrested recently pose as active,"clean" drug smugglers as part of their plea bargain agreement with the District Attorney's office to avoid long prison terms. Their job is to bring drug dealers to the negotiation table and to acquaint undercover agents with the Colombians so the agents can infiltrate illegal operations. I was afraid Goldberg was one of those turncoats. Why else would a wealthy man like Goldberg, who had indicated he had already retired from the business, meet with us? My mind raced; I needed reassurance if I was to meet this man.

"Wait a second!" I complained, "you must be out of your mind to believe that I would meet a total stranger to discuss cocaine business!" My tone of voice was getting louder as my nervousness grew.

"Shut your fucking mouth and just listen," said Archie, getting up from his bed. "Goldberg is a millionaire with ruthless ambition...I'm sorry...listen Carlitos, I am sure Joe has checked this man inside out and he cleared."

"Why don't you go and meet him yourself if you're so confident, you fat shit!" I was so furious by this time I forgot the proximity of Archie's gun.

"Well — simple...I don't speak English."

I couldn't argue with that, so I had no choice but to go and take the risk. At least Joe, not Archie, was master-minding the encounter. Archie tried to placate me as he suggested that I take Cristina along to meet with the Goldbergs, and from there enjoy a jaunt to the Bahamas while Ed and I conducted our business.

Once back at home I decided to make a few phone calls on my own, based on the information I was given about Goldberg. I called directory assistance and his number was unlisted, but that only meant smart. No one in the drug business puts his number in the phone book. Secondly I phoned the Chub Cay Yacht Club in the Bahamas to ensure he was the president in charge as well as its owner.

Both my inquiries were confirmed. I felt better I By the time I had made my phone calls, Cristina was up and out of the shower and ready for the new day. Our two year old daughter slept peacefully in her bedroom, totally unconcerned with her daddy's worries. Cristina looked relaxed from a good night's rest but as much as I wanted to make love to her that very minute, my mind told me I had limited time for sex.

Lately our relationship had been going through a series of radical changes, due to my continuous traveling abroad. I knew she deserved more attention and I felt guilty for my neglect and preoccupation. I wished she understood the pressures I faced. She dressed quickly as I informed her of our plans to travel to the Bahamas. We had to wake Lisa so she could stay with her grandmother until we returned from our short trip.

Cristina pulled on slacks that fit her just perfectly, outlining that sensuous figure that always drove me nuts. Her hair was short and with a quick comb-through it fell into place. It took only forty-five minutes to drop Lisa off in Davie.

It would not be wise to be late to the Howard Johnson's in Pompano, in case Mr. Goldberg and his wife were already awaiting us.

The Howard Johnson's on Federal Highway was situated on a corner just across the street from the Pompano airport. We were there in plenty of time to order breakfast, and as Cristina and I ate our way through scrambled eggs, home fries and sausage, we commented about the gorgeous day ahead of us. The sun was bright and the light began to filter through the window next to our table. It was nearly May, but it felt like late July. Our small talk covered up the anxiety we both shared, waiting for Mr. Goldberg.

We only had a sketchy portrayal given over the phone of the color of his car and his approximate age.

We knew our destination was to be the Bahamas, but it still remained a mystery which of the many islands. This did not bother us, since heavy precautions in a high risk venture are standard.

The Goldbergs arrived in their 1984 Dodge Le Baron convertible, just as it was described to me. It was obvious

Goldberg had also been given a description of us, since he very casually walked into the restaurant and sat right down at our table. After a very cordial good morning with a firm hand shake, and smiling, he started conversing between bites of his own scrambled eggs, as if we were friends of long standing...I was impressed with Ed.

He was well dressed in a sporty but classic Polo shirt and pants, but more importantly he gave an impression of a well educated, polite and most charming gentleman.

Peggy, his wife, was perhaps twelve years younger than Ed, in her late twenties or early thirties. Her personality was very likable and the tone of her voice so high that it sounded childish, amusing and cute.

Ed went on to explain his position straight forwardly,

"Listen Richard, I have no idea who your boss is...you don't have to tell me. I am here to take you to my island so you can look and see if something there is of interest to you." He paused for a few eternal seconds, "However, just remember, I never met you, and you have never seen my face nor my wife's ...understood?"

"Understood, Ed," I told him, "I like your style, and I am looking forward to spending a very comfortable day with you and your family."

As we ordered more coffee, Ed visibly relaxed. Peggy and Cristina were chatting amiably. Ed had expected to have met a more Colombian profile in me. He confessed his stereotype of a rough looking Hispanic with dark complexion, a mustache and of course a poncho! I was wearing a light sport suit and my appearance is definitely Anglo. We were enjoying our compatibility of characters, and although we'd just met, we both felt like old buddies within minutes.

Seemingly heedless of other diners, Ed wove colorful tales of his adventures as a drug smuggler out of Jamaica,

Haiti, Colombia and the Bahamas. One familiar story is documented in the archives of Barranquilla, Colombia. Ed Goldberg single-handedly flew to that city to rescue his son who had been caught trying to fly out in a plane loaded with marijuana. Ed did not succeed just by bribing the Colombian authorities, but by physically breaking into the prison where his son was incarcerated. After a short daring gun battle, he had his son over the coast of Colombia and flying home free to the United States. Needless to say, the publicity of such an event caught the attention of the media, and soon the name Goldberg became known as a folk hero. The Colombian Cartel began to seek after him for help in the drug trade. Their promises of great wealth were impossible to refuse.

It was then that Carlos Lehder heard about Ed, checked his credentials and ordered Archie to set up this breakfast meeting. Since Goldberg needed neither money nor work, he made Plain from the beginning of our conversation that he would welcome my friendship but would turn the other way if he were to witness any illegal activity. "I will help you set up your operation... but I have no interest in taking a direct part in it."

We all left the restaurant and drove straight to the airport in Ed's car, leaving my car parked at Howard Johnson's. In a matter of a few minutes we were in front of a private hangar, and Ed got out of the car to pull open the wide door that unveiled his personal 1980 Aerostar twin engine airplane. Beige with a brown accent stripe from nose to tail, the plane looked beautiful. Ed was definitely very proud of his toy. "This baby will get us there in no time," he spoke as he ran a rag over its nose to remove a thin film of dust accumulated overnight. We all volunteered to push the airplane out of the hangar into the open air, and once the door closed behind us, we climbed into our seats. Ed and I were at the front, with Cristina and Peggy respectively behind us. Ed pointed to the headset by the co-pilot*s seat so I could wear it and listen to the communications from the control tower. After a few minutes of warming the Aerostar's engines, clearance came loud and clear for our taxiing onto the runway. The Aerostar was in immaculate condition inside. The only evidence of a decade of use were a few of the armrests; everything else about the plane seemed up-to-date and well maintained.

In spite of Ed's vast expertise and experience in flying all kinds of private airplanes, he surreptitiously wiped a little nervous perspiration from his face.

"You don't look so well...are you all right?" I asked him with hesitation.

"He is fine," answered Peggy from behind, "he always gets a bit nervous every time he flies. I'm the one who's not doing so well. I hate flying; normally we take "Easy Street." Flying is a terrifying experience for me."

I turned around to respond to Peggy and saw a frightened woman holding tight to Cristina's arm as if it were her first time ever on an airplane. Later on Ed told us how afraid she was of flying in spite of all the many times they had flown together.

"It gets worse by the minute," he said, "it is an incurable phobia." The waiting in-line for take-off was minimal, and the Aerostar took off with incredible ease leaving behind a bright postcard of the city of Fort Lauderdale under our wings. In a few seconds we were flying over the coastline of Florida due east to Freeport and then to Chub Cay.

Our landing on the island was smooth and Peggy's face regained its natural color once the wheels of the Aerostar touched down. Ed taxied close to a small hut bearing a faded wooden sign on its roof that read "Customs." As we came to a halt, Ed advised us to have our documents ready. All we needed was proof of American citizenship in order to comply with Bahamian authorities, and be granted a tourist card, which entitled us to remain temporarily on the island. When the engines died, we left the aircraft and walked to the Customs house, where a couple of uniformed police officers cheerfully welcomed Ed and his guests. I was impressed with the way the Bahamians treated Ed Goldberg... no one requested identification from us; his presence was enough for the guards to issue the respective documents. Right outside Customs, an old van waited for us and two native men deferentially helped the ladies on board. The ride through palm trees along blue waters was very brief in spite of the bumps in the dirt road that led to our destination. The van pulled next to a row of yachts' and came to a final stop. An unkempt old man who resembled Hemingway, opened his arms and from a distance shouted: "Welcome to Easy Street."

Easy Street's late model luxury 120 foot yacht shone among older yachts and smaller pleasure boats docked near the same pier. With a cabin of fiber glass, the luxurious Chris Craft was another toy in the list of Ed's collection of expensive assets. A fleet of four Suzuki motorcycles was parked next to the yacht, for transportation to the island and for the pleasure and recreation of his guests.

"Hi Uncle George," responded Ed to the friendly man with the white beard. We followed Ed and Uncle George on board Easy Street where a lunch of native fish, tropical fruit and a few cocktails made us feel like carefree jet setters.

Chub Cay is one of the Berry Islands in a series of small cays just north of Andros and New Providence. The population of Chub Cay is transitory since most of its inhabitants are American tourists and rich foreign families with hold-ings in the island. The native population totals perhaps 85. The island's main attraction is the Chub Cay Club offering scuba, tennis, swimming pool, a beach and all the fishing anyone could want.

Although Chub Cay is also a private club, it welcomes a limited number of nonmembers.

The reason for my visit was not the Chub Cay Yacht Club nor its beautiful waters, nor deep sea fishing. I was there on a mission. Thousands of kilos of cocaine waited in a remote section of the Amazonian jungle, and it was my duty to move them out of the country to avoid serious confrontations between my boss, Carlos Lehder, and the other families of the Colombian Cartel. We, the C.C.Q., were in charge of transportation for the Cartel and as of this day we were at least three thousand kilos behind schedule due to the blockade of Norman's Cay by American and Bahamian authorities. I had to find alternative routes to unload and refuel our airplanes. The pressure from Colombia was becoming unbearable and Archie had dropped the responsibility into my hands.

Goldberg did not want to be a direct party in any involvement in the event of accomplishing something together through Chub Cay. He was willing to introduce me to the right people, but it was up to me to put together the necessary ingredients and to negotiate the loose ends without his taking part. His reputation in the Island was to be respected and protected, although, he would get a substantial sum of money if I succeeded in putting through a deal. All he had to do was "turn his back and keep quiet."

Peggy and Cristina relaxed by the bar enjoying some cool drinks while Ed and I sat with Uncle George on the open deck.

"Uncle George...please go out into the island and find Chief of Police Johnson and also look for Brian," instructed Ed, "tell them we have someone I want them to meet...don't be obvious, but give them a hint of the nature of our plan so they'll hurry coming here."

"Be back in twenty minutes," replied uncle George getting up from the canvas chair and mounting one of the motorcycles outside the yacht.

Once uncle George was out of sight, Ed pulled his chair closer to mine in an effort to have a very secret almost whispered conversation.

"Let me give you some advice about my people here," he said slowly, choosing his words carefully.

"Brian is a young Bahamian boy, probably not twenty years old yet. I care very much for the kid, we've both come a long way together and he is trustworthy. Brian is adventurous and likes money. He is very mature for his age and he is the man you can rely on here to bribe customs and immigration." He paused looking up to the sky as if for inspiration. I just listened intently, as I saw how serious he was.

"I do not want any Latins or Colombians on my island," he ordered. "Should you be able to put something together, it will be YOU in charge and the locals here." He expressed that sentiment very clear, by pointing his finger at my face.

I understood his concern and shared his reservations. In the past few years Colombians had created a very negative image in the islands, and every time a Colombian was spotted in a small island like Chub Cay, he was immediately suspected as a trafficker up to no good.

"You are entirely right Ed, and I assure you that I, and only I, will supervise and control this operation with the help of your people."

"Good," said Ed with relief on his face.

Deep inside I knew that Archie would want me to put our own men in Chub Cay for radio communications and for rehearsals before the actual plan went into effect, but I was prepared to go directly to Lehder, if need be, to avoid difficult confrontations. Anyway, this was my show and I was going to call the shots — no matter what!

"Let me take you on a tour of Chub Cay" suggested Ed pointedly. "By the time we get back George should have some news for us."

"I'm ready" getting up from my chair and gladly breaking the tension of our discussion.

We advised our wives that we were going for a few minutes, they were so deep in conversation that our words were totally ignored.

Riding the motorcycles we set off to a location Ed obviously wanted very much to show me. I followed him as he took me along a dirt road to a house near the airport a few yards from the beach. The house was deserted and hidden from the road by tall palm trees. A one story brick construction with wide glass windows leading to a wood deck just above the water, it was what he called "my personal retreat."

"I own this house in partnership with a man from New England who only comes here for a few weeks each January." It was the ideal place for a get away from civilization. The interior was tastefully decorated with pastel colors, functional furniture, a wet bar and all the appliances of today's modern living.

"I recommend this house in the event you have to get your pilots to a safe place should anything go sour. From here you can arrange for a speed boat to whisk them out of danger."

It sounded perfect, but my mind was trying to evaluate

how much I should offer Ed for all his tools if I managed to put my plan into action.

I left Ed at the dock while I walked the perimeter of the house, imagining the scenario of a police raid on our airplane and thinking of my safety and route of escape by measuring in my mind the distance between the airport and the house.

There was a sacred order of priorities ordered by Carlos Lehder in the event of trouble with local police or Federal Agents:

> *(1) Save the pilots.*
> *(2) Save the load.*
> *(3) Save the airplane.*
> *(4) Save yourself.*

I personally put #4 as priority #l, but that was a secret I kept to myself.

I returned to the house after a quick inspection of the grounds and found Ed already heading for the motorcycles. "I like what I have seen so far," I confessed. "Let's hope Mr. Johnson and Brian are agreeable to my requests."

"They're good people, Richard," said Ed with confidence.

"Let's go back to the airport strip. Can we?"

"As a matter of fact this is the perfect time to go there," said Ed, "because the Customs officers close the airport to air traffic for a whole hour for lunch break." The time was one thirty p.m. Indeed the airport looked deserted and the Customs house was closed. No airplanes were allowed to land in Chub Cay for that hour .

We drove the motor bikes all the way to the end of the air strip and I was satisfied with its length, which measured more than two-thousand feet according to my conservative estimate. I knew I could have my men land our airplane from Colombia with just enough room for a safe touch down. The problem that first came to my mind was refueling. I took Polaroid pictures of every detail that could be vital to determine the "go ahead" of such an operation, but there were many obstacles yet to be solved before I made a decision to hire any personnel. I made some brief notes regarding the house near the airport and the lunch hour of the officers, both of which I thought were significant elements to keep in mind.

Ed watched from a distance as I got off my motorcycle to inspect the thickness of the air strip and the tolerance we would have in case we had to dynamite the whole air strip. This extreme measure would be necessary should Coast Guard or DEA planes attempt a landing in pursuit of our cargo. It would be the only way to gain sufficient time to evacuate the island and get our men to a safe location.

"We'd better get going, Richard, I don't want people to see us here asking all kinds of questions."

"I am sorry Ed, I guess I got carried away."

"No problem...Let's go," he said.

We returned to Easy Street and the sight of Uncle George's motorcycle was a message that he had come back, hopefully with good news. As we boarded the yacht, I noticed Uncle George sitting next to a huge, black Bahamian who looked like Idi Amin, and next to him a teenager I presumed to be Brian. Ed stretched his arm to greet Mr. Johnson and introduced me without giving much importance to the younger man.

"Mr. Johnson, this is Richard-a good friend of mine from Colombia; but not to worry, he is an American Citizen and no one knows he is on the island." I was surprised by all the explaining he had to do, however, I approached the big gorilla and shook his sweaty hand. "Hello Mr. Johnson, I am very pleased to meet you sir."

"Likewise" he responded, not getting up, but sliding his huge 45 caliber pistol to the other side of his belt so it wouldn't pinch his disproportioned figure.

I proffered my hand to greet Brian, since Ed seemed to have forgotten to introduce us. Very politely the young Bahamian stood up and in a polished British accent said: "It is a pleasure sir."

Uncle George went to the sliding door leading to the cabin and made sure it was closed, shutting out Cristina from the reach of our voices.

"Mr. Johnson, Richard works for a corporation that I guarantee is professional and serious," Ed started his presentation as he paced back and forth on the open deck. "They need to make one or maybe two drops of about 550 kilos each, one right after the other...and that's it. I've told Richard about your quality of work and he is aware that you are expensive, but before we get into details I need to know if you and your people are interested in making some extra cash in, let's say... two weeks." I admired the coolness and the persuasiveness of Ed's words, and could see the respect and admiration with which the Chief of Police listened.

"What kind of plane do you have, Richard?" asked Mr. Johnson, looking straight into my eyes.

"Well, I always operate with Rockwell Turbos because of their range and spread; besides it gives us more interior room for the load...is that any problem?"

"The only problem is that Turbos are very noisy, and since no Turbos land on this island at all, the local people will get curious and may even go to the airport to see what's happening." His logic was good and I pondered the obstacle he brought up. "Mr. Johnson, with all due respect, I would like to come to an understanding with you of how much this is going to cost me before I reveal more about my equipment," I hedged, feeling slightly uncomfortable.

"Well, this is going to require the participation of all my men in the island and they all want some decent money..."

"Wait," I interrupted, "I do not want a breakdown of details of what you have to do; just give me a flat figure and your word that I and my men, as well as my load and airplane, will have all the necessary protection. Then the rest we'll discuss later." There were, long seconds of silence before he replied.

"Because you are a close friend of Mr. Goldberg, I am willing to drop my fee to a minimal...$80,000.00, and I'll take care of my men." I was aware that Ed, Uncle George and Brian were watching my reaction closely.

"That amount is no problem," I told Johnson, "but let's talk about how it is going to happen before we make it official... What is your plan?"

"How long does your Turbo take from its destination in Colombia to this island?" Johnson asked me.

"Roughly about seven hours," I told him.

"Well, have your pilot take off from Colombia around three in the afternoon so we'll be ready to welcome him around ten p.m." said Johnson decisively.

"You must be crazy, Mr. Johnson, as I understand your airport closes at six thirty p.m. How are you going to justify a plane landing at ten p.m. when most of the natives are asleep and our airplane is one of the noisiest made by Rockwell? No way, sir."

I continued, "It has to be done at the time your Customs men take an hour for lunch in the afternoon. That would give us just enough time to unload, hide the cocaine, refuel and get the hell out of here before they return to their posts." The scraps of information I had noted were already proving useful and adding to my authority.

"I can distract them so they take longer returning to the airport," said Brian with excitement. "I can invite them to lunch at the Club, that way it takes about twenty minutes just to get served before they start eating... besides they always stop at their houses to see their families before heading back to the airport."

"Wait a minute, wait just a fucking minute," shouted the huge police chief. "You seem to forget I am in charge of my men on this island," he said glaring at Brian.

"Take it easy Mr. Johnson," intercepted Ed, "I believe Richard's plan is safer than having to land a big plane in the middle of the night when nobody expects it."

I realized Mr. Johnson's reaction was not a result of my proposition, but a childish outburst of anger at our over-riding his control.

"Another thing Mr. Johnson," I told him, "I do not operate without a plan 'B,' and I must inform you that I have already chosen Whale Cay as an alternate place to drop my plane in case something goes wrong before landing in Chub Cay."

Whale Cay is an island one quarter of a mile west of Chub Cay with a short landing strip, but it could be used to save my pilots in case of an emergency. The little island was uninhabited and I needed a boat sitting nearby in any event.

"No problem, I can have a speed boat circling around looking for your plane in case it needs to land there."

"Wonderful" I told him..."There is however, the biggest obstacle not yet solved!"

"And what is that?" asked the Chief of Police.

"Jet fuel," I answered flatly. "I need at least 500 gallons of juice for my plane to get back to Colombia in one shot."

"You are right, Richard," said the big man, "that is a major problem, because no one on these islands uses jet fuel. Most people fly propellers. If I try to purchase jet fuel from Nassau or Freeport, I'd be raising suspicion."

"I could try telling my people in Colombia not to put many kilos in the plane, so we'll have a longer range to drop off and maybe could fly to Eleuthera to refuel..but I doubt my boss would go for that."

"I understand your point, Richard," said Ed. "Why don't we leave it at that for now? I think in principle the plan is feasible if we can bring in the plane at the lunch break," he paused. "By the way," he went on, "I have taken Richard to my retreat house near the airport where we can hide the cocaine overnight until his American plane comes to pick it up the following noon and take it to the States."

"It sounds perfect," agreed Mr. Johnson.

"OK gentlemen," I said, getting up from my chair and extending my hand to dismiss both Mr. Johnson and Brian. "I will be back in Chub Cay next week and by then I should have a solution for the Jet Fuel situation. If I manage to get all my needs fulfilled, I will bring you $40,000.00 in cash, and the balance upon completing a successful operation."

"That sounds dandy to me," said the big black man smiling and shaking my hand.

Once they both had left, Ed an I joined our wives without mentioning a word to them of what had transpired outside those glass doors.

We dined inside Easy Street. Goldberg and Peggy proudly showed us an array of antique China sets they had bought in Spain, plus other collectables of fine taste and historical value.

I insisted on flying back to the United States that same evening. Lisa was waiting at my mother-in-law's, and further international drug business would just have to defer to my two year old child. Uncle George drove us to the empty airport and shortly after warming up its engines the Aerostar took off on a direct course to Fort Lauderdale International Airport.

Peggy again closed her eyes and held tight to Cristina's arm as Ed kept cruising smoothly northwest. Twenty minutes into the flight Ed contacted Fort Lauderdale's control tower to get an update on the weather.

"Fifty-four mile winds N.E. with heavy showers and hail." Thank God only Ed and I heard the report through the headsets, otherwise I was sure Peggy would have gone into a coma. A few minutes later the weather report was proved accurate as strong winds and heavy rain started hitting the aircraft. The Aerostar began to shake like a toy plane in the fury of turbulence. When hail piled up on the side windows, Ed reached for the deicing button to avoid accumulation of frozen hail on the front wind shields. Again and again he pushed the knob that should have activated the system, but the ice kept accumulating until we lost view of the outside clouds and the windshield wipers died in the obstruction of the thick hail. Ed could no longer cover up his increasing panic.

"Fort Lauderdale...Fort Lauderdale ...this is Nancy Niner Niner four zero two miles northeast of Chub Cay over Alice Town requesting guide by instruments. Our deicing system has failed and our visibility is nil."

"We hear you Nancy Niner Niner four zero, keep same altitude and speed until further notice...do not change frequencies!"

Peggy turned waxen but thank God, was speechless. I

glanced at Cristina and I saw her courageously trying to hide her fear. I tightened my seat belt and silently said a prayer.

Perhaps God would hear me for Lisa's sake, if not my own.

Ed, with sweat running from his forehead, kept a continuous conversation with the Control Tower while I tried hard to divert Peggy's attention from the crisis by telling her stories I knew she wouldn't hear. The following seven minutes became an eternity.

At last the storm seemed to make a sharp turn and through a little crack on the ice covering the windshield we saw a touch of blue sky only a few clouds away. The heavy rain had ceased, and the warm temperature deiced the built up film of hail. Suddenly, we had left the black skies behind us and the coast of Fort Lauderdale shone ahead bringing us back to the peace that comes with survival. Fort Lauderdale International gave us immediate landing clearance after Ed radioed the identity of the Aerostar passengers by reporting to Immigration authorities the numbers of our passports and dates of birth. We landed smoothly and taxied straight to the private Aviation Customs building for their brief inspection of the aircraft's cargo area.

Once outside the airport, my wife and I hailed a taxi to take us back to Pompano to pick up our car, while Ed and Peggy stayed on to take care of matters related to their airplane maintenance. I promised Ed to keep him posted on my progress in putting the Chub Cay operation together.

After tucking Lisa in bed that same night, I summoned Colorado, who lived in Denver, and Gaviota from Medellin to fly to West Palm Beach and to meet me the following afternoon at Wildflower. I always kept at least twenty dollars in quarters in my car to make all my phone calls from payphones, thus avoiding a possibility of tracing. I had decided not to tell Archie about the meeting with both the American and the Colombian pilots, because I didn't want to put in jeopardy my plane in Chub Cay. If Archie intervened by appointing Colombian citizens to do the communications, protection and other important tasks on the Island, their presence could be disastrous. I intended to report to him early the following morning, show him the Polaroid pictures and even discuss my recommendations, but I would under no circumstances let him know that I intended to carry out the operation without Colombians. The time would come when I would have to break a cardinal rule, by contacting Lehder myself to advise him of my intentions. Both Gaviota and Colorado offered me their support and silence, but at the same time pressured me to rush the plan through before Archie could suspect our moves and cause serious problems for the three of us. I knew I needed the Colombian-based crew to collaborate[1] with me in case I appointed a Bahamian at the radio controls, but at that point it seemed like mission impossible since Lehder would probably refuse to let a foreigner take part in any phase of the Chub Cay plan.

If I could personally and successfully accomplish the importation of some 600 kilos of cocaine within the next two weeks. It would make Lehder look very good in front of his partners within the Cartel, and would easily give me "Carte Blanche." I was willing to work with Archie, but not under Archie. I had an underlying motive; perhaps the most ambitious of my desires. I wanted to show my esteemed friend Carlos Lehder that he had erred in not coming to me directly. By hiring me with lies and misrepresentations he had made a grave miscalculation, and it rankled me. If Carlos Lehder was prepared to deny the existence of Carlos in his organization, I was going to make very sure he was aware of my existence! And yet I'd promised Archie not to betray his confidence. All this furtiveness...but I could sense there might have to be a shattering of subterfuge if I were to obtain my goals for Chub Cay.

Early next morning, I found Archie in his bed sound asleep. I had entered the house through the garage by using the automatic opener he had given me. This concealed my car every time I went to see him by closing the door once I was inside.

I hesitated for a minute and finally decided to wake him up by knocking hard on his partially opened bedroom door. The reflexes of his massive body amazed me. In one smooth flash of action, he rolled over to the edge of his bed, let his body fall to the far end of the bedroom, and reappeared with a machine gun pointing at me. The thick mattress served as an arm rest for the heavy weapon.

"DON'T FIRE!!!" I yelled, "It's me. Itos . . . Carlos . . . your friend!" I threw myself to the floor hoping his brain would deliver the message to his firing arm in time.

"You scared the shit out of me!...Don't you believe in knocking?" he growled angrily.

"My God, you could have killed me and you still have the nerve to get mad?" I complained.

"When are you getting that maid from Colombia so she can wake you up, and run for her life every morning?...It was your idea that I should walk in at any time and rouse you, if I considered it important. THIS is important but as of now don't count on me to enter this house again unless you can arrange for a person without terminal paranoia to open the door."

"OK, don't make such a big deal out of that. As a matter of fact Maximiliano, my personal body guard and radio expert, is arriving from Colombia today along with Juliana. She'll take care of the house and keep our style of living more like a family for the sake of the neighbors... they'll see her in and out and we'll be looking like the next door All-American family: the wife, the man of the house...I might even buy a puppy and teach it to bark m English so our high class neighbors will see us as a new breed of Yuppies."

"You should be the one learning to bark in English" I muttered under my breath as I listened to his ridiculous idea.

"How did it go with Mr. Goldberg?" asked Alvaro, getting down to business.

"Great; I am very impressed with his connections on the island. He is a man of influence with the Chief of Police, and although Chub Cay is not the most appropriate place to land a load, I think we can squeeze in one or two if we play our cards right."

I went on to explain why I had reservations about the island based on the minimal time to get in, unload, hide the load, refuel and leave again during the brief closing of the airport, for the Customs lunch break. He listened attentively without interruption.

"The Chief of Police is definitely eating out of Goldberg's hand, so that puts us at a great advantage in the event of needing protection during evacuation."

I brought out my Polaroid pictures and proceeded to describe each in detail, making color markings of the precise location of each shot on a big map of Chub Cay. With the help of a stop watch I explained to Alvaro the approximate timings of the several routes and the alternatives we could take. I recommended Whale Cay as the perfect location for plan "B" and also suggested we use Goldberg's house to store the jet fuel and the cocaine. It would be a great asset in our favor, due to its proximity to the airport and easy access to a quick escape by boat. When I finished my presentation, he took the pictures, the map and some notes he had written and put them inside the top drawer of his desk. He first looked thoughtfully into my eyes and then by rotating his chair, looked out of the window. With his back to me, and after a few seconds of profound silence, he said: "Do you think you can put it together?"

I didn't reply; somehow I needed to see his face to answer that question. He, victim of my deafness to his question, swung the chair 180 degrees. '

"Well...can you do it?"

I was faced with a question that could have been answered in two ways. First, I could have said: "Yes...a piece of cake, call your men and let's be careful!" or "Archie, the only way I can do it is if you let me run this show on my own...I don't want your intervention!"

I went for the latter response.

"The power is going to your head you son of a bitch!...Get out of my house...You're finished. I hired you for your intelligence but you over estimated yourself, you motherfucker!"

I met his angry gaze. The man was in a rage but I did not fear his tone of voice nor his language and efforts to intimidate me. I knew how Alvaro Triana's mind functioned. He had not changed in ten years.

"Fair enough, Mr. Antonio Jimenez (I insultingly called him by his Venezuelan name). I'll leave now but we are not finished." He knew I was not a man of physical aggression, although I could hardly control an urge to break his face.

I left his house, agitated, but mindful of the meeting coming up with Gaviota from Colombia, and with Colorado from Denver. There were still two hours to our meeting, but

I went ahead of time to Wildflower to buy myself a double scotch on the rocks and to allow myself time to put the scene at Archie's behind me and calculate my next move.

I sat by the mezzanine to have ample view of the first floor and each patron who walked into the restaurant. Colorado appeared wearing jeans and a 'T' shirt. "I like to keep a low profile" he once told me referring not just to his style of dressing but also to the automobile he drove. Here was a man who had earned two million dollars in 1982 working for Lehder and yet drove a dented pick up truck and did not even wear a watch.

I waved and he acknowledged me with a nod, but instead of walking upstairs to meet me he wandered around the restaurant. I realized he was checking every face to make sure Wildflower was a safe place to have our conference.

Colorado was a man of few words, so it didn't surprise me when he sat down at my table without even saying hello.

"Thanks for coming," I spoke in a low tone.

Colorado had flown his own airplane for our meeting and I offered to compensate him for any related expenses.

"Let's order some food while we wait for Gaviota to join us," I continued my monologue..."his Lear Jet should be touching down any minute now at Boca's air strip just a few minutes away from the restaurant next to Florida University."

"I know the place" said Colorado, breaking his silence.

We were half way into our French Dip when. Gaviota joined us. His presence brought a refreshing tone to the sour atmosphere and without further ado we went to work.

"First of all I must advise you that Archie and I had a falling out a couple of hours ago, and I am not sure about the future of our relationship. However, I am going ahead with my plans as if nothing has happened."

"We all knew you guys would soon have serious problems," said Gaviota, "and that is why I didn't mind meeting you without his consent. Lehder knows I am meeting you since I had to justify the use of the Lear Jet."

"I never understand Lehder," I told Gaviota petulantly. "One day he orders Triana to hire me with a special emphasis on not letting me know the order came from him, and now he gives you his personal Lear Jet so you can be here on time to meet my demands!"

"Lehder thinks Archie is taking an active part in this meeting" explained Gaviota, "Maybe that is why he didn't object to your orders to have me here today."

Gaviota made sense and I thanked the two men again for keeping our meeting just among the three of us.

"OK gentlemen, I just* returned from Chub Cay yesterday and tend to believe that I can score with two loads as soon as two weeks from now, depending on putting together a few loose ends. The most important will be managing to put my hands on 500 gallons of jet fuel for Gaviota to fly back to Colombia."

I shared with both men all the specifications of my plan hoping they would coordinate their roles without objections.

"I don't like the idea of having such limited time to get in and out," complained Colorado.

"I don't see why you have to worry about that...if any one should be worried it is Gaviota, who has to fly the Turbo, refuel it, and take off again, all before the cops return from their lunch break!" I argued. "Besides," I continued, "You, Colorado, will go there the following day during the same lunch period, but you have the advantage of more time because you won't need extra fuel to return to the USA...your cargo will be waiting for you at the end of the runway and I estimate... at the most twenty minutes to put those bags inside your Beechcraft, and off you go!"

Colorado listened carefully. He knew Chub Cay inside out so there was no need to go through maps or pictures, and even if they wanted to see them, Archie had kept them in his desk.

"I am the one who is getting the short end of the stick here," said Gaviota, who now looked very concerned.

"The Turbo Commander is very difficult to refuel by hand because of the position of its fuel nozzles by the wings." Gaviota spoke in a near whisper as he made a drawing on a paper cocktail napkin of the wings of the airplane, which were above the fuselage instead of in the middle as in most airplanes. "I am really afraid of the brief time available...many times most of the fuel is spilled on the ground no matter how carefully your men try to feed it. With no way to hose it in it becomes a fight against gravity."

I took every word into consideration. I was anxious to put this plan to work, but not ambitious enough to put Gaviota's life on the line for it.

"What is the range of the Commander; let's say with 500 kilos?" I inquired.

"I can leave Colombia with 550 kilos and a co-pilot and have just enough fuel to make it to Chub Cay. but you have to understand that I must have at least another 50 gallons, as a safety measure, to reroute or to go to Plan B."

I started to get nervous about the whole operation, but I insisted on exhausting all the possibilities before erasing it from the board.

"Any suggestions?" I asked Colorado.

"I can have the Commander fixed in a way so we can put an extra fuel tank either in the nose or somewhere else."

For a minute I thought he was kidding, but I realized he

was serious when Gaviota rebutted his idea with the obvious argument that it was wasteful to add weight to a space better used for cocaine. "Besides," added Gaviota, "we would need to leave the plane in Wichita Kansas for at least a whole month to get the job done. Let's put aside for a minute the possibilities of adding tanks or even buying new equipment; obviously there is hardly any time to do either. Why don't we try to put this operation together with what we've got and let's see if the three of us can solve the problems that are more crucial, like the fuel situation? Give me some background of how you have treated this crisis in the past." I nodded to Gaviota.

"Well, if we manage to bring a load into Chub Cay as you have been planning, that would mark our 97th successful H. H. into this country," said Gaviota proudly. "Fuel has been the number one problem for every load every time we embark on a run through the Bahamas. There were instances when we were allowed us a stop-over in Santiago de Cuba under Fidel's wing and protection, but since we learned that "Cara de Piña" was selling secrets to the DEA, we decided to forget about Fidel's help and turned to the Sandinistas. Managua was by far the best place to refuel. We were greeted by military escort, driven to our hotel and the following morning we would find the Commander, not only topped with jet fuel but reflagged from HK to N. (2). However, good things don't last and after only four loads through Nicaragua, Lehder was notified by an envoy* from Ortega to halt all shipments until further notice. That was the end of Central America for us." Gaviota's memories of previous H.H's, with the help of foreign heads of state were most fascinating. I listened with undivided attention as he continued.

"Later on we started working with the government of

Mr. Pindling in Nassau and he agreed to turn his back while we refueled on several islands. But in the last year or so Pindling came under fire by the DEA and the Americans and we lost his direct help; in fact he even pledged to help the DEA in enforcing stricter laws to fight drug smuggling. That did not stop us from flying to the Bahamas for the first leg of the trip, but it put a dent in the chances of flying out once the load was dropped for the American plane. We just didn't have enough juice to take us back to Colombia." He He paused to have a sip of water.

"I was assigned by Lehder to check every island and make an inventory of all the fueling stations in the Bahamas. I took the Cessna 410 and spent a whole week touching down on every single strip shown in the pilot's manual to the Bahamas. I discovered that there were maybe a total of 15 operational fueling pumps through out the islands, out of which 10 were privately owned and operated, but none of the fifteen with the exception of the ones oper-ated by Bahamas Air offered jet fuel."

"So how have you managed to get about four loads, since the closing of Norman's Cay?" I asked, anxious to know the answer.

"It was through that inventory assignment that I landed in the northern part of Andros near a place called Nicholls Town where I met a man by the name of Harry Treco. Harry was at the time owner of Texaco's franchise for the whole island. I made notes of my findings and a few weeks later Lehder hired a Bahamian to approach Treco with a proposal to supply us with the necessary fuel, using hfs Texaco fran-chise as a front to cover up any questioning by the Bahamian government or DEA."

"Well...then, if Mr. Treco is still alive why aren't we going to him right now!" I asked excitedly.

"He is alive and well," responded Gaviota. "But Texaco in the USA began to ask why Andros, an island with no need for jet fuel for private aviation, was suddenly consuming 1200 gallons every month. When DEA heard of Texaco's investigation, they moved in and Treco gave up his franchise before things got ugly."

"How-much was Treco making besides the cost of the fuel?"

"Oh, I guess $70,000.00 per H. H." answered Gaviota. There were a few seconds of silence as both Colorado and I looked to Gaviota for answers.

"There is nothing we can do with Treco right now," he said. "The old man no longer has access to Texaco's gasoline."

"Are you in good terms with Treco?" I asked.

"Well, I have not see the man in about a year; I am sure he misses our profitable visits."

"O.K., guys," I said getting up from the table, "you stay here for a few minutes," I said to Colorado, "while Gaviota and I make a couple of phone calls."

"Take your time," responded Colorado. Gaviota followed me outside the restaurant to a nearby pay phone.

"Let's call Harry Treco. Tell him that I need to meet with him ASAP!"

"Whatever you say!" answered Gaviota with an encouraging smile.

(*)"Cara de Piña" is the nickname for General Manuel Antonio Noriega — Commander-in-chief of the military in Panama. (**)

(**)H.K. are the call letters assigned to Colombia to identify the aircraft under its flag.

N. identifies aircraft flying under the United States flag.

6

APRIL 28, 1983

H arry Treco agreed to meet me in Nassau the following morning. As much as I anticipated the encounter, I was in a turmoil about meeting Treco without Alvaro Triana's consent. Taking matters into my own hands was probably very brash, but after all Alvaro's insults I felt too proud even to speak to him—and I certainly didn't want to humble myself to ask his permission for my activities. Archie was rapidly becoming an albatross around my neck; and a very fat albatross at that. This might be the golden opportunity to show Carlos Lehder I was more than a puppet on Alvaro's string—or I might be winding that string around my own neck. I knew that sooner or later I'd take that chance, and it might as well be now. So, I ordered Gaviota to fly me to Nassau first thing in the morning, while Colorado was instructed to stand by in Florida in case I needed him at short notice.

By now it was late afternoon, and I headed home to spend a few hours with my family. Alvaro's car was parked in my driveway! I tried to respond warmly to Lisa's shouts of "Daddy, Daddy!" but my attention was centered on the bulky figure lumbering up from the couch in my family room.

"Hi, Itos," he said ingratiatingly, holding a cup of coffee.

"What are you...?"* I didn't get a chance to finish my sentence.

"Listen...I am very sorry! Please don't quit this job. I need you to help me run the organization."

"Sit down, Archie," I ordered as I helped myself from the coffee pot. He must have sensed the new strength I'd gained from the decision I had just made, because his eyes never left my face.

"I am not quitting the organization...I am quitting working under you, and I guess the only way to do that is to go directly to Carlos Lehder for his approval."

"No, please don't do that!" he insisted nervously, "It'll cost us both our jobs if you do that!"

"Alvaro, for heaven's sake listen to me and listen very carefully; you and I are simply not compatible enough to work together in this organization. I have already mastered what it takes to accomplish the goals, but so long as you keep making the decisions we are not getting anything done!" I started pacing as I tried to make my position clear to Triana.

"I am calling Lehder today...I don't even know where to start looking but I am going to find him, and then Lehder and I are going to have a little talk. I still believe that you and I can belong to the C.C.Q. and work towards obtaining the goals of the organization, but not under this arrangement. I need autonomy in this job for best results. You and I can coordinate certain functions, but when it comes to major decisions like Chub Cay I want to be in full charge. It'll be Carlos to blame if we lose, but it'll be a triumph for both of us if I succeed!" Alvaro listened. He could tell I was not giving him bullshit, but a carefully thought out plan to further both of our careers with the C.C.Q.

"OK, Itos,"assented Alvaro, getting up from the couch, "but let me call Carlos Lehder and present him with the whole plan before you call him. It will help if he understands we're in agreement."

"Fair enough!" I said, "Let's go to a pay phone right now; I have plenty of quarters in my car!"

"No! I will either go to Colombia to meet with him in person, or he might want to meet us both somewhere else..."

"Fine with me, but let's go to the phone and set up the meeting!"

"All right! Let's go call him," he agreed.

We drove together to the familiar pay phone on Glades Road. Archie dialed a number, and after introducing 36 quarters for the first three minutes, he had Lehder on the other end of the line.

Alvaro's conversation with Lehder was brief, but I was impressed with the respect and reverence with which he addressed his boss—it was not just respect, it was sheer intimidation and fear! In spite of all the years that had passed since the last time I met with Carlos Lehder, I could not see myself quite so awestruck if the time came for me to speak to him on the phone or even meet him in person. I didn't underestimate Lehder's power and wealth, but in my mind he was still just my childhood buddy instead of a world famous terrorist. I recalled the many days that Carlos and I refused to take the school bus home. We risked our parents' wrath, but we were two mischievous little boys who loved to sneak over the local convent fence to fill our pockets with stolen mangoes.

When Alvaro handed me the receiver I didn't hesitate to

greet Carlos Lehder with genuine enthusiasm. It was like old times...I was happy to hear his voice.

"Joe?" I asked.

"How are you doing, my friend?" responded Lehder warmly.

"Great!...Now that I can talk to you without mysteries."

I sounded a little bit sarcastic. I knew I had to be very careful with what I had to say over the phone, so I limited my conversation to the issue of the day.

"So, do you have any objections to my working as a 'free-lancer,' reporting only to you?"

"I am meeting with Archie the day after tomorrow. I'll have an answer to all your needs by then." He cut the conversation short.

"Fair enough, Joe...I hope you and I can meet soon!" I pressed.

"It'll be sooner than you expect, Carlitos!" and he hung up.

Alvaro waited inside the car during my brief conversation with Lehder. I got in the car and started driving back to my house without saying a word.

"Well, are you happy now?" Archie broke the silence.

"I feel a lot better; I understand you guys are meeting the day after tomorrow," I said.

"Yes, I am flying to Port-au-Prince, Haiti, where Joe is getting his divorce. Lehder said that after I meet with him, and once I return to the USA, you must fly to Haiti to see him before he flies back to Colombia."

"That is fantastic!" I exclaimed. "I think there will be a lot of good coming out of our meetings. At least I can assure you, Alvaro, that it'll be easier for you and me to communicate and work together once we coordinate our job descriptions under Joe's direct supervision."

Alvaro knew that I was right, and he seemed relieved that we had made the positive move.

Upon arrival at my house, Alvaro declined my offer of lunch.

"You go ahead and continue your so-called "secret" meetings with Gaviota and Colorado!" was his parting shot as he drove away.

"Shit!" I said to myself, "He had me followed!" I felt embarrassed at first, so I decided to catch up with Alvaro and explain my activities. But as I drove after him I began to grow angry as I realized how I had been followed and watched. I felt my privacy had been violated, and now I was the one who wanted an explanation. I drove faster and faster, and I finally caught up with Archie at the intersection of Glades Road. I blew my horn as I approached his car waiting at the red traffic signal.

"Pull over for a minute!" I shouted, rolling down my window. He nodded, turned, and stopped a block away west on Glades. I followed* and parked right behind him on the grassy shoulder of the road.

"What's all the excitement?" he asked.

"Since when have you had me spied upon? You have no right to do that!" I demanded.

"I am just doing my job, Itos." His tone was friendly as he shrugged his shoulders. His comical expression broke my anger.

"Let's go to your house and we'll talk there," I smiled as I got back inside my car. Archie's car trailed mine to his house.

"Who's car is that?" I asked when I saw the red Camaro parked inside Archie's garage.

"Juliana and Maximiliano arrived this morning from Medellin, they will be living with me."

I knew about Juliana. She had been a close friend of Guillermo, my brother, when both of them worked at *La Posada Alemana*, Lehder's Alpine-type vacation resort, between the cities of Armenia and Pereira. Juliana had been the hostess in charge of the John Lennon discotheque while my brother was in charge of entertainment and beverages. Juliana, a twenty-five year old native of Armenia, was the steady girlfriend of Jorge Forero, Lehder's number one pilot. She had been working for Carlos Lehder for several years in various jobs and on this day she had fulfilled the dream of most employees of the C.C.Q. She had been assigned to the United States on a permanent basis. Becoming part of the American crew was a special recognition only afforded to Colombian's of exceptional loyalty and dedication. The opportunity of earning the almighty American dollar, and the chance to live among the rich was a coveted prize. Juliana, a well-educated college graduate, was too pretty and intelligent to become just a maid for a Colombian 'mafioso'. She knew that, but she also knew that by sacrificing a year or two under the suppressive mandate of Alvaro Triana she could save every cent of her three thousand dollar, tax free, monthly salary. All her living expenses, including transportation, would be taken care of.

Her role was to be the helper in Alvaro's house, cooking three meals a day, doing his laundry and remaining in the house at all times to guard the large amounts of cash usually on hand. Her room was upstairs next to the large walk-in closet where Alvaro and I had set up the HF radio on a small table. It was Maxiliano Garzon who would spend twenty-four hours a day. seated by the short wave radio monitoring all conversations between the four bases of the C.C.Q.–Medellin, Armenia, Los LLanos and the Bahamas.

Juliana's bedroom was furnished with a single bed, night

stand, dresser and a color T.V set. Her duties were light, making breakfast by seven in the morning, swimming from ten to eleven, serving lunch at eleven and tanning by the pool most of the rest of the day. Dinner was usually brought in from Albertson's deli or from other local restaurants. Juliana knew Alvaro Triana. She knew the man was not to be trusted and she had never liked him.

"This fat asshole tries to make a move on me and before he knows it I kill him!" she told me one day after Alvaro had made seductive remarks to her. She was tough, and Alvaro knew he had to be very careful. If something happened to Juliana while in his employ he would have to answer to Jorge Forero or even Carlos Lehder himself, who thought of Juliana as "one of the best elements within the C.C.Q."

Juliana was very pleased to meet Cristina later on. In Cristina she found a-friend—someone to ease her loneliness in the United States, and to confide in and rely on. I had not met Juliana until this day but I was aware that everyone who knew her in Colombia had nothing but words, of praise and admiration for this young girl.

"Oh my gosh...you look just like Guillermo!" exclaimed Juliana, as I stepped out of my car.

"Juliana, I am very pleased to meet you!" I shook her hand. God had gifted Juliana with a well-proportioned petite figure, luxurious black hair and expressive features. Her good manners and sparkling personality brought a refreshing refinement to Alvaro's house.

"I am also a good friend of Clemencia and your two beautiful children, Andres and Juan Carlos," she continued.

Clemencia was my ex-wife with whom I had two boys, and Clemencia and Juliana had worked together at *La Posada Alemana*. We all walked into the kitchen and sat down to have some freshly brewed coffee while Juliana captured my attention with anecdotes of my family in Colombia. She knew I was especially touched to hear stories of the children whom I had not seen in several years.

"Archie, Archie!...There is someone from Medellin on the line!" The voice came from upstairs. It had to be Maximiliano calling Alvaro for his immediate attention to the Colombian party waiting on the other end.

"Come on, Itos, it's time you get familiar with our communication codes and radio personnel in the other bases." I followed quickly as Alvaro rushed to the second floor to receive the coded message from his Colombian partner.

"Golden Eagle, Golden Eagle this is the Commander calling from Ohio...can you read me?" The voice came amid much interference from other parties on the same frequency, preventing proper reception of the man calling himself Commander.

"Golden Eagle here...we can read you, though not clearly. Please call back at seven tonight, Florida time, and make sure you cash a check for eight hundred five dollars and seven cents first...can you read me Commander?"

"We read you very well. We'll send someone to the bank right away to get you the funds." A whistle like noise followed the Commander's acknowledgment. The whistle signal was the identification of the C.C.Q.'s operators, and its unique tone made our radio operators a breed apart among other groups using the same frequencies all over the world.

"What was that all about?" I asked Alvaro who sat at the communications panel holding the microphone in his hand.

"I'll explain in a minute; this man ... is Maximiliano Garzon. He flew in with Juliana this morning and from now on he will be our radio operator."

"Hi Maxi, my name is Richard."

"Hello, I have heard a lot about you." Maximiliano was a shy man in his thirties. His reputation as an unscrupulous killer contrasted with his polite and even timid personality.

Maximiliano and I started a conversation about his four years of dedicated work with the C.C.Q. He spoke so proudly of Carlos Lehder that I wondered whether he had been brain washed.

He seemed obsessed with the *Movimiento* and its causes. Here was a man who would literally kill anyone, anywhere with no hesitation should Lehder give the order.

"Carlos Lehder is the answer to the future in Colombia; we must work very hard to produce the necessary funding for the *Movimiento* to succeed not only in Colombia but in all of Latin America. Lehder will be the new Hitler of the Western World!"

Maxi spoke with eloquent pride. What a job Lehder had done with the poor man. And I had heard that there were perhaps another three hundred thousand followers with the same mentality.

I knew Carlos Lehder had always admired Adolf Hitler and denied the existence of concentration camps, but I never imagined he was setting himself up as a reincarnation of the dictator. His intense Nazi doctrines evidently were shared only with his close workers, and not in the open political arena. I was aghast as I listened to Maximiliano, but I knew it would be useless to attack the absurd philosophy.

"OK Maxi, let's talk about that radio message Archie conveyed to the party in Colombia. What is the meaning of cashing checks and Golden Eagle, and Commander?"

"Well, Golden Eagle is Alvaro Triana, and Commander is Diego Vasquez in Medellin, Colombia. You will be Silver Star from now on." Maxi read from his little note book as he translated some of the 100 codes for radio communication. I couldn't repress a chuckle as he assigned me the name of Silver Star ... Twenty-five years ago Carlos Lehder, Alvaro Triana, Carlos Echeverri and I called each other Golden Eagle and Silver Star...how ironic!

"The check for eight hundred five dollars was the radio frequency at which Commander is to tune his HF to call back at seven tonight," explained Maxi, "Normally those frequencies are not SO busy at that given time." Maximiliano then went on to teach me how to whistle as only C.C.Q. members knew how. It took some twenty minutes of repeated drilling before I mastered the unique identification noise.

I had a busy day ahead of me. I wanted to have a second meeting with Gaviota and Colorado before my trip to Andros to meet Mr. Treco and most importantly, I wanted to have a quiet session with Alvaro Triana before his trip to Port-au-Prince to meet with Lehder.

7

MAY 10, 1983

Harry Treco was a perfect example of a well educated, polished Bahamian man.[1] At the age of fifty-five years, he kept himself in great shape, and his British accent made him even more distinguished. We exchanged anecdotes of past times in the United Kingdom, a country where he had spent many years going to school, and a place where I had worked and studied on different occasions.[2]

He spoke proudly of his children and told me how hard he had worked all his life to obtain the vast properties he owned on the island of Andros. We instinctively refrained from discussing the real purpose of our meeting. We knew there had to be a common ground of understanding before the issue of smuggling was brought up. Finally it was time to approach the subject obliquely.

"Well, Harry, I would really like to visit your island soon, and especially have a chance to meet your family."

"I would like to have you over any time. I came to Nassau to make it easier for you, but if you wish I can have someone fly us there right away!"

"I would be delighted!" I answered enthusiastically.

We left my room at the Playboy Hotel and headed to the private aviation building at Nassau's airport. A young Bahamian waited for Harry next to a twin engine Beechcraft and after a brief conversation I was invited on board the plane. The flying time to Andros was only twenty minutes. Harry instructed his pilot to circle the big island at low altitude as he explained the different characteristics of each town, their distances from each other, and most important to me, the length of each airstrip.

We landed in San Andros at the northern tip of the island. The pilot was ordered to wait for us. Harry's pick up truck had been left at the airport so we started our tour right away. The first stop was only three-quarters of a mile from the airport. By an unpaved road, we arrived at a house that Harry explained had been used in the past by the Lehder people.

"I have a number of guns and radio equipment that was left behind, and since you are now in charge I'd like to ask you what to do."

"Well, Harry it all depends - I am here to see if we can have your cooperation in helping us move at least 2000 kilos from Colombia."

"Oh, that is bloody hard to tell! Things have really changed in the Bahamas since two years ago when it was a simple matter. We have to sit down and study all the available channels."

Breaking the ice and discussing the real issue, and getting Treco's commitment, was the hardest part. Now we were ready to sit down and negotiate.

"OK, Harry, I have visited Chub Cay. A man by the name of Ed Goldberg has offered to introduce us to the right people there so that we can land a couple of loads as early as next week..."

"I've heard of Mr. Goldberg, but I don't see how you can operate in a place such as Chub Cay." I explained my plan to Treco but he kept warning me how risky and dangerous Chub Cay could be. "We can do it here in Andros, but this time we have to avoid a lot of the mistakes we made in the past!"

"Tell me how you would do it, Harry!" I pressed.

"What kind of equipment is Lehder using now?"

"He now flies Honeywell Turbos from Colombia to the Bahamas, but for the second leg of the trip we'll have American-flagged twin engine Cessna's to pick up the load."

"That is the problem!" said Harry, "Turbos are too noisy and fuel is hard to come by."

"Harry, I am well aware that you no longer have access to Texaco, but are there other avenues to purchase jet fuel...let's say, fifty gallons today and another fifty gallons tomorrow?..." Harry laughed. "Richard, you seem to have an answer to everything, but let me first show you around before we begin to get excited here."

The house was a one story brick structure with what looked like a concrete roof. It had a modern kitchen, and its three bedrooms, living room and lounge areas were tastefully decorated. An extensive collection of English literature occupied the bookshelves on one side of the walls and a grand piano and some easy chairs filled the sun porch.

"This is an inspiring place; I never thought that a house with this kind of Victorian decor could be found in as remote a setting as this."

"You'd be surprised, Richard, there are homes in this island that are little museums. There are a lot of British millionaires who have retired to the island. This house was built by a writer from Wales maybe forty years ago. When he died ten years ago, I bought it from his estate. I have no idea what this stuff is..."

I ran my finger through some of the books, they were immaculate from centuries back. There were facsimiles of British currency, both notes and coins, and legal documents dated from the 1800's. I was fascinated by the look of a classic Knightsbridge house.

Harry asked me to follow him to the backyard of the house. The mango and grapefruit trees were blooming in spite of the weeded garden at their feet. A few feet away there were several rocks, very huge in size.

"Under those rocks there is a little cave; there I have hidden the machine guns, the grenades and short-band radios."

Harry pointed to the rocks. I had had no idea there were weapons or ammunition on the island, and I am sure Archie was unaware of their existence.

"Well, let's take a look." I was curious to see the real thing. Harry removed the top stone making just enough room for his arm to reach inside the cave. First he pulled out a heavy bundle wrapped in towels and put it by his feet. Again he reached inside and pulled out a second package, just as heavy. The first one contained two Uzi machine guns; the second had six clips for .45 caliber bullets and four hand grenades.

"How long have they been here?" I asked Harry as I held the machine guns.

"Oh, maybe a year and a half, they were left here by your boys who never came back for them."

"What are the hand grenades for?"

"They come in very handy when we need to destroy air

strips in case the DEA or Bahamian planes want to land right behind our cargo."

I gingerly put each weapon back on the towels and Harry tucked them back inside the cave.

We walked into the house and began to discuss the possibilities of an early operation on the island of Andros.

"What kind of money are we talking about?" Obviously Harry wanted to know how much he was to profit from this new venture.

"Harry, before we get into the money aspect of it, can we do it?...I mean, is-there a chance that we might be able to work in Andros?..."

"I think so, but I don't want to make any commitments until I know how much I and my people will get." Harry was straight forward in his concern. "Last time I lost a lot of money , and at the end everybody disappeared leaving all their belongings behind."

"I understand your worries, Harry, but this time I will be here on the island supervising my people and the radio communications, and I personally will guarantee your pay."

"How much jet fuel do you need?"

"At least 460 gallons to make it back to the north coast of Colombia."

"I can have my boys get the jet fuel in drums of five gallons each and hide them in the bushes until we have completed the 460."

"And how do you intend to buy 460 gallons, five gallons at a time, without being questioned?"

"Let me worry about that, Richard." Harry seemed assured of his ability, and the fact that he didn't want to share his secrets didn't really matter to me. So long as he and his sons got me the fuel, I was willing to ignore its origin.

"Now, to answer your question, I am going to give you the money for the fuel today. Once you have talked to your people, let me know how much they want."

"They would require at least fifty-thousand up front for the police and some people in Nassau." The price sounded right, but I still did not have a figure for Harry's fees.

"I will take care of police protection, transportation of your pilots, fueling of the airplanes and all expenses to have your men here as long as necessary prior to the operation. One hundred thousand will cover me and my people."

At that point I didn't want to make any promises to Harry.

"That figure sounds fair, however, I will have an answer for you once I speak to my superior later tonight." Alvaro Triana was supposed to be on his way to Port-au-Prince to meet with Lehder so I intended to have an answer for Harry after Carlos Lehder and I had our own meeting the following day.

"Fair enough," agreed Harry. "Let me take you to the air strip and explain to you how I believe we can pull it off!"

The drive to Nicholls Town took longer that I expected. Andros was bigger than the small spot of land I saw from the air. Miles of wooded areas dominated the scenery from San Andros to Nicholls Town. The narrow road seldom had traffic in the opposite direction and every time a vehicle approached, both Harry and the passerby would slow down to exchange salutes by waving their hands or even coming to a full stop, just to say hello. Everybody knew Harry Treco. The Treco family owns vast properties in the northern part of the island. Agriculture and cattle are their main interests, and their wealth included many houses, hotels and obviously airplanes and machinery.

After a few hours Harry and I felt very comfortable with

each other. There was a special understanding between us and that made our working relationship very smooth. The prospects for a healthy and very profitable alliance were cemented with a handshake of mutual trust.

"The airstrip I intend to use this time is at the local airport and is used by Bahama Air four times a day, but it is the best alternative to the private airstrips that are frequently monitored by Drug Enforcement and Nassau police."

We drove to the front of Nicholls Town airport. There was the usual traffic of a few natives waiting for a flight from Freeport, and we sauntered around the terminal as if we also were waiting for the incoming flight. Harry briefly said hello to the Bahamas Air local manager and introduced me as Richard, an American who wanted to buy one of his houses in San Andros.

"James, I want to show my friend Richard the terminal and the private aviation facilities, he wants to fly his own plane and leave it here from time to time." James, a pale and thin Bahamian had been assigned to the post of airport manager only a few weeks before. "He owes me a favor," explained Harry, "my daughter Laura got him this job "

We followed James through the gates past the signs that read AUTHORIZED PERSONNEL ONLY.

"O.K., James, I'll take it from here!" James immediately turned around towards his office after Harry winked at him. It was all understood. James was in on it!

I followed Harry to a Cessna 410 that was parked at the right hand side of the runway among other twin engine private planes.

"Let's take her up just once around the area so you can estimate more or less how I intend to bring your cargo in."

I listened and followed his directions. We boarded the

Cessna. Pointing to the South end of the strip, Harry explained the position in which our Turbo was to land and taxi to a final stop.

"Your plane will be landing at approximately seven thirty, right after the last commercial flight of Air Bahamas lands, unloads and returns to Nassau. I will have a car parked at that end of the strip to flash its lights to your pilot once we are clear of any danger." Again Harry pointed, this time to the North side of the airstrip.

"How are we to keep people from coming to the airport?"

"There is no reason for anybody to show up here after The last flight of the day has left. However, to be perfectly safe, I'll have the police block all access to the terminal so, should someone try to drive in, they will be stopped and told that there is a 'drug bust' taking place at the airport. Most people do not want to get into that kind of situation. They just turn around."

"How long do you estimate the operation of landing and unloading to take?"

"In one hour we must have the plane fully unloaded, parked by that fence with an 'N' on its tail, and your men safely at a location where they can get at least five hours sleep. For secrecy you should send your boys in the middle of the night to refuel it."

Harry was indeed an expert in this kind of planning. I had no need to ask any more questions because even the smallest of details had been anticipated by him.

The Cessna took off for a short flight over the airport grounds and facilities. As Harry circled the area we had in front of us a view of the airstrip.

"Right here is where your pilots must switch from HF frequencies to the walkie talkies!" There was perhaps a mile between us and the terminal. "I will have the frequencies scrambled at this point, but you must remember that here there is no turning back!"

What Harry meant was simply that at that point our airplane would be so close to the airport that no order from me to abort the operation could be obeyed. Moreover, there would not be enough fuel for the Turbo to reroute.

"I guess that is when the machine guns and hand grenades could come in handy."

"You've got it," answered Harry.

Every piece of information that Harry explained fell into place like pieces of a jigsaw puzzle, revealing what I considered a very smart and well planned operation.

"Harry, I am very satisfied with what I've seen so far. I will fly to the States as soon as possible and get the O.K. to pay you one hundred thousand dollars. When can I send my boys to set radio transmissions and rehearsals?"

"As soon as you like," answered Harry. "I can have a preliminary meeting with the police as early as tomorrow "

"Fine, let's go back to San Andros and the sooner you can fly me to Nassau, the better."

Our drive back to San Andros was very pleasant. We put aside the concerns of a smuggling operation and just enjoyed our opinions on a variety of topics. Upon our arrival in San Andros, we discerned a young Bahamian girl waiting outside Harry's house.

"Who's that beauty, Harry?" I was very impressed by her uncommon blend of Anglo and Bahamian negro.

"Oh, Laura's..." Obviously Harry was happily surprised to see her again. "She's my daughter. She just came back from London."

Laura was moving rapidly towards Harry's truck. She had on a blouse that was gaping open down the front, revealing her breasts. She wore pink shorts that were very loose and floppy in the legs but exceptionally tight across her buttocks. I stared at her appreciatively. She stared back and smiled tantalizingly. It was a confident, unabashed smile that as much as said, "Hi! We like each other don't we?" So frank, so eagerly immodest.

Harry abandoned his truck and ran to embrace his daughter.

"This is Richard, a business associate," he said to his daughter, who extended her arm to greet me.

"Hello, Richard, how do you do?"

We all walked inside the house to make arrangements for my return to Nassau. While Harry made some phone calls, Laura told me about her business school in London and briefly explained how she and her brother Keith were born of a different mother from her two other brothers, Robert and Michael.

"My mother is white British and separated from my father long ago," she told me. Now I understood the green of her eyes and the olive tone of her skin.

"O.K., Richard," said Harry, calling me back to business.

"One of my sons will fly you to Nassau in a couple of hours." From Nassau I would ask Burt Gordon to fly me back to the United States.

8

MAY 13, 1983

J ust before my arrival at Fort Lauderdale Executive Airport, my pager went off. The number 13 which appeared on the display of the digital beeper meant the Ochoa family wanted me to call them. From the first pay phone in the terminal I phoned Jairo Ochoa, who indicated that he had a package for me.

Normally, he would have called Archie, but in his absence he knew I would be the one to handle cash pick-ups.

"Hi, Richard," said Jairo, "I have 375 invoices for your accountant; can we meet somewhere between Dade and Broward?"

I was very tired. The long day with Harry Treco and all the work we put together had exhausted all my energy, but the call represented 275 thousand dollars urgently needed for operational expenses in Fort Lauderdale, as well as the 100 thousand for Harry. Nevertheless, I decided to go home, take a shower, and just relax for a few hours with my wife and daughter before driving south to pick up the cash. I had been looking forward to having Archie out of town so I could put business aside, and I didn't want to let this call spoil my family time. Normally, we worked seven days a week, twenty hours a day. Handling vast amounts of cash was all in a day's work to me.

Cristina, Lisa and I spent precious hours at home. Later in the evening Lisa fell asleep and we carried her to bed.

Cristina and I went out for dinner and drinks, calling on Archie's sister to babysit. My wife made me forget the worries of the day.

Her beautiful smile and irresistible sex appeal made it easy for me to ignore the insistent calls of Jairo Ochoa to pick up the cash. He could wait until morning; I had better things to do.

The following morning I left home to meet Jairo Ochoa at the place we had agreed upon. Jairo's white Nissan Maxima was already at the Burger King parking lot. I parked next to his car.

"Hello, *hermano!*" Jairo jumped from his driver's seat as I woke him from a brief snooze.

"Hi! Richard!" He got out of his car and we both went inside the restaurant to have a milk shake.

"I have the money in the trunk of my car," explained Jairo, "but the problem is that I haven't had a chance to count it."

"But Jairo, you told me last night you had 375 invoices."

"Well, that is the figure I was given by the people I collected from."

I could not accept that cash unless it had been counted by the Ochoas. Never in the past had we had a problem and I trusted their word, but this time the money came from an unknown source to me and I couldn't take any chances. We had to find a safe place to count it, but where? I thought of going to the Marina Bay, my tennis club only a few blocks away, but still the risk was great. It was C.C.Q.'s policy never to reveal to any member of another family in the Cartel the sites of our residences, but nevertheless...I decided to drive Jairo Ochoa to my house in Boca Raton, count the money with, him and send him back to Miami. I had no fear of Jairo's knowing my place of residence, but I requested that he keep it just between us. I trusted him very much.

Twenty-five minutes later we were in front of my home. Jairo and I went to Lisa's room and slowly and carefully counted the cash. There were five thousand dollars missing from the 375 . It proved again the need for constant vigilance, otherwise I would have been responsible for the shortage.

Jairo, a young Colombian in his late twenties, was a very polite, well-mannered man. He shared coffee with Cristina and our conversation was pleasant. But this was the day Archie was due to return from Haiti so I cut our conversation short and Jairo promised to keep our meeting secret.

I put the cash away in a safe I had in my closet. The rest of the afternoon I relaxed at home making some preparations to meet Carlos Lehder in Haiti early the following day.

Archie arrived from his own meeting with Lehder late that evening. He sent Juliana to advise me of his arrival and ask me to come to his house right away.

"How did it go with Joe, Archie?"

"Very well; he is very pleased with the fact that you went to meet with Harry Treco; the rest you'll know when you see him tomorrow." It was obvious that Archie did not want to share the details of his meeting with the big boss, and I didn't insist on getting any further information.

"I had you come over so you can tell me how it went with Harry Treco."

"It went better than I expected. If Joe has no objection,

I'll have one thousand kilos on the island in a couple of weeks."

My words to Archie were calculated. I was indicating to him that I was going to sidestep his views in my quest for Joe's approval of my plans. Tomorrow's meeting with Carlos Lehder would mark the end of my reporting to Archie; I made that very clear. We covered the last of our business technicalities as I explained to Archie about the money I had collected from the Ochoas.

"Take one hundred thousand of that money to Harry Treco, and divide the rest between Red and Colorado." It was a good decision. Both Red and Colorado were growing impatient and if we lost them due to non-payment I could never find better men to move the loads of cocaine from Andros to the United States.

I left Archie and returned home. Burt Gordon waited for me there to plan our trip. Burt was well established in Port-au-Prince as a respectable businessman. He managed a water treatment plant, and was a sought-after member of Haiti's social circles. Although he spent a great deal of his time in North Miami Beach, Burt owned a residence in Haiti and frequently traveled back and forth.

"Just prepare a flight plan straight to Port-au-Prince," I directed. Previously I had expected to fly to Andros first to drop off Harry's cash, but now I was most eager to face Carlos Lehder.

As the time to depart grew closer, I grew even more anxious. Meeting Carlos Lehder was very important in terms of work, but my feelings of anticipation were, of a more personal nature. Time and distance had kept us out of contact, but at last I was en route to be reunited with that brother. There was also a desire to exchange stories of the tumultuous events of the past few years. Lehder's incredible success, his future plans, his political inclinations, as well as where I fit in, were on my agenda to discuss. Before my departure I telephoned Harry Treco to advise him that I would stop in the Bahamas on my way back from Haiti to advance him one hundred thousand dollars so he could start the preliminary tasks for our load 98.

The flight to Port-au-Prince was smooth and enjoyable with the exception of some dark clouds and turbulence some forty minutes into our flight, but it cleared over the island of Anse a Galets before our descent to the capital city. The weather in Haiti as per the control tower in Port-au-Prince was 78 degrees with scattered showers and a humidity of 98%. Upon landing we were greeted by a couple of Immigration offices who, instead of asking for our passports, requested we follow them through a door that led to the airport's parking lot. The tourist cards had already been issued. A friend of Burt's waited in a station wagon. "Was everything all right?" he asked Burt.

"Sure, but we didn't need to skip customs and immigration; both our papers are in order."

"Well, that is the way Joe wanted it."

Going to Haiti was routine for Burt, but I did not need my passport stamped with an entry.

This was my first trip to Haiti. I always believed that French would be heard everywhere; instead Creole was the language most Haitians spoke. There seemed to be a lot of discontent with the government of Jean Claude Duvalier and the graffiti on the city walls spoke loud and clear. Unemployed men and poor living conditions were common sights on every street

We were driven through the center of Port-au-Prince to a three story building where Burt had his company. The offices were modestly decorated affd there seemed not to be much activity. A Haitian bilingual secretary welcomed us in perfect English and then handed each of us menus so she could order lunch from a local restaurant. Burt's office was the largest of the three. It had a full size executive desk, a credenza and a pair of chairs.

"Joe should be coming here shortly," said Burt, "I think he wants to fly tonight."

"That's too bad," I replied disappointedly,"I was hoping to spend at least a full day with him."

"Well, he is trying to get Fidel Castro[1] to see him in Cuba before he flies back to Colombia."

"But—isn't Cuba out of the way to Colombia?"

"It's only a few minutes from here and I think it would be very profitable for the two of them to meet."

"How close friends are they?" A knock on the door interrupted my questioning. Burt's secretary had a tray with a variety of Haitian dishes. Steamed fish, green plantains, rice and beans were all in the same dish. "O.K., gentlemen, enjoy!" she said as she laid the tray on Burt's desk. The Haitian who had driven us from the airport brought in two bottles of beer. I was extremely curious about the relationship of Carlos Lehder with Fidel Castro, so in between bites I probed: "How well does Carlos know Fidel?"

"Oh, I think they go back some seven years since the time when Vesco lived in Norman's Cay. It was Robert Vesco who actually introduced Joe to Fidel." Burt paused to take a spoonful of rice and beans. I waited impatiently.

"As a matter of fact, back in 1978 Joe knew Fidel's birthday was coming up, so he asked Ken Reed to help him find an amphibious airplane to send to Castro as a birthday present. Reed found a brand new twin engine Sea Hawk in Wichita, Kansas, and bought it for Joe. We had tried several times to fly cocaine in it to the Bahamas but the son of a bitch just wouldn't take off with more than two hundred kilos and the crew, so Joe decided to send it to Fidel because it had not paid its dues!"

"Who flew the plane to Cuba?"

"I did!"

"What did Fidel say?"

"He was excited; he sent Joe a warm letter of gratitude and ever since they've exchanged a letter and a visit every now and then."[2]

We finished our meal. There was a sudden knock on the door and. Carlos Lehder entered accompanied by Jorge Forero, his private pilot.

"Hello, Burt!" said Lehder, opening his arms to Burt.

"Carlitos, *cómo estás?*" he roared as he turned away from Burt extending his arm.

"*Muy bien, hermano!*" then we both hugged.

"Burt, please send your secretary home and make sure we have privacy while we meet here."

"Sure, Joe." Burt got up from the desk, offering his seat to Carlos Lehder, then walked outside to make sure we were alone and safe.

I kept my eyes fixed on Carlos Lehder. It had been almost ten years since the last time we met. He looked great; I suppose his fame and fortune kept the wrinkles away while most of us in the mid and late thirties begin to show age here and there.

He wore a short-sleeved sports shirt, jeans and deck shoes. His face looked full although not a trace of fat was noticeable on his body. He had certainly kept good discipline in the gymnastics department, since his arms were solid muscle. Lehder had not lost his charismatic personality. He was warm, sincere and genuinely glad to see me again.

"So, Carlitos, what's happening!... I understand you married again and have a daughter?"

"Yeah, a beautiful wife and a precious little girl!"

"I have seen your other children in Armenia several times, they both look very much like you." I knew that Lehder was close to my ex-wife's family and he had on several occasions spent time with my two sons. Our conversation went on for at least an hour, mostly about our families, the old country and people we knew in common, until the telephone interrupted our reminiscing.

Lehder spoke to what seemed to be his divorce attorney and told him to go ahead because he wanted to be out of Haiti that same evening.

"Carlos, can you stay longer, so we can really go through a number of items regarding our operations in Florida?" He looked into my eyes and said, "No, honest, I have to be out of here tonight, but I had a meeting with Archie yesterday and I think I know what the problems are."

"Well, based on what Archie told you...what do you think?"

"I think Archie is afraid of you, I think you pose a threat to him only because you are more adventurous and more of a go-getter than he is; but I don't want both of you fighting because I need you both!"

"I understand, Joe," it was the first time I called Carlos Lehder Joe and it came out very naturally, "but I cannot operate positively if I have to report to him; the man is not ready to take some necessary risks, and I need to take those risks to get the loads out of your hands!"

"I agree with you 120%, Carlitos, but Archie is good for other things. You go ahead and tell me what you have in mind; if I like it you don't have to go to Triana for anything!"

I proceeded to tell Lehder about my meetings with

Harry Treco and how I intended to bring at least one thousand kilos through Andros within the following weeks. He listened carefully making notes of my plan.

"Well, Carlitos, if you succeed with those loads in Andros, I'll have a premium of one hundred thousand dollars for you on top of the salary Archie is supposed to pay you!"

It was a good incentive and I knew it could be done.

Lehder then asked me to take notes on a number of tasks he wanted me to do upon returning to the USA.

"First, I want you to call Ken Reed and try to get the Turbo Commander released from him. That plane was sent for repairs and additional fuel tanks and it's been, four months already. If he has sold it please collect the proceeds, then see if you can find me a Merlin. Once you find it, call me and I'll give you instructions. Now, there is the plan with Ed Goldberg. Meet with him and see how we can have a sale of the island on paper where my two corporations. Air Montes and Titantic Aircraft, sell the Norman's Cay hotel to Goldberg, so he can be the 'front,' operate it and open it to the public. I want you to be in charge and responsible for the negotiations with Goldberg. I want to purchase his ranch in Okeechobee as a possible landing spot for your loads from Andros."

I wrote my notes as fast as possible, not wanting to miss any details. Lehder got up from his chair and started to pace back and forth. I interrupted his concentration with the inevitable question I had been waiting to ask.

"Why did you go through Triana to hire me?...It never made any sense to me!" He stopped abruptly, stared at me and then smiled.

"I always believed you had the ingredients to get the island back into operation, but at the same time I was afraid you would reject my offer because of my reputation. I knew that sooner or later you would know I was behind it all — but by that time you would be too involved to go back!"

I could hardly believe his frankness.

"Carlitos, listen, Alvaro Triana is not the man to run my interests in the United States. You are the man, just hang in there. Don't tell Archie what we have discussed today, but I firmly believe that in a matter of six months I'll have Triana back in Colombia and you in charge, making a quarter of a million dollars a year!"

Lehder was very eloquent. He sounded genuine, but I wondered if those were the same words he had used with Alvaro Triana the day before when my name came up. I played the game..."Sure, Joe, I can't wait!" Lehder grinned and put his arm over my shoulder.

Carlos Lehder was a dreamer, and now he started to share with me his plans for a world dominated by the Lords of Cocaine. He believed that cocaine would solve the problems of all Latin American nations and that his political party, though only a movement of a few thousand at that time, would reach international attention and become the party of all nations on earth. His hero was Adolf Hitler. "Adolfo was the greatest warrior of all times!" He talked about revolution, and perhaps taking over Colombia for himself. He wanted power and more power. He told me how he was linked with influential people all over the world, people who intended eventually to destroy American democracy and terminate what he called "imperialist" rule.

"Cocaine is the stepping stone to wealth and to power. We are not hurting America's moral fiber; America has no morals! We are using her decay to set up our own system of helping the downtrodden of the world. I want you to be part of the bonanza, Carlitos!"

I was immobile. Somehow I began to believe that he could successfully accomplish each and everything he just told me. He had a way of mesmerizing his listeners. It was very scary.

Lehder then asked me to give him an account of how things were being handled in Florida. I was relieved to get back to business, and gave him a detailed break-down of all the activities, funds, etc. He listened, making only a few notes.

[Text missing] {He?}[3]

would give some cash to my children in Armenia as soon as he returned.

He insisted on my silence regarding the contents of our meeting. He then handed me a list of items to be dealt with upon my return to Florida, and repeatedly asked me to avoid using public phones when calling him in Colombia. "Do your best to get me on the HF frequencies, unless it's a life or death emergency!"

The phone rang again, Lehder listened to the party on the other side, then, with a wide smile, reflected a great sense of satisfaction.

"Well, it seems like good news!" I had a deep desire to know the nature of his call.

"Fantastic ! Mr. Castro will see me for lunch tomorrow!" Jorge Forero who had been sitting mutely in a corner of the room glancing through every magazine as we spoke, got up from his chair as he heard about the trip to Havana.

"Do we need a flight plan?" he asked Lehder.

"No," he replied, "we'll notify Mr. Castro of our arrival time and there won't be a problem with Haiti's airspace."

"Joe," I interrupted, "I would very much like to meet Fidel! "

"Well, I need you to get back to Andros and take care of

Mr. Treco, maybe I'll bring you along on my next trip to Cuba."

Lehder started to gather all his paper work as if ready to leave. It was about four-thirty in the afternoon and if I left right away I could fly to Andros, meet Treco briefly then fly back to the United States

"Jorge, please find Burt for me and tell him we're leaving for the Bahamas in half an hour."

Jorge left the office to locate Burt. Carlos Lehder and I hugged again and I promised to visit him in Colombia once my first operation with Treco was accomplished.

"We'll celebrate at *La Posada Alemana*," he said. A few minutes later Jorge returned with Burt and we had one of the Haitians drive us back to the airport.

My meeting with Carlos Lehder was over. I left Port-au-Prince with an uneasy feeling. Lehder was bullshitting me and he was bullshitting Archie. But I was determined to carry on with my commitments. "I'll stick around until I make at least one million dollars in the next few months," I said to myself, "if all Lehder's grandiose illusions about destroying democracy become too uncomfortable, I'll just take my money and run."

As I left Haiti I had no idea that US Attorney Robert W. Merkle was on his way to hold a secret meeting with Colombian officials in Bogota to urge Lehder's extradition on a 1981 Jacksonville, Florida indictment.

9

MAY 15, 1983

J ust before leaving Burt Gordon's office in downtown Port-au-Prince, I telephoned Harry Treco in the Bahamas to meet me at the airport either in Nicholls Town or San Andros.

"I'll have one of the boys bring you over to the house," replied Harry.

I didn't want our airplane parked in San Andros while I met with Treco, so I asked Burt to drop me off, go to Freeport or Nassau then pick me up at 7 p.m.

Robert Treco waited outside the terminal by the runway. I deplaned and followed him through a fence on the side of the building. Immigration authorities just looked and nodded in approval. We drove about twelve miles into the island to the Andros Beach Hotel where Harry, seating on a rocking chair enjoyed watching as the peaceful waves washed the white sands of his ocean front property.

"Welcome, Richard."

"Hello. Harry, I don't have all the time in the world, so tell me how things look," I took a chair next to him. Robert left us alone.

"Things look very favorable to do something next week."

"That soon?"

"Well, I can have your radio set up over night. From there it's all up to you; my police officers are notified and all they need now is twenty-four hours."

"Fantastic," I replied. "I'll have my radio men here in a couple of days; you go ahead and set up the antennas. Expect me back in four days. I'll stay for the duration of all the radio transmissions before the operation, and I will personally supervise the unloading and refueling of the planes as well as the security of our people."

"That's great; for the first time we'll have someone responsible in charge. In previous operations there was no organization and things were improvised at the last minute."

"How is the fuel situation, Harry?"

"I have already five hundred gallons of jet fuel committed to me. I'll have them transferred to this island in five gallon drums in 48 hours."

"O.K., I brought you one hundred thousand dollars in cash."

I opened a Hartman leather bag. Under a few personal belongings, underwear, shirts and a pair of sneakers I had ten bundles of ten thousand dollars each. All one hundred dollar bills. I handed the money to Harry. Harry inspected the cash by running his fingers through each bundle, then called his daughter, Laura.

I had no idea that she was still in town. Our last encounter had left a lasting impression.

"She is at the store," answered Robert, "I'll get her."

Laura walked in looking more beautiful than the first time I met her. The Bahamian sun had taken away the pale-dry look one gets after living in London for a year. Now her skin had darkened to a bright copper. She was stunning.

"Well," she said, "I hope this time you're here to stay at least overnight."

"Hello, Laura."

"Hi, Richard." We shook hands.[1]

"Laura, take this money and put it inside the safe at the store." Harry handed her the cash. Laura took the wads of bills and strolled nonchalantly away. Her off-hand manner intrigued me.

"O.K. Harry, please have someone clean all the weapons and make arrangements for three men and myself. We can house them together, but I'd rather be in a separate place on my own, so long as I can have transportation to see them every morning."

"No problem, I'll take care of all their needs. As a matter of fact I'll send my son to do grocery shopping in Miami for the two weeks."

"Why in Miami?"

"The food here is very expensive and hard to find. A steak could cost fifty dollars. Milk, beef and good canned food comes from the States and we'd better be prepared to feed you guys properly."

"Thank you, Harry."

We sipped tea which Laura had offered us on a silver tray. I asked Harry to have someone drive me to the airport before seven to wait for my ride home. As I walked into the house to use the bathroom, I ran into Laura in the kitchen.

"Are you staying tonight, Richard?"

"No, I can't, but I'll be back next week for maybe ten days." She gave me a look that was just irresistible. I walked closer to her. "Would you visit me while I am on the island?"

"Sure, you bloody fool!" Suddenly her arms were over my shoulder running her fingers up the back of my neck. I was just about to pull her closer when Robert walked in.

"Just let me know when you're ready and I'll drive you to the airport." I was embarrassed. He had seen us, but he politely disregarded our flirtation.

I returned to the porch. Harry and I were optimistic that the operation would go without fault. It was almost six-thirty and I had to be at the airport at seven. I got up and said good bye to Harry. On my way towards the front entrance I shook hands with Laura. Through her hands I could feel the vibrations of two people in lust. "See you next week, Miss Treco."

"I shall be here, Richard!"

During the first few minutes of our drive, Robert and I didn't talk. A couple of miles from the terminal Robert broke the silence.

"Laura really likes you, Richard."

"She is a beautiful girl." Nothing else was said.

Our airplane was touching down. Burt taxied to the end of the runway where I waited. Without much delay Burt turned around and in a matter of seconds the jet-prop was en route to Fort Lauderdale. It had been a long working day and I collapsed in the rear of the plane preparing my agenda for the next few days.

My first task was to send some Colombians to Andros and start communications with Los LLanos and Medellin aiming at importing the first 550 kilo load in six days, and another 550 in ten days.

The radio equipment that we had installed on the second floor of Archie's house on Andora Place had been transferred from the house where Cesar Londoño had it for a couple of years and although we used it frequently to communicate with Colombia. I decided to update it by adding new pieces that could improve the quality of our transmissions.

I went to the only store in Fort Lauderdale that special-
izes in Ham radio operations, on State Road 84, and bought
two mobile transmitters, two antennas with spring mount
and capacitance hat, two ground grid amplifiers for 432
MHZ and two 13.8 volt, 5 ampere switching power supplies
for use with the transmitters.

Everything was bought in pairs so I could take one of
each to Andros and have Balin, our Colombian radio engineer, work on the installations. Balin, a friendly fellow[2]
from Armenia, had graduated from college as an engineer
specializing in RDF (Radio Direction Finding). Right after
college he was hired by Carlos Lehder to handle all communications both with aircraft and land bases.

I telephoned Harry Treco and asked him to fly to the
USA to pick up the radio parts I had bought. Only Harry
could bypass customs with that kind of equipment without
being questioned. That same afternoon he flew to Fort
Lauderdale to pick up his package. I radioed a message for
Balin to fly from Colombia to the Bahamas to set up a trans-
mission base. He flew in the same afternoon via Panama.

In a matter of twenty-four hours after my arrival from
Andros, all the radio network was installed and fully operational. Maxi Garzon started having daily transmissions with
Armenia, Medellin and Los LLanos to agree on the frequencies that would be used before and during the operation.

Three Colombians[3] were also flown to Andros to reside
in one of Harry's houses for the duration of the operation.
One was to handle radio communications, the second one
to serve as an arms expert and the third to aid the Treco
family in refueling the airplanes. They were there to assist
in any aspect, including but not limited to protection,
weapons, communications, surveillance or even flying an
airplane if needed. They were experts in the territory and

knew the ways to escape from the islands in the event of an emergency. None of them spoke fluent English, but I would join them in a couple of days to supervise their operation.

Radio communications were sporadic at this time In the plan but seventy-two hours before the green light to take off from Colombia, the radios would be tuned to the same frequencies day and night. The status of the airplane sitting in the Colombian jungle, weather updates, FAA reports, constant monitoring of Coast Guard, DEA and Bahamian Police operations were to be followed every thirty minutes day and night. Any possibility of failure due to interception or poor weather would become sufficient probable cause to abort the whole show until such anomalies were corrected.

I personally made it my task to keep contact with the ranch in Ocala, Florida where the load was to be flown from the Bahamas. Men were assigned to monitor the local sheriff radio frequencies two days before the operation. An insider[4] working for the Drug Enforcement Administration in Miami was to inform Red, the American pilot, of any possibility of the Federals' learning of our program. And FAA employees[5] were paid to monitor Red's flight from Andros to Ocala keeping him informed how to avoid detection.

Since my return from Haiti I had seen little of Archie, especially because one of his girlfriends from Montenegro, Colombia was visiting and he had decided to take her to Disney World for a brief tryst. His absence made it possible for me to operate more freely in putting things together. He knew I no longer had to report to him, and needless to say he knew of my plans in Andros.

The time came for me to go to the Bahamas, not to return until I had successfully accomplished my goals. This time I flew Eastern Airlines to Nassau and was picked up by

Robert Treco for my final destination in San Andros. The house that Harry owned, only a few miles from the airport, was set up as the communication center. The three Colombians were already in the house and all radio equipment was operational. Balin had just left for Medellin the day before.

I greeted the fellow Colombians in Spanish and we had a productive meeting basically discussing our individual job descriptions and making sure each one understood every aspect of our presence in that island. They were all very jovial and there was no need to be bossy or even demanding. Those men were well trained by Carlos Lehder and they knew the discipline required while on the island.

The Trecos had brought enough groceries to feed them just about any thing they desired, and a local woman had been assigned to take care of their laundry and other housekeeping tasks. I decided to spend the night with them in spite of a separate location previously arranged for my stay. I needed to size-up those men and to see what made them tick.

We stayed up all night talking about each other's families, friends, Colombia and even playing a few games of poker. Every now and then we would run to the radios to answer the whisper code that identified the members of the C.C.Q. calling from overseas. My emotions were running high and I could sense the Colombians were also charged up despite their experience with operations of this kind.

Our Colombian party was periodically checking to make sure we had all channels open and an available operator was there at all times. Early in the morning, Robert Treco came to the house to offer to drive me to the place where I was to stay for the next two weeks. I had been up all night and a few hours of quiet rest would suit me perfectly.

My quarters consisted of a two-bedroom one bath hut in an isolated water front property about six miles away from the radio baseband maybe seven or eight miles from the Treco's residence. The old construction provided me with a small kitchen with an electric stove but no refrigerator and an old fashioned bath-tub with a toilet bowl next to it. The water tank hung from the ceiling and a metal chain dropped on one side. The red lettered sign by the corner next to the toilet seat read "Pull the chain."

Apparently the hut had been empty for a while. A water bed from the Andros Beach hotel had been set up in the main bedroom together with a dresser, a desk and chair. On one side of the bedroom, a door led to the beach. The high tide gently washed two of the four concrete pillars that held up the front porch over the beach.

"I'll bring you a T.V set and a radio...I know it's not as luxurious as we'd like to offer you, but..."

"This is perfect!" I interrupted Robert. "Forget about the TV set and radio, this hut is the perfect retreat."

"There is no one living on this beach and it gets pretty dark at night but it is a very secure place for you. I'll get two-way radios and you just call us anytime day or night."

"Robert, this place is unique, it's just what I always wanted. Away from the noise of civilization."

The place was indeed away from the world. The wooded area shielded the hut from the main road and by the water front I could see miles of sand and blue waters without a soul in view.

"Well, Richard, I know how you feel about this spot. It has always been a favorite for friends that want to come to Andros and feel free to walk naked and have total privacy."

"Just get me some books from the main house; I think I'm gonna love it here!"

"We'll leave a motorcycle for your use but we'd rather have you call us if you need anything. It's not wise to have you going to town at all unless there is a real emergency."

I understood Robert's concern and I fully agreed with him. "O.K, Robert, I'll get a few hours rest; what about meals?"

"I can have someone come and cook for you every day, or I can pick you up to have meals with us."

"No, thanks. I must remain here. Just get me the radios and I'd rather you send someone to help with the meals, although I don't mind doing my own cooking."

"Fine, I'll see you later.*

"Bye, Robert."

Once Robert was out of sight I took a close inspection of my new residence. The house was at least thirty years old. The walls didn't have a definite color. The original paint had faded away and all that remained were the shadows in places where pictures once hung. The floor tiles covered the entire area giving it a very tropical ambiance. The porch by the water-front had a single rocking chair facing the ocean. "This is magnificent!" I exclaimed out loud.

I don't remember falling asleep. The sun came in hot and bright and a gentle breeze rocked the window shutters making a squeaky noise disturbing my rest. I looked at my watch. It was one thirty in the afternoon. I had actually slept five hours. I jumped to my feet to find a pile of towels and linen over the desk. The door that led from the bedroom to the living room and kitchen was closed but I could hear noises coming from behind.

Slowly I approached the door and turned the knob. Laura Treco and another older woman were puttering in the kitchen. A love seat had been placed in the empty living room together with a coffee table. The place looked nice, a little bit like a home.

"Hello" I announced before coming out.

"Hello, Richard, we have lunch for you."

"Hi, Laura"

Laura met me half way into the living room and gave me a warm embrace, kissing me on the cheek. I reciprocated.

"Well, what do you think?" Laura pointed at the love seat and showed me a pile of books she had gotten from the other house.

"Marvelous, thank you very much."

"Come here, Richard, I want you to meet Lena; she will come every day and take care of your meals."

I followed Laura to the kitchen where Lena, a lovely Bahamian lady in her late fifties, chopped a conch over the kitchen counter.

"Good afternoon, sir"

"It is a pleasure to meet you, Lena."

Laura then showed me the shower curtain she had placed on one side of the bath-tub. She had used a long string nailed to each side of the walls. It was crooked, and besides I didn't need a shower curtain because there was no shower. "It's ...nice." I didn't have a better comment.

Lena served Laura and me lunch on the coffee table. A fresh conch salad, vegetable soup and steak sandwiches were more than sufficient to please my hungry appetite. Laura told me about her business school in London, about her plans for the future and about a boyfriend she had just broken up with. It amazed me how much she knew about me. She knew I was married with a little daughter and it was no secret to her why I was present on the island.[6] I helped to carry the dishes back to the kitchen. Lena asked Laura for a ride back to town.

"What is your schedule, Richard?"

I didn't have one planned. Later in the afternoon I intended to go to the radio base to check on the situation in Colombia and to role play our moves with my men. I felt tempted to ask Laura to come to my hut later that evening, but the words just didn't come out. Laura and Lena left. Lena promised to be back at seven-thirty to have dinner for me.

"Mr. Richard," she said, "if you are not in the house I'll just prepare dinner and leave it for you inside the oven."

"Thank you Lena, that is fine."

Laura grabbed my hand and pulled me towards her. "Walk me to my car." I did.

"Please, Laura, have someone drive me to the radio base later on today."

"I'll drive you."* She smiled and drove away.

It could not have been a better time to go for a swim. The temperature was in the eighties and the aqua color of the waters made my private paradise just perfect. I hesitated for a minute, then in a sudden impulse I took off my clothes and ran naked to the beach. What a feeling...I felt as if I were the sole human being in the whole island. After a few minutes in the water it felt natural. Later on I walked around the beach totally nude as if I had never known any other way.

At around six-thirty I returned to the hut. On the way I collected a few conch shells and I also found a big coral ornament. I dressed and started reading one of the books, a best seller from the sixties, while waiting for Laura to take me to the other house. If things were in order, I didn't doubt that by the following day I would give the green light for the Turbo Commander to leave Colombia. I was happy with my progress. If only my friends could see me now.[7]

I heard the noise of a vehicle approaching the hut. I presumed it was Laura to pick me up but instead it was Harry. "Hello, Richard, everything all right?"

"Hi, Harry, everything is just perfect"

"I want you to go with me to Nicholls Town and meet with the chief of police. I have been to the radio base and everything is under control. Your men have been on the radio with your Colombian bases and they tell me that they're just waiting for you to give the signal."

"Well, Harry, all I need is to verify the existence of the extra jet fuel and to meet with the police...are you ready to bring it in tomorrow night?"

"I think so," answered Harry, "have them take off around one in the afternoon, that will put them over Bahamian territory by six p.m."

I got in Harry's pick-up truck and we drove to Nicholls Town. The chief of police lived in a very small house, maybe no bigger than the one I was staying at by the water. A table in the center of the living room had a bottle of Jamaican Rum and a few empty glasses. The huge man saluted us warmly and invited us to share his rum. Harry, the chief of police and I took straight shots bottoms up of the liquor; then we all moved to the table.

A blueprint of the airport facilities was opened on the middle of the table. The bottle of rum was placed on top of the print to keep the wind from blowing it away. A uniformed Bahamian officer was ordered to keep surveillance outside the house while we held our brief meeting. The place was in total disorder. The kitchen had piles of dirty dishes and as I got up to use the bathroom, I felt nauseous when confronted with a toilet bowl that obviously had not been flushed for weeks. The smell of urine and human feces was just unbearable.

The chief of police gave me his promise that there could not be a chance of raising suspicion and that he and his men would block every entrance and access to the airport. He showed me where I was to instruct my pilot to park our plane, and meticulously explained the positions where his men were to be assigned. It all sounded perfect in theory.

"Let's do it tomorrow at sunset."

We shook hands and left the house. A quarter of a mile down the road to San Andros I asked Harry to pull over. I vomited excessively. The smell from that house had clung to our clothes.

"I know just how bad you feel; do you still want to go to check the fuel?"

"Yes, please Harry."

First we drove to the airport, but it was dark, so I decided to wait until the morning to evaluate the scene of my first operation. We went on past the airport to a wooded area. The pick-up truck came to a halt and Harry asked me to follow him into the woods. Some twenty-five feet away from the main road we ran into a mountain of metal drums.

"There it is! 500 gallons of jet fuel."

The one hundred five gallons drums were piled up in rows of ten each and a large canvas covered most of them. A police officer in uniform guarded the fuel.

I walked around and on top of some of the drums. There was no need to inspect their contents. I was satisfied.

The men at the radio base were all playing cards when we arrived. As if they were to be penalized they nervously gathered the cards and put them away when they saw me walking in.

"Hi, Richard how're you doing?" said one of them.

"Fine, how's everything here?"

"The load is already inside the plane, all Cachona needs

is for you to give the green light and the plane will be airborne."

"Get me Los LLanos on the radio." I wanted to verify the status of the plane and the load.

The radio transmitter was placed on top of a small wooden table inside the bathroom by the main bedroom. The frequency was set at 167.9 and the voices of what seemed to be seamen communicating to other bases were coming in loud and clear. I turned the tuning knob to 189.0 and by putting the microphone close to my lips I began to whistle in the style that would identify me as one of the C.C.Q. operating bases. I persisted several times but it appeared that either I had tuned to the wrong frequency or Cachona was not at the radio at the time of my whistling. I gave up. As I walked out of the bathroom the whistle signal from Colombia came through with difficulty due to excess interference,

I ran back to the radio and grabbed the microphone before I could lose the chance to whistle back to my Colombian colleague.

"*Positivo, positivo, este es El Paisa hablando desde la capital de la arepa.*"[8] The voice was coming from Medellin. We were finally in contact.

"*Por favor avísenle al jefe que estamos TR-24 en la gerencia.*" My message was coded but for El Paisa it meant: "Please tell the boss that we are ready in the island."

"*Positivo, positivo, le avisaremos, espero que tengan suficiente gaseosas para tomar en esos calores.*" replied El Paisa. He just told me that he hoped we had enough pop-soda to quench our thirst in such hot weather, meaning, "I hope you have enough jet fuel."

"*Positivo,*" I answered, "*Notifiquen por esta misma serie de chequera que el partido lo jugaremos mañana a partir de la una de la tarde en dos tiempos, y que los árbitros ya estan listos."* My message was to let them know that the soccer game was to begin the next day at 1 p.m. in two halves, and that the referees were ready. We cut off by adding: "10-4 and out," simultaneously. I returned the microphone to German Escobar, one of the young Colombians assigned to me.

"Let's get a good night's rest," I ordered, "We have a hell of a day waiting for us tomorrow!" I explained to them how I intended to give Lehder the green light to have the Turbo Commander leave Los LLanos at 1 PM, and that if things worked out, we would be unloading five hundred kilos by midnight the following day. "We're more than ready," they all answered with a wide smile.

To those men, the successful accomplishment of our operation would mean financial prosperity but more pleasing was the image they would enjoy in their homeland among their peers and co-workers. They would return to Colombia as heroes of the C.C.Q.. Women would run to their side and their virility would be unquestioned. In Armenia days of wild parties and sex would justify all the risk and discomfort they suffered. *La Posada Alemana* would be the arena for all their uncontrolled appetites.

The next morning, after a full breakfast with eggs, home fries, sausage and bacon, a long walk along the beach and a back massage from Paula's long sensual fingers,[9] I left my cottage to join the Colombian team for the final preparations. The time was 10:00 AM on a Friday. The radio transmissions had improved in quality and the feedback was clear as the whistle code.

I was informed by El Paisa that the airplane was fueled and ready to take off at 1 p.m. from Arauca in the eastern plains of Colombia. An estimated six hours of non-stop flying would put it over the Bahamas at approximately

7.p.m; perfect timing for the last Bahamas Air commercial flight to unload its passengers and fly back to Nassau, leaving the airfield to our private benefit.

Three Colombians were ordered to drive to Nichols Town to set up ammunitions and weapons to resist any possible raid . I held a meeting with Harry Treco and the chief of police to insure the safety of my men, the pilots and the way out in case of emergency. Everything appeared to be acceptable. A call from one of my men by walkie talkie confirmed again the existence of the jet fuel. I was ready. At exactly one o'clock in the afternoon, I picked up the microphone and ordered the release of the aircraft. "Green light, all systems go!"

The hours between one and seven were aid full of tension. Jorge Forero, PIC (pilot in charge) kept me posted of his position every hour on the hour. The plane was crossing without any inconveniences.[10]

Once Jorge had reached the island of Andros, and was flying over Mangrove Cay or Northern Bight, we were to switch from the aircraft's HF Radio to high power walkie talkies with scrambled frequencies already prepared by Balin, our technician.

The time was 6:48 p.m. As I sat on the bed of a pick-up truck holding the yellow portable radio in one hand, and the binoculars on the other, the whistle sound from Jorge Forero came loud and clear. Bahamas Air had already landed and was again taxiing to take off ; suddenly Forero's voice came in with urgency "620 TR, 620TR, 620 TR!!" he repeated.

I froze. The code meant either a DEA or a Bahamian police aircraft pursuing our load. The order of priorities immediately came to mind: SAVE THE PILOTS, SAVE THE LOAD, SAVE THE PLANE. I could feel the blood gone from my face and I knew that my panic was visible. Any thing I said to Jorge Forero was under a scrambled frequency, so there was no need for secrecy in my response. My fear was that he would crash trying to find a place to bring theAir Commander to the ground. He had already been flying for almost the entire seven hours of its range and the fumes were drying in his tanks.

"Jorge, do you read me?"

"Yes, there are two black DEA helicopters flying this area."

"Have they intercepted in any way?"

"No, but I fear they are waiting for us to land."

My mind raced for an answer. Several lives were at stake and I was in charge. I could not give way to my fright.

"Drop the load, and fly to Exuma Sound; do what you can."

"I'll try to make it," he spoke through tight lips.

Jorge Forero was the best pilot in the Lehder organization. Not only had he vast expertise in flying over these islands, but he knew how to keep his composure under tight demanding life-threatening circumstances. He knew that in Exuma Sound we had friends that would get him out of danger in a matter of minutes after his landing, and if time permitted even the plane could be saved from the authorities. There were George Town and Williams Town. Either place could offer safety to our men.

I switched the radios off and officially cancelled H.H 98. Harry Treco made arrangements for us to travel to The Exumas immediately. It was a fifteen minutes flight that seemed like an eternity. As we approached the coast of Rolleville, I started to look for our plane. Thank God, there was no sign of any crashes or forced landing. I began to regain my faith.

Later that evening we learned that Jorge Forero had successfully landed in George Town and gotten enough fuel to make it safely to the coast of Colombia. It was a good feeling to know we had not lost our men nor our load or plane. But I felt defeated. I was tired. "Let's go back to Andros," I requested.

10

JUNE 16, 1983

After the frustration of having failed in my first true test, a new dimension of work awaited me. My first meeting with the money launderers was due that morning.

Upon arrival from Medellin on Avianca's flight 066 to Miami at noon, and after the customary inspection by the authorities, Jota arrived looking fresh and alert. His immaculate shirt appeared to have been pressed and starched one minute before landing. Not only had he extraordinary taste in clothes, but his courtesy and cultured manner of speaking made him a likable and welcome business companion, unlike many of the Colombian mules[1] with whom I normally dealt.

Jota was a graduate of St. Thomas University in Bogota, where he had earned a degree in Economics, with Honors. He was the son of a well-educated upper middle class Colombian family, and the proud brother of Clara Helena who had been the first runner-up in a beauty pageant for the title of Miss Colombia in Cartagena. But above all his academic credits and proper upbringing, there was one factor that gave him even more prestige — he was Carlos Lehder's cousin, economic advisor and confidant in matters related to money laundering–perhaps the most delicate function of the C.C.Q. organization.

"Welcome to sunny Florida, Jota," I greeted him with honest pleasure.

"Love to be here," said Jota with a broad smile, "if I could only stay for more than a couple of days." He was affectionate and trustworthy. Talking to Jota, one could absorb his down-to-earth candor.

The ride to Boca Raton would take roughly one hour, which offered enough time to gossip about our mutual friends in the old country, but instead we got into a heated conversation about President Belisario Betancourt. We had diametrically opposed views. I strongly criticized Betancourt's conservative and oppressive policies towards imports of foreign goods in a failed effort to boost the Colombian-made industry. In contrast, Jota applauded the President's every move...but then again, how could I be critical of his loyalty and admiration to the Chief and Commander when he, Jota, was one of the President's close friends?[2]

In any event, it was a pleasant and refreshing experience to share some time with Jota before settling down to discuss his official visit and put our agenda to work. This time Lehder's instructions to me were not typed on a small piece of paper as customary. As my guest unpacked his few belongings, just the necessary toiletries for an overnight stay, he handed me what looked like an old-fashioned table top microphone.

"Is this a joke?" I laughed.

"Some kind of souvenir...most people from Colombia bring their friends a pound of Armenian coffee or aguardiente; and you of all people bring me a six-pound rusty microphone!"

"*Maricón!*" he said. "Inside that microphone there is a mini-cassette with a message from Joe...and you better play it before it s too late." Just like a *Mission Impossible* script.

A few screws held the top of the microphone attached to a screened filter and right beneath a thin layer of sponge and paper there was a tiny mini-cassette waiting to be played.

"Good morning, *hermano.*" said the undistinguished voice, "There is a gentleman in Miami representing a local bank from Bogota. There is no need to describe him. Jota has already met him here in Colombia. You must not reveal your name, and only what is necessary shall be discussed. Your duty is to provide him with all the cash you can collect from the Ochoas as soon as possible. Good luck! *Todo por el Movimiento Latino!!*"

The next day I set off early to meet again with Jota, who had been with Archie since early morning. Jota gave us directions to the condominium where the banker would join us. The building stood in a neighborhood called Hallandale; an area of retirees with money, retired seniors queuing to get the early bird special and risking their lives by jay walking across congested Hallandale Beach Boulevard. The modestly decorated apartment was leased on a short term basis only for the purpose of holding this kind of meeting. No one lived in it; however, it was properly equipped with cooking utensils, linen and a full line of appliances to be ready for use at any given time in case emergency shelter was needed.

The telephone rang a couple of times. It was the intercom.

"Is Jota there please? Is this Jota?"

"No, please hold on," I said, "I'll get him for you." Obviously it was a Colombian, his accent was familiar to my ears, so I handed the receiver to Jota.

"Doctor, please take the elevator to the sixteenth floor, and as you get off turn, left for apartment 1603." said Jota politely, putting the phone back on its place.

Two middle aged white Hispanics were standing by the door.

I noticed Jota's hesitation to welcome these individuals, since we were only expecting one banker. The older one, dressed in a three piece suit, extended his hand for a greeting while the second, wearing tennis shoes, shorts and an oversized Lacoste shirt, waited timidly a few steps behind.

"Don't be concerned, my friends," the first said apologetically. "He is one of my associates here in Miami. Believe me there is nothing to worry about."

For a second I was afraid of an unpleasant surprise. Ordinarily this never happens, so I looked for Jota's approval; his eyes clearly told me it was O.K.

Both men were shown to the living room where, after a brief exchange of small talk, we got to work.

"This time we might be able to offer you a better deal than ever before," said the banker with an ingratiating smile.

"We will need of course at least $250,000.00 to honor our special rate of exchange." He paused as if to allow us time to digest his bargain of the day.

"Otherwise," he continued, "it will be $140.00 Pesos instead of $160.00."

By the time he finished his brief proposal, his smile had been replaced by a sour grimace — just like a banker! Jota's calculator was already displaying multi-digit figures so it was not long before he got up from his chair, and without further ado dismissed the banker.

"Jorge," said Jota in an angry tone. "You're so full of shit that you stink all the way from here to Bogota." I wasn't really sure what triggered his reaction, obviously he knew something I didn't.

"Go tell your board of directors that we have put more cash into your banks between 1982 and the remainder of this year than Benjamin Herrera and the Botero brothers combined. So take your ridiculous proposal somewhere else!"

I was impressed with the way Jota dealt with the two bureaucrats although I wasn't sure about the strength of his position. I didn't want to seem naive, so with braggadocio, I added: "That's right, you guys, I felt all along this meeting would be a waste of time. I think I'll take the cash back to my house." I turned to Jota, whose eyelids twitched in surprise. We both knew I had no money with me. Both men got up deferentially and tried to give us what sounded like useless rationalizations of their rates of exchange and commissions.

"Listen señores, you seem to underestimate our roles; the President of Colombia is ordering the Banking Superintendent to audit all suspicious income and to search for undeclared capital. We have to split fees with Noriega's[3] group in Panama, and to make matters worse Miguel Cardona has already given notice that he is leaving his post as President of Banco de Colombia. He is the only person who can really help us. We do not know what new face will be assigned to his desk."

The voice of the older man was almost quivering, but seeing Jota's stern face I knew all his rationalization was in vain.

As the men were escorted to the door they urged us to reconsider their predicament, and meet their terms. We could barely hold back our smirks as they departed formally. With no rehearsal, we had supported each other's bluffs.

Once we were left alone, however, I said to Jota: "Somehow I don't really understand why you turned them down...it sounded like a decent offer to me."

"My dear Carlos, I make a percentage on every dollar that leaves the United States for Colombia. If I can get them to go just three pesos higher, that represents a small fortune to me. Besides," he continued, "you grab a man by his balls...and his mind will follow."

"You couldn't be more eloquent," I agreed. Jota was entirely right. They would come back. They would not abandon a profitable opportunity, or disrupt a multimillion dollar relationship over a matter of a few pesos.

I went downstairs to the 7-11 to telephone the Ochoas and arrange delivery of $250,000.00 in cash. A pager number and a code were both necessary before one of their members would call back.

The reply came in within three minutes from my call.

"Is this Richard?" asked the voice at the other end.

"Yeah, please tell Jairo I need 250 'invoices' right away."

"Let me get Jairo for you...Jaaaaiiiirooo!" he shouted as if Jairo were not within normal sound of his voice.

"Hi, Richard, what's up?" I recognized Jairo's voice.

"I want you to meet me as soon as possible and please bring the 250 'invoices.' Make sure they belong to the hundred series."

Jairo knew that each 'invoice' meant a thousand dollars and the hundred series was my demand to get us denominations of one hundred dollar bills only.

"I haven't had any lunch, so why don't you come to Kendall and we'll meet at a restaurant near by," proposed Jairo Ochoa. I disliked the way he always insisted on our going to Miami to receive money, and I was fed up.

"No way!" I told him, "I've had it with your laziness in putting us through the risk of driving to Miami to pick up that paper work. It's not just the distance, it's the heavy traffic and all the state troopers looking for speeding vehicles. And remember that delivery of those papers to our office in Fort Lauderdale was part of our deal from the beginning."

Jairo Ochoa knew what I meant. He knew I was refusing to drive with that amount of cash, and he knew I hated to work in Dade County - perhaps the most dangerous place in the world to do any kind of drug transaction.

But he owed us that money, so I demanded that he have one of his men bring it up to Broward County.

"O.K., help me, I don't want to send my man to Boca Raton." He didn't know that I was calling from Hallandale, so I said: "I'll come half way. I'll drive south from Boca Raton to Hallandale, and you have your man drive the invoices to the Denny's Restaurant by the intersection of Interstate 95 and Hallandale Beach Boulevard."

There was a pause, I imagined he was writing my directions, then he came back: "O.K. Richard, thank you for coming all the way south to Hallandale. Next time I'll deliver anywhere you say. My man will be driving a white Nissan Maxima, he will park at the back of the restaurant at a place with enough space for you to park next to him. He will get out of the car leaving the keys in the ignition. You'll do the same with your car. Once you have spent a few minutes at the restaurant, you guys walk out and switch cars. Tomorrow we'll switch back!"

It was the standard procedure and I was uncomfortable that he explained it so clearly over the phone. Although pay phone calls are not easily traceable, I was a bit paranoid about someone listening to our conversation. In any event I agreed and went upstairs to notify Jota that the money was on the way.

"Great!" he said, "let's go get some lunch. How long do you think they will take from Kendall?"

"If they have the money already counted, no more than one hour."

"In that case let's go eat at Denny's and wait for them."

We locked, the apartment and drove a few blocks to Denny's for BLT's, fries and Coke (as in Coca-Cola). The table at the restaurant offered a good view of the parking lot, so we waited patiently for our contact, also planning to make sure he would not bring a 'tail' behind him.

The brand new Maxima drove in and parked just as we expected. The driver did not leave the vehicle while he waited for my car to pull up next to him, so I left Jota while I went to switch my car to the spot next to the Maxima. I recognized the face of the young Colombian from previous deliveries, although. I had never known his name. We both looked at each other, smiled, then at a distance of maybe ten feet apart walked into Dennys. He sat at the counter and I went back to the table where Jota and I were still half way through our BLT's.

After a quick cup of coffee, the Colombian left Denny's without glancing in our direction. I watched him get into my car and drive away without obstacles of any kind. We finished our lunches leisurely, and I got into the driver's seat of the Maxima with Jota as my passenger. I drove around the block a couple of times to make sure no one was follow-ing, then went back to the condominium to verify the delivery. Three supermarket brown paper bags contained the money.

A few groceries such as canned food, a head of lettuce, a loaf of bread and a dozen eggs hid the cash. We divided the bundles of hundred dollar bills that were tightly wrapped in rubber bands and started to count. After an hour of a careful count and re-count we were satisfied.

"Let's have one of your men come over and keep guard on this money while I locate the bankers," suggested Jota. I went downstairs once again and placed a phone call to Max's pager. He was our radio man stationed at Archie's house, a monotonous job compared to his other occupation of hit man.[4]

"I'll be there in forty minutes, Richard." To leave his post in Boca if only for a few hours, was Max's highlight of the day. Normally[5] his job was to sit by the HF radio 24 hours a day in case Lehder called from Colombia or one of our bases tried to contact us.

Upon Max's arrival about an hour later, Jota and I left for Miami to find the bankers.

The Fontainebleau Hilton had been redecorated since the time I took my wife to a New Year's party the year before. Its entire furnishings were more contemporary and even the shape of its swimming pools and outside grounds had been rebuilt. The two bankers were playing tennis at one of the courts and in their concentration on their semi-professional game they were oblivious to us by the fence.

Both Jota and I watched the two men competing with all their might and techniques to win a match that seemed a tie. When the younger shouted GAME! I considered it a proper moment to get their attention.

"O.K. Mr. Ashe, can we have some of your precious time?" The two men came towards us, shook our hands and asked if we minded waiting by the pool while they showered and changed clothes.

"Take your time," said Jota, and we ordered two rum and Cokes.

The two men returned dressed in the same clothes they wore when we'd met them earlier, and sat down at our table.

"I have $250,000.00 in cash waiting for you at my apartment," Jota told them.

"But I don't want you to waste our time with sad stories of how you have to split your profits. You either give us the three more pesos per American dollar on top of what you already offered, or you leave me no other option but to call some people from Banco Cafetero and get it over with!"

"Can you gentlemen excuse us for a minute?" requested the older man.

"Of course," responded Jota. The two men walked away from our table and went towards the swimming pool to have their little chat. In a couple of minutes they returned and with broad smiles said in unison: "It's a deal!"

"You go with Richard to pick up the money," proposed Jota to "Mr. Ashe," "while I make a phone call to Bogota and order your bank to deliver $41,000,000.00 pesos to Carlos Lehder immediately." I left with the man who wore shorts, and Jota stayed with the one we'd been calling Jorge.

Those forty-one million pesos were to be distributed into bank accounts in Armenia, Medellin and Bogota under corporations with different names; one of them the central account for the *Movimiento Civico Latino Nacional*.

A few hours later I phoned Carlos Lehder in Medellin who had been satisfactorily notified by the local bankers of the deposits. Just before leaving the Hilton the Colombian banker asked me, "Richard, does someone in your family in Colombia need a state-of-the-art refrigerator?"

"I am not sure...why do you ask?"

"Well, all this cash will be hidden inside four Whirlpool double door refrigerators and I thought you might want one...once we take the money out."

I thought of my mother, but then I was afraid that in case of an investigation they could trace that equipment, so I declined. "Thanks, but no thanks." I chickened out. I resolved that my mother would get her new refrigerator someday, but only when it could come with no risk attached.[6]

The preparations for load 99 were well under way. This time I had held several meetings with Bahamians police officials to avoid situations such as the one we had a few weeks back.

Another fifty-thousand dollars was given to Harry Treco so he could insure the cooperation of Bahamian traffic controllers in keeping us informed of the activities of DEA's surveillance helicopters. An additional four hundred gallons of jet fuel were purchased and positioned in Inagua and The Exumas to guarantee the safety of our pilots in the event of last minute necessity to return.

Carlos Lehder's reaction to the aftermath of load 98 came as a total surprised to me. I feared he would be very upset to find out about the tight situation in which Jorge Forero, his plane and his load had been placed. Contrary to my fears, I was congratulated for my controlled emotions under pressure, and Carlos himself praised me for what he called: "The smartest way to handle such an emergency. Once again, Carlitos you have shown that you and I were made to be partners in the greatest venture of our times." Carlos was always eloquent, and his words boosted my ego.

Andros was again the base for our planning. Our strategy remained the same and our M.O. had not been altered one bit. Two weeks of preparations, meetings, rehearsals and verification went fast. Finally, on July 25, I contacted El Paisa and let him know I was ready to welcome the 650 kilos the following day around 7 PM

The next day at approximately 1 PM I gave the green light for the load to take off from the southern plains of Colombia[1] with a final destination of Nicholls Town, Andros, Bahamas. In the United States Thomas Jerry Penton, a.k.a "Red," one of my pilots, was making all the arrangements to have the load flown from Andros to Ocala early [text deleted] morning. Normally he himself would fly to pick up the cocaine, but this time he had decided to send two of his most trusted men to fly the cargo back. Red would supervise his pilots and once the cocaine had arrived in the United States, he would fly counter-surveillance over the two transporting vans.

The counter-surveillance would keep the ground team informed of any possible obstacles on the way to South Florida.

The same group of Colombians were assigned to their posts as first arranged. Communications, weapons, transportation, refueling and other tasks had been secured with the supervision of the local police. This time we were even more cautious, more alert and more defensive.

At six-thirty that evening, Bahamas Air landed on schedule. The police were waiting for the passengers of that flight to leave the terminal in order to close the airport for public use. Road blocks were in position to bar all access to the airport using the excuse that there was a big drug bust taking place. Bahamas Air was to depart for Nassau at six forty-five according to their schedule. I walked inside the terminal playing tourist as the passengers deplaned. Only two or three had relatives or friends waiting for them at the terminal.

The rest, some fifty native Bahamians were members of the same church and apparently had come to Andros for a religious convention. I noticed the three police officers in our payroll patrolling the grounds and they winked at me to acknowledge my presence. The group went inside the terminal building and took every available seat. They sang hymns and praised the Lord. I was the only American or white man among them and obviously sooner or later they would notice that I had no business being there since they knew there were no more commercial flights in or out of that airport.

"Excuse me, brother" said an elderly lady as she approached me friendly, "have you been here long?"

"Not really; I've been waiting for a friend of mine flying from the States on a chartered flight."

"Did you see a bus outside the terminal when you came?"

"No, what seems to be the problem?" I asked

"Well, they were supposed to pick us up and they're not here," she complained.

The worst was happening. My plane was to touch down in twenty-five minutes, and there were at least fifty people around us to witness our forbidden operation. I contacted one of the police officers and informed him of the situation.

"Get the chief and tell him what's happening here. We must find transportation for this people to get them out of the airport."

The officer, who had a walkie-talkie radio, passed the

information to his boss who was at the airport entrance detouring traffic back to town. Five minutes later we learned that the bus for the religious group had broken down four miles away from the terminal but thanks to the C.C.Q. several vehicles were made available to transfer the passengers.

I hurried to the runway to look for signs of our plane. At first I could see nothing but then, far in the horizon, I spotted the unique shape of the Rockwell Turbo on its final approach. This time there was no way out. I hurried to the jeep I had driven and picked up the yellow walkie-talkie.

"Jorge, Jorge, do you read me? This is Richard."

"Go ahead, Richard, you're coming loud and clear."

"Bring it down northbound and taxi behind a blue Jeep. I'll take you to a stop position. We had a last minute problem with passengers of a commercial flight, so stay inside the plane until I tell you."

"10-4" replied Jorge.

I drove the Jeep to the end of the runway and waited for our plane to touch down. As customary, due to the loud noise of a turbo-jet landing, we had instructed Jorge Forero to cut off the engines a few seconds before touch-down to avoid a lot of attention from the natives, but for some reason, the airplane came down roaring like a lion[2] which brought every member of the religious convention to the outside of the terminal building to see the noisy bird.

Forero taxied according to my directions and parked on one side of the terminal building between other private airplanes. The letters HK identifying the aircraft as Colombian could not be seen from the building. Feeling a little better I walked inside the terminal.

"Is that your plane?" asked one of the curious spectators.

"Yeah, he finally made it." I answered with a sigh of relief.

I went back to the plane and asked Forero to remain in the cockpit for a few minutes while we tried to get rid of all the Bahamian Air passengers. When I returned to the terminal a van, two Jeeps, and three pick-up trucks showed up at the front of the building.

A uniformed police officer gathered the group and informed them that their bus had broken down and to please excuse the inconvenience having to travel to town in those vehicles. They all joyfully praised the Lord for answering their prayers by providing alternative ways of transportation, and gratefully mounted all seven vehicles singing loud songs of praise. I was thankful to see them go. Once I had known the words, to their hymns, and something within was urging me to run pell-mell after them and away from this filthy business.[3]

Jorge Forero and Crispeta the co-pilot had been cooking from being closeted inside the plane. I drove them to a house which the chief of police had arranged for their overnight stay.

The place, in a lonely part of the island, was nothing more than a hut with two beds, a bathroom and running water. Several men in plain clothes guarded the house while our pilots ate and rested. I returned to the airport to wait for a suitable time to unload and take the cargo into the woods.

Once the sun had gone and darkness was thick, I ordered three Colombians to unload the plane's cargo on two pick up trucks and to drive to a location already chosen by Harry Treco. From a distance and using Army night vision binoculars, I watched the unloading of our plane.

I followed the two pick-up trucks to a remote location in the woods where Harry waited with other Colombians heavily armed, their only job was to protect the valuable packages before they were to be taken back to the airport upon arrival of the American planes at around four-thirty in the morning.

We all took turns trying to sleep curled up on top of the cocaine after the long exhausting day but both the heavy smell of the chemical powder and the millions of mosquitoes flying over our heads made sleep impossible . Every time my eyes started to close, the paranoia images of a DEA raid and the noisy firing of automatic weapons in a bloody battle would bring me to my feet as a survival instinct.

It seemed an eternity until one-thirty in the morning finally arrived. Keeping my plans under tight schedule, I ordered German Escobar and the other two Colombians to help Robert and Keith Treco refuel the Colombian jet plane.

The gas had been transported in drums of fifty gallons each and placed under its wings. The refueling process was awkward and dangerous. Much of the jet fuel was lost in the process for the lack of an automatic pump device. It all had to be done by hand with the aid of a couple of flashlights; a time-consuming and wasteful job.

At five-thirty, before the opening of the new day, I sent Michael Treco to rouse the pilots. It was time for them to fly out of the island back to Colombia. The plane had been properly refueled[4] and this time they could reach the Colombian coast in less time thanks to the benefit of having no cargo on board. I would later advise the Colombian base of its departure.

Jorge Forero looked relaxed and rested.

"Please, Richard, tell Juliana that I miss her and that I'll be seeing her soon."

"I will," I assured Jorge. Juliana was back in Boca Raton and I would be seeing her late that evening upon my return to the United States. Jorge and I embraced briefly and I wished him good luck. The Turbo Commander took off without any problems.

I kept my eyes on its silhouette until it disappeared over the horizon. In a half an hour Red's pilots were due to land. This time there was no need to refuel their plane since the distance back to the States did not override the plane's range. The twin-prop Cessna made contact, asking for clearance ten minutes after Forero's departure .

At the end of the runway we had a truck with its headlights on to guide the aircraft to a side of the landing strip where the cocaine waited on the rear of the pick-up trucks. Time was tight. We had one hour to load the plane and to dispatch it. The interior of a Cessna is much smaller than that of a Commander, so we had to pack every bag very tightly from the end of the tail all the way to the immediate back of the pilot's seat to make it fit.

Once loaded, the Cessna taxied to one end of the runway to build speed. The engines roared with all their torque and power to lift the fuselage and its heavy load. It hesitated, then finally, just when there was no more gravel under its wheels, ascended in a forceful effort to make it over the tall trees that surrounded the landing strip.

Mission accomplished, I said to myself. I had done my part successfully. It was time to go home.

12

AUGUST 25, 1983

A rturo Botero had grown a beard and had gained some weight since I had last seen him. As a skilled attorney with special training in International Law and Diplomacy, degrees he earned at Universidad Javeriana in Bogota and at Oxford University in the United Kingdom, he had been retained by Carlos Lehder. I only knew his job concerned confidential matters in Western Germany in relation to the *Movimiento Cívico Latino Nacional*. His stopover in the United States was for the purpose of meeting me in Miami Beach and using that opportunity to deliver a written message. Lehder had insisted it be put in my hands personally.

The previous day I had been advised of Botero's arrival via HF radio. My meeting with Botero was to be held early in the morning so he could make a flight connection to New York in the afternoon, and later that evening from New York to Frankfurt.

I reserved a room at the Doral so Arturo could freshen up and get some rest between flights.

The typed, white letter-size bond paper contained a long specific straight message:

"Richard:

As soon as you get this message, please fly to Nassau and contact attorney Nigel Bowe. You'll find his phone number listed in the book. His office is right downtown off Bay street. Do not disclose to him your identity until you meet him face to face. Mr. Bowe has stolen more than a million dollars from me in cash and assets. Arturo Botero will give you all the details of goods and monies Nigel owes me. Please be firm with him. He will try to intimidate you with threats of putting you out of the country or even throwing you in jail...if that is the case, remind him of the emerald and diamond bracelet he was supposed to give to the Prime Minister's wife, but 'by accident' it ended around Mrs. Bowe's neck! Also, make him aware of the DC-3 incident; we know that he managed to get it back after it was seized by the Bahamians, and that he then sold the plane and kept the proceeds.

I am hereby sending you a power of attorney to fire Mr. Bowe as attorney and counselor for all my corporations and holdings in the Bahamas, and to retain the services of Mr. Turnkuist who I've been told is an honorable and well respected man inside the chambers of the Bahamian Parliament. There is a small balance of maybe $60,000.00 at the Bank of Nova Scotia which Turnkuist will be able to withdraw as initial retainer if he agrees to represent us in future ventures. You will of course let him know that if he accepts the job the rate for his professional fees will be honored.

I have some ideas that I will disclose to you very soon related to Mr. Goldberg and the possibility of reopening

Norman's Cay. I wish you a lot of luck with Nigel. The man is a beast so do not expect a warm welcome!"

LEHDER'S LETTER ended with his signature which by the way did not offer a clue of his name. A crooked single horizontal line in the following style:

UNDER SEPARATE COVER a memo from "Joe Lehder" to Nigel Bowe read:

"I am sick and tired of your lies and dishonest conduct. The man who delivers this memo to you will request all the files you have in reference to any previous cases. Also, please, give him back the diamonds you have stolen and the valuables you never returned.

If my memory serves me right we're talking of monies due to me since the Vesco days.

A substitution of counsel and other pertinent motions are in order for you to surrender all documentation at once to my envoy Mr. David Jones."

AGAIN LEHDER'S scribbled signature appeared at the bottom of the Memo. There were other legal sized papers that had been prepared by attorney Botero and signed by Lehder to speed up my mission.

Botero and I sunbathed by the pool as I read the letters carefully and discussed other specifications surrounding the Nigel Bowe issue.

Late that afternoon I drove Attorney Arturo Botero to Miami International to board a flight that would take him to Kennedy and then on to West Germany.[1]

For the first time since I joined the C.C.Q. I arrived home early. When my daughter jumped into my arms I realized how little I had noticed what a beautiful child she was becoming. I disciplined myself to put aside the concerns of my new job and give my family my undivided attention—at least for this one evening–I could see in my wife's appreciative response how much the business of working for Carlos Lehder had deteriorated the quality of our relationship.

I had become involved so suddenly in all phases of his operations, and now I felt trapped and short-changed. I looked back at the Carlos I knew God was proud of creating and I saw a Dorian Gray face concealing the greed and selfishness at the core of my being. But as always I put aside these flashes of conscience and gave myself to an evening of togetherness with my wife. Cristina knew I'd be on a plane bound for Nassau first thing in the morning and she had already learned that her questions about my mission would fall on deaf ears, so she just prayed for my safety and hoped for the best.

Morning came all too early, and I knew Burt Gordon would have the plane I requested ready. He was meticulous with the maintenance, and with his paperwork if a flight plan was required by the FAA. I would find him at Executive Airport with both engines running and all tanks topped to capacity even if our flight was just a short hop to the

Bahamas. A pioneer in flying those routes to the Caribbean, Burt made the time a relaxing experience. He never took any short cuts in basic routines either with the FAA regulations or with the aircraft's checklist and instrumentation before taking off. He was polite and respectful to those — in the control towers — in contrast to some arrogant pilots I had met who believed they owned the skies.[2]

This day we cruised at average altitude with the winds at our tail, making record time to Nassau. After the routine clearance, we landed and taxied to the private aviation section a few blocks away from the commercial terminal.

"How long do you estimate to be here?" Burt asked me as we left the airplane.

"Oh, not knowing what I am running into this time, I suggest you go to Paradise Island and reserve a couple of rooms for the night, just in case."

Paradise Island was always crowded with American tourists so Burt suggested we go to a hotel near the airport where the Playboy Club had closed and the Cable Beach Hotel and casino opened a block away.

I telephoned a man everybody in the C.C.Q. called "Borns" whose job was to provide ground transportation when one of us visited Nassau. Borns sent a young cohort to drop off a Toyota-automobile at the airport for my use while on the Island.

On my way downtown, I stopped at the Cable Beach Playboy Hotel to make some phone calls and to prepare my agenda for the day. First I called solicitor Turnkuist's[3] secretary and requested an appointment to see him that afternoon.

"May I ask your purpose in wishing to see Mr. Turnkuist?" she asked politely.

"I am interested in opening a corporation in the

Bahamas and wish to retain his services," I circumvented her question so as not to disclose the true motive of my appointment.

"Mr. Turnkuist has a court hearing at one-thirty, so he can only see you after four p.m. Does that present a problem for you Mr. Jones?"

"That is just perfect, thank you. I shall be there at five o'clock!" On a piece of paper I wrote his address—North on Bay Street.[4]

Burt Gordon had presented me with a new passport and other documents to support my identity. "I have been ordered to give you these. Just make sure you leave your wallet and other papers with your real name inside the plane." A manila envelope contained an American passport issued by the American Embassy in Bogota, Colombia, and a voter's registration card from Dade County, Florida.

The passport physical description was in accord with my picture, and the voter's registration card held the same information with the crucial difference that under color of skin it read "Black male." Thank God I picked up the startling discrepancy so I could destroy the voter's registration and keep only the passport. It doesn't pay to be careless, and my story had to withstand scrutiny. I worried how I was to support my identity with the power of attorney under the name of David Jones, but I didn't ask any questions, trusting that perhaps Borns was the man to straighten out that part of the mission.

I left the hotel and drove to downtown Nassau leaving the car parked by the curb outside the old Holiday Inn building.

Nigel Bowe's office was only a couple of blocks away in a narrow street right off Bay. The three-story building had a glass door entrance but offered no elevator to Mr. Bowe's office on the second floor. A door with a smoked glass portion in the middle had his name painted in black bold letters:

Nigel Bowe
Solicitor at Law

I ENTERED the office without knocking and found myself in a small reception area containing a couple of old leather chairs.

Some out-of-date periodicals rested, on top of a wooden coffee table at the center of the room. An unattended desk with a black old fashioned telephone and some messy piles of paperwork stood next to some glass partitions framed in dark wood. The voices of two women could be heard from behind the glass partitions but I could not make any sense out of their conversations. There was a half open door a few feet away from the reception desk.

I cautiously walked towards it and saw someone who I believed was Mr. Nigel Bowe. He seemed totally involved in the reading of a thick manuscript and I knew he had not seen me. I walked back to the reception area at the front and knocked on the door as if I had just arrived and never been inside at all.

"Come in!" said a feminine voice as I turned the knob and let myself inside.

"Good morning Miss, my name is Jones. I do not have an appointment with Mr. Bowe and I apologize for not making one in advance. I just got in from the States and it is very important that I see him." She started to write with a pencil on a legal pad she picked up from the old desk.

"David Jones. J - O - N - E - S," I spelled it carefully, annoyed that Burt had given me a name starting with J, always hard for me to pronounce.

"Mr. Jones, if you don't mind just waiting a second I'll see if my husband can see you today."

So she was Mrs. Bowe. I was surprised. She seemed too nice a woman for the kind of man I already suspected was unethical and rude. My early assessment was too mild, as I later got to know him as a loathsome disgrace to the cause and profession he practiced with the blessings of the Bahamian courts. I sat down, but while pretending to read a magazine, my mind was rehearsing my entrance, salute[5], and the speech that I knew would make Mr. Bowe a very angry man.

Time seemed to come to a halt. It was a long forty minutes before a huge black obese man in a grey suit and navy blue tie stepped out of his office.

"Mr. Jones?" he asked me, smiling ingratiatingly.

"Attorney Bowe?" I asked him returning his artificial smile.

"Please step into my office."

His wife held the door to his office as I followed Nigel Bowe. In a very calculated move to display good manners and respect, I waited for him to sit at his desk until he invited me to take one of the chairs across from him. I believed that diplomacy was the most important ingredient to gain ground in the war that was just about to unfold, and I made it my job to choose my words very carefully.

"Mr. Bowe, I am the legal representative[6] of a client of yours whom you have not seen for a number of years. and due to the fact that he has tried to reach you by means of telephone calls and written correspondence without obtaining your attention, he has decided to send me."

I uttered every word slowly in a firm deep tone of voice and never relaxed my gaze from his eyes. I rested my elbows on the rim of his desk and clapped my two hands under my chin as I leaned forward at the edge of my seat. I remembered the old lessons on body language at a famous sales seminar and put them to the test.

"And who may that client of mine be, Mr. Jones?" He remained stolid. The man was not easy to shake.

"Doe's the name Joe Lehder ring any bells Mr. Bowe?" As I showed my hands I leaned back and waited with a sarcastic smile for his reaction. If I had not been working for such a powerful man as Carlos Lehder, I wouldn't have had the guts to be so arrogant and cool with the big attorney.

I had information as to how influential he was, but the C.C.Q. had by this time built an imposing image and a man with the power of attorney I carried was not just a mule. Mr. Bowe knew that, so I didn't feel at a disadvantage at any moment during our meeting.

At the mentioning of Joe Lehder, Nigel's face changed completely. He stopped being relaxed and, as if trying to conceal information from me, he got up and started to collect the paper work scattered all over his desk and throw it carelessly inside the middle desk drawer. He got up and closing both his fists in an obvious fury, let them drop on top of the desk producing a loud noise that startled the two women in the other room.

"Is everything all right Mr. Bowe?" they asked at the same time from the other side of the door. Nigel Bowe paid no attention to the women's concern and just kept his glinty eyes on me.

"Who the hell does Joe Lehder think I am? His puppet?" he exclaimed, raising his hands in the air.

"Mr. Bowe here is a letter I must give you," and I handed

him the single page containing the angry memo from Lehder. As soon as he grasped the meaning of the message, he tore the paper into small pieces and threw them at my face.

"I got the son of a bitch out of jail, protected his interests for all these years, I bailed all his men out with my own wallet, I provided him with protection while he lived and worked in these islands," he paused to catch his breath, "and he has the fucking nerve to call me a thief? I do not owe him!" Nigel Bowe was shouting in an uncontrollable rage.

I sat there immobile, listening in shock. I had expected a bad reaction, but not this serious!

I dared not interrupt. I waited for his tirade to wind down so that I could interject a few words to ease the hurricane I had started.

"Mr. Bowe, I have not been present at the negotiation or legal transaction you and Mr. Lehder had through the years. I know Mr. Lehder is a very intelligent man and I have no doubt he made the right choice when he hired your services. Mr. Lehder himself briefed me on the pending issues, however, he praised you and does not deny that on many occasions you have done an outstanding job for his organization." Nigel Bowe sat back on his chair, somewhat mollified, and to my surprise, listened with concentrated attention.

"Sir," I continued, "here are a series of documents that authorize me to collect from you all the papers you have in this office pertaining to every case you held on behalf of Mr. Lehder or his corporation in this country."

The lawyer took the motions and power of attorney and after a silent and careful examination of their contents he put them on his desk.

"Are you the Mr. David Jones appointed herein?" he asked pointing to the power of attorney that had been notarized at the Embassy of the Commonwealth of the Bahamas in Bogota, Colombia.

"Yes indeed! And here, Mr. Bowe, is my passport to verify my identity." I showed him the passport, but made sure it did not entirely leave my hands. Just a precaution in case a close look at the passport could give him and opportunity to discover any possible anomaly. He looked at the picture and made a positive match with my face.

"I am satisfied!" he said.

So far so good, I thought. But I still had 50% of the worst part of my mission, the request for the 'stolen' items and monies. I hesitated for a few seconds trying to find the right words to call him a thief without using that word.

"O.K. Mr. Jones, you have to understand that I have represented Mr. Lehder for more than six years, and the amount of paperwork for all the cases both civil and criminal is so big that it is not all stored in this office. I will need time to summon all that information for you."

"I understand Mr. Bowe. Perhaps tomorrow in the afternoon you might be able to give me the files?" I asked him.

"No, Mr. Jones, there are documents and law research that I will not release. They are my property. I only intend to give you what I consider relevant to his new counselor, and it will take me weeks of work to prepare that material. Are you willing to pay me $200.00 per hour for my fees in collecting that information?"

He had no idea of the great favor he had done for me, by mentioning fees. He himself had opened the door for me to drop the bomb he never expected.

"You have some nerve to ask me for fees!" I exclaimed

getting up from my chair and again resting both my hands on his desk .

"You owe Mr. Joe Lehder about one million dollars, not including a diamond and emerald bracelet, and ahh...let's see, a Douglas DC-3 that just disappeared after it was released to you by the courts in 1977, and do you want to talk about monies from the six corporations that were taken out of the banks for legal fees never accounted for? Should I go on Mr. Bowe?" I raised my voice as each item of his alleged misconduct was mentioned. He looked and trembled with anger.

"Get out of my office!" his hands tried to get my throat, but I was only a third of his size and I was agile enough to duck his grasp. In a second I was by the door defensively watching his every move so I could avoid death by strangulation.

"Get OUT!" he shouted again, "before I kill you." He meant it. The man was totally out of control. Today, as I write about this incident, my mind has no recollection how I ended up walking to my car, but all I can say is that I left that building just in time.[7]

I decided to go inside the Holiday Inn and have lunch by the patio facing the sapphire water that separated Nassau from Paradise Island. I enjoyed watching the big pleasure cruisers as they anchored and the hundreds of foreign tourists disembarked for a few days of fun and tan. Every now and then an airplane of Chalk's Airways[8] would lightly splash the blue waters of the bay in attempting to land before letting down its full weight, making high waves against the walls of both islands.

Over a conch salad and a fresh broiled snapper I began to unwind and recover from the upsetting events of that morning at Bowe's office. I had a few hours to kill before my appointment with Mr. Turnkuist, so I decided to do some personal shopping through the narrow alleys in downtown Nassau. The small shops offered some exceptional values from solid gold Rolex Watches to genuine coral ornaments and jewelry from the deep reefs of the Bahamian waters.

As I entered a men's Italian clothing boutique, I noticed a familiar face reflected in a mirror in front of me. I wanted to turn around to verify my curiosity, but decided not to do so when I realized I was being followed by the woman who earlier introduced herself as Nigel's wife. I pretended to continue my shopping by going from section to section and asking questions of the sales people, but all the while I was aware of Mrs. Bowe's presence in the ladies' section of the store. Coincidence?

Maybe!...But my antenna was up. I bought a sport blazer I didn't really need. I wanted to have a valid excuse to linger and see if she would buy something or leave. The store was small so it would be easy to flush out her motive if she overstayed her time as a browser.

It worked! She saw that I had spotted her and she looked flustered as she rushed out the store. I left the shop leaving my blazer and even charge card on the counter in an effort to catch up with her.

By the time I reached the door, Mrs. Bowe was out of sight. I ran to the bottom of the street but she had vanished in the crowd of tourists and daily traffic. Frustratedly I gathered my charge card and purchases and walked back to where I had left my car so I would be ready to meet Mr. Turnkuist.

The yellow Toyota was gone!

I checked the signs on the sidewalk and there was no evidence that I had parked illegally or in a tow away zone. I looked around to double check but that was indeed the place where I left it from the beginning.

"Nigel Bowe!" I thought to myself..."the son of a bitch!" I believed Nigel Bowe was behind all this and I knew this trip to Nassau had just offered me the tip of the iceberg in terms of surprises .

I called Borns and advised him of the disappearance of his car. I didn't offer any details of what I believed to be a conspiracy, but nevertheless, I asked him to please put a body guard at my side every minute for the remainder of this trip to the Bahamas. Borns was a loyal, long-time employee of Carlos Lehder and had learned the discipline of taking orders without asking many questions regardless of the situation.

"I'll have someone meet you at the entrance of the Bank of Nova Scotia in twenty minutes," he said. "The man is a Bahamian wearing a yellow sleeveless shirt and blue shorts...he will give you a weapon if you want one, although I would prefer not to have you carrying arms while on the island."

"I don't want a gun," I interrupted Borns. "All I want is someone to make sure I get off this island in one piece!"

"I understand," he said, "go over to the bank now." He ended the conversation.

The Bank of Nova Scotia had its branch only a few minutes walking distance from the public telephone I had used to call Borns. I did not go right to the front door but waited across the street to make sure the man in the yellow shirt was indeed available.

Borns might have shown my guard a picture of me because the minute I started to cross the street towards him, he did the same and we met in the middle of the road.

"You are Mr. Jones, is that right?" he said, pushing me away from the traffic.

"Yes, please don't be too obvious. I am going to walk to the office of Attorney Turnkuist. If you see someone following me, just do something to get rid of her or him and then get me out of Nassau!"

"I can get you off the island right now, Mr. Jones."

"Thank you, but I have to see Mr. Turnkuist before I leave." I took a piece of paper from my pocket and wrote the following note:

Burt;
    Have the plane ready at seven o'clock and meet me at the airport.
    We must get out tonight!
    D. Jones

"ONCE YOU HAVE SEEN that I am safely inside Mr. Turnkuist's office, I want you to go to the Playboy Casino and personally deliver this note to Burt Gordon in room 406." I explained as I handed the Bahamian the note. "If you do not find Mr. Gordon, leave the message for Borns to give him and then return to Mr. Turnkuist's office. I will not leave until you come to get me."

"Yes, sir," he said respectfully and followed me into the reception area of Attorney Turnkuist's office. He left once he saw that I was admitted to the lawyer's private chambers.

"Mr. Jones, may I offer you some tea or coffee?" offered the secretary charmingly.

"No thank you, perhaps later," I responded.

Mr. Turnkuist's office, was. entirely different from the

one I had seen earlier during my unpleasant visit to Nigel Bowe.

The highly polished French desk rested in the center of a lush navy blue area rug. The remainder of the office was tastefully decorated with a small grouping of couch and chairs some ten feet away from the desk. The richly mellow parquet floor gave the room the ambience of an old Victorian mansion. On one side a collection of framed titles, diplomas, degrees and citations, including one large picture of Mr. Turnkuist[9] next to Her Majesty Queen Elizabeth in Buckingham Palace.

"Thank you, sir, for seeing me on such short notice; I will try to be as brief as possible." I told him while shaking his hand.

The distinguished attorney listened carefully as I began to present my case.

"I've come to ask you to represent Carlos Enrique Lehder as his attorney in all pending and future matters related to his assets and interests in this country." There was a moment of silence.

"I have never met Mr. Lehder, but have known of him and of his activities in the Bahamas." The attorney's voice became tightly controlled and distant.

I could sense his negativeness and I felt compelled to interrupt him before he could dismiss any proposition in regard to Carlos Lehder. Here was a conservative man of outstanding reputation and impeccable image as a law maker and politician, and any relationship with the already infamous Lehder could only taint his noble career.

"Forgive me sir for interrupting. There is a misconception about the man once known as a drug smuggler and law breaker as most people here remember him. Mr. Lehder is no longer interested in the Bahamas. You may be aware that he is an active political figure in Colombia, his native country, and his only goals are to rule his land under the *Movimiento Cívico Latino Nacional* and to help the people of his country."

Turnkuist listened politely.

"We want to sell his island not only because he is no longer welcome in this country, but also because Mr. Lehder needs the proceeds of that sale to support his political ambitions," I lied.

"I understand Mr. Nigel Bowe has been his counselor for years," countered Mr. Turnkuist.

"Not any more, sir." I told him smiling. "This morning I had a meeting with Mr. Bowe and he has been advised to release all files to me along with some properties and other assets of great value." I paused to see his reaction. His face remained passive but his eyes flickered with interest.

I gave Mr. Turnkuist a brief account of the events that took place at Nigel's office together with the incident of my encounter with Mrs. Bowe at the clothing store and the disappearance of the vehicle. I was relieved to see him begin making notes on a yellow legal pad. It was a sign that he might take our case.

"Now Mr. Turnkuist, I'd love to have that cup of tea, if you join me!" I felt more relaxed. We had tea and biscuits while I related to him the whole story behind the monies Mr. Bowe owed the C.C.Q. and about his misconduct in general. I could see growing fascination in Mr. Turnkuist's face as I went on with my story.

"Listen, Mr. Jones, you leave this power of attorney with me together with the substitution of counsel papers. I will call Nigel and speak to him."

"Are you agreeing to represent us, Mr. Turnkuist?!" I pressed.

"Yes, but only in matters that are protected by the laws of the Commonwealth of the Bahamas." I understood his message and I promised to abide by his rules.

The attorney got up to signal the end of our meeting.

"What about fees? How much do you need to start?"

"Call me in a couple of days...in the interim I want to do some investigating and see how we can sue Nigel to get some of your property back...all right?" I was just about to leave his office when his secretary walked in abruptly.

"Mr. Turnkuist, there is a man in the reception room insisting on seeing Mr. Jones, right away!"

"Are you expecting someone?" asked Mr. Turnkuist, with a hint of surprise.

"What does he look like?" I asked the secretary.

"Oh...maybe in his late twenties wearing a bright yellow shirt and blue shorts."

"Please let him in," I requested, "he is working for me!"

The Bahamian came inside the office where Mr. Turnkuist and I stood ready to leave.

"Sir," he said to me, "there has been a slight emergency and I must see you in private." Immediately the attorney offered me the use of his library by showing us a door next to his office.

"You must leave the country right now!" exclaimed the Bahamian, who obviously had been running and needed to catch his breath.

"Why, what happened?"

"Nigel Bowe has found out that your real name is not Jones, and he has the Immigration authorities ready to arrest you at the airport if you try to leave the country with that passport."

"Holy shit!" I said out loud.

"You must come with me right now, please!" he insisted.

"Did you find Burt Gordon?" I asked the Bahamian.

"Yes, and he has already been notified. He is flying to Freeport and he will wait for you there. I'll take you to Freeport by boat and then from there you'll be able to leave without Immigration Inspection." It was a well thought out plan for such short notice.

"O.K., wait outside. I'll be out in five minutes."

I did not tell Turnkuist what had happened and he did not ask any questions. I tried to conceal my haste under a cool professional demeanor. I promised to call him in two days from the USA

A car with its motor running waited for me outside the office with Yellow Shirt behind its wheel.

Two and a half hours later I landed safely at Miami International Airport.

13

SEPTEMBER, 1983

I felt weary. The anxiety, the excitement and the lack of sleep had taken their toll. The small Cessna piloted by Robert Treco shook as we approached turbulence near the coast of Pompano. We had been cleared for landing at Pompano Airport and in spite of all the need for rest, I looked forward to meeting with Archie. I had just delivered. I had proven myself. I was the man of the hour. In my mind echoed the words of Carlos Lehder when we had met in Haiti: "You are the man!" he insisted, "you'll make at least a quarter of a million dollars this year." Now it was a reality that I had the right stuff to do the job and to do it right.

"Twelve hundred pounds of the finest Colombian cocaine must be in their way from Ocala to Fort Lauderdale," I gloated. I could see the two identical Volkswagens heading south on I-95, one driven by El Monstruo and the other by one of Red's men.

The first would serve as a decoy in the event of police trouble while the second would find a way to escape. El Monstruo would have a woman as a companion and their souvenirs from Disney World would be visible from the outside of the van to avoid any suspicious profile and to convince patrols that the couple were just returning from a week-end at Disney's resort.

The instructions to the driver of the van without the cargo were to divert any state trooper or police vehicle that tried to stop van No 1. Should van No 2 spot a police car pursuing van No.1, van No 2 must immediately crush his vehicle against the police unit.

This action would disable the authorities allowing van No. 1 time to find a detour and hide the cocaine. Red himself would follow van No 1 flying at a very low altitude. He would keep constant communication by two way radio from the air, with Maximo Garzon in Boca Raton and with the driver of van No. 2 to inform him of the existence of any remote danger.

It all represented a well-developed plan. I had no doubts in my mind that the cocaine would reach its buyers that same evening.

But the plan was not conducted as I had arranged. Taking advantage of my absence, Alvaro Triana had instructed the men in this operation to seize my wife and child from my home in New Floresta and to drive them to a house he had rented posing as Carlos.[1]

The Colombians suavely but firmly asked my wife to leave our house only bringing with her the necessary clothes for a few days. Upon questioning such an unexpected move, Cristina was told that Archie had reasons to believe that we might be subject to a DEA investigation, and that for her safety and that of our child's, it was best for her to leave immediately.

Needless to say, Cristina didn't hesitate and was escorted out of the house within minutes heading to the undisclosed location. It turned out to be a quiet, remote area of old Fort Lauderdale just off the Intracoastal and New River.

Unaware of the events that were taking place, I happily cleared Customs and Immigration and proceeded to the National counter to rent a car and rush to my wife and daughter. After all the danger I had just gone through I needed to hug them and to tell them how much they meant to my life.

As I pulled into the driveway I did not see Cristina's car, but I assumed that she had parked it inside one of the garages. I parked next to the service door and entered by the hallway that led to the kitchen. The click of my key going into the lock triggered a nerve reaction in the men Archie had ordered stationed inside my own house.

From behind the kitchen counter a Uzi machine gun pointed at my head. The man behind the weapon was obviously Colombian but his face was not familiar to me. The other two men held hand pistols and one of them yelled "Drop your weapon motherfucker!" I did not have a weapon, but I dropped my bags to the floor and instinctively raised my hands and begged. "Don't shoot!" I had no idea what in the world was going on. I glanced crazily around as if to verify that indeed I was in my own house. I was.

The thought of Lisa and Cristina rushed to my mind with panic and rage. I dropped my hands, and blinded with anger I charged towards one of the pistol-holding Colombians.

"Where the hell are my wife and child?"

"Usted es Richard?" Thank God he understood that I was Richard, and in a loud tone he ordered the other two men to drop their guns.

"I am sorry sir, we expected you tomorrow, not today"

"Who are you guys? And where is my family?"

"We are here to protect the load; Archie has taken your wife and daughter and you're supposed to spend the night at the Holiday Inn."

"What load?" I could not believe that Archie had taken the load, the same load that I had put in a plane early that morning and had stashed it in my own house exposing me and my family to the utmost danger. He had kidnapped my family and had turned our home into a front. His abuse violated every rule of friendship or business conduct, even among the drug trade.

I began to perceive the smell of cocaine. The air conditioner was operating at full capacity and several boxes of air freshener paste had been opened ail over the house to cover up the powerful odor of chemical solutions. I walked past the man with the Uzi towards the guest room. The closet had been emptied of our belongings and filled up to the ceiling with bags of cocaine. In the master bedroom a machine gun and several rounds of ammunition rested on our bed.

"Get this weapon out of here!" I ordered.

"I am going to find my family; I intend to be back with my wife and daughter before this day is over and I expect each one of you to be out of here by then, with or without the coke."

They listened and nodded.

As I prepared to leave, Cucho, one of the men working for the C.C.Q. in Ocala and my trusted friend, walked into the house.

"Richard, I am sorry. We tried to warn Archie not to do this, but he ordered us to do it."

I could see that Cucho was telling the truth. He was frightened.

"Cucho, where is my family?"

"Archie would not tell us where he took them; all I can tell you is that he called your real estate agent and told her that you were out of town and that you needed a furnished house right away. That was yesterday morning. This morning I took him to the Holiday Inn where he met the agent and she gave him some keys, but I have no idea where they went."

"What happened next?"

"He had those men in your house staying at the Hilton Hotel since yesterday. They came from Colombia the day before."

A raging uncontrollable urge to find Archie and have it out with him washed over me, but I had to find my family first.

The easiest method obviously was to locate my real estate agent and ask her for the address of the new house. I left Cucho by the driveway and gave him the same ultimatum I had given the other men. I drove to the nearest public phone and called the real estate office.

"Florida Coastal," answered the voice at the other end.

"I need to speak to Phyllis, please."

Phyllis, a lady in her late forties had been very helpful in obtaining the houses I needed to set up the employees of the CCG. My generous payments for her services kept her lips sealed and my unspoken orders warned her to keep her questions to herself. She had made a great deal of money with me and I knew she would not jeopardize that fountain of income foolishly.

"Good afternoon, this is Phyllis." She was always pleasant, courteous and a great PR lady.

" Hi, Phyllis this is Carlos," forcing my voice to be casual.

" Carlos, darling, I understand you have been to Brazil."

"Yes, who told you?"

"Well, this partner of yours, Mr Antonio Jimenez, told me when he came to bring the power of attorney you had given him for the house in Victoria Drive."

"Of course, Phyllis, I really want to thank you for being so efficient. I understand you found my associate the house that I needed."

"Well, Carlos, that house does not meet your standards but with such a short notice it was the best choice for a fully furnished four bedroom near the water."

"As a matter of fact, Phyllis, that is why I am calling, I just got off the plane from Rio and I didn't get the address of the house from Antonio, could you kindly look up the files and tell me how to get there?"

"Of course, darling, hold on just one second." I waited impatiently, thumping my fist against the ledge.

"Hi, you're still there?"

"I am here Phyllis."

"Take Broward Boulevard east of I-95 past US 1 all the way to the end of the road. Make a left at the bottom, then take the first right over the bridge. The house has a circular driveway and it is the second on the right hand side. The mail box says Santos. That is the name of the owner who lives in New York."

I wrote the directions as fast as she dictated them. I remembered to thank to Phyllis calmly and drove back to my house, not calm at all.

Cucho came outside as I blew my horn.

"Cucho, get me a weapon, one of the pistols your men in there have."

"Where are you going? Do you need me for protection?"

"No, Cucho, I'll be all right. Thanks."

Cucho came back in a minute with an automatic .45 caliber and two clips loaded with nine bullets each.

"See you later, Cucho."

I drove south on I-95 from Glades Road. As much as I wanted to get to Broward Boulevard as fast as possible, I knew I could be stopped for speeding and not being able to explain the possession of that gun could be the end for me. I drove at the top of the speed limit.

The house was an old brick structure with an iron gate and high pine trees at the entrance of the circular driveway. The white facade was more impressive than the other neighboring dwellings. The place was at least forty years old, and although well kept on the outside, the inside was dingy and poorly furnished.

Archie's blue Cressida was parked outside, and next to the garage were two other automobiles that I didn't recognize. I thought for a moment. Should I be diplomatic and avoid a lethal confrontation for the sake of getting my family out of there, or should I just push my way inside once the door was opened and grab my wife and child out without any questions asked? I felt more than prepared to face any resistance, but then, why would they resist? I decided to play it cool and be naive about the whole situation.

I rang the bell twice.

"Who is it?" that sounded like Juliana.

"Richard."

The door opened and Juliana didn't hesitate to ask me in.

Archie, who had been sitting in the sun room all the way at the end of the house had obviously not heard the bell. His surprise at seeing me was written all over his fat face. He got up from the chair and approached me. Lisa, my daughter had heard my voice and ran out of one of the bedrooms shouting "Daddy is home, Daddy is home!"

I held my little girl in my left arm and put my right arm

over my wife's shoulder, ignoring Archie who was standing in front of me.

"Congratulations!" said Archie offering an embrace with open arms. I looked disdainfully into his eyes one step backwards to avoid his hug.

"I want that cocaine out of my house by three o'clock in the afternoon, otherwise I will personally call DEA and deliver it to them myself."

Neither my tone of voice, nor my anger were signs that I was bluffing. Archie ran both his hands over his head down to the back of his neck.

"Fine, and who do you think is the first to get arrested?"

"Not me, Archie; besides, do you think I care about a six million dollar load when my family's at stake? The feds would be glad to have you and Carlos Lehder handed to them on a silver platter."

I was not just bluffing. I was playing the strongest card I had.

"Are you OK sweetheart?"

"I am fine," answered my wife and then she motioned to me surreptitiously. I followed Cristina to the kitchen leaving Archie in the living room. On the way we ran into Max Garzon who apparently had transferred the radios from Andora Place to one of the bedrooms in the old Spanish house. Both Juliana and Max had tried to stay away from the scene of the arguments by going to their respective bedrooms.

Once out of reach of Archie's ears Cristina explained to me now she had been tricked out of her own home-and forced to move to that place. She could do nothing without Archie's consent. "We're prisoners here; I cannot even go to my car."

"Stay here for a minute," I said to my wife.

I went back to the living room . Archie was waiting in one of the chairs. My eyes adjusted to the sight of his impotent presence.

"Itos, please understand, all these things are done as security measures."

"Shut up you little shit, I am taking my family with me and if you interfere I'll kill you."

"Cristina!" I yelled. "Get all your things. We're going."

"You work for me and if you go back to that house or touch that cocaine, you are fired," shouted Archie.

"Fuck you Antonio." I pulled my gun and pointed it at his face, "Don't pull any tricks, as of now we are enemies and I don't work for you any more. If I work for someone, that someone is Carlos Lehder and I hope he finds out what you have done."

As I started to hurry after my wife and my daughter, a loud knock on the door stopped me. The noise was more like someone kicking the door with rage.

"Cristina, take Lisa back to the kitchen," I ordered.

My first thought was of a raid. I looked at-the boat docked at the back of the house, then waited tensely to see who was behind the door. What a trap I had set for myself, I wondered.

"Archie, you motherfucker, open this door."

The voice was Red's. Thank God. But why was he so angry?

I went near the door.

"Red? Is that you?"

"Yes, it's me, let me in."

Before the front door was fully open Red pushed himself in and demanded to see Archie. When I turned around, Archie had disappeared into one of the bedrooms to find protection behind Max's gun.

"What is the trouble, Red?" I queried.

"This asshole knew that I would do this trip only if I were to be paid upon returning from Andros. He sent me to Miami to meet the Ochoas and to collect one million five today. I just came back and all they had was 300 thousand."

"Holy shit." I had witnessed that promise we made to Red but I had no idea Archie had failed him.

"Let's go, Red, I'll pay you."

"You?...How?"

"Just follow me."

I went outside the house to the driveway and explained to Red how Archie had kidnapped my family by trickery and had used my residence as a *caleta*.[2] He listened intently.

"I will pay you with cocaine. I want that cocaine out of my house and by giving it all to you I am giving you the power of six million dollars in collateral to collect the money they owe you and me."

"Fantastic, let's go for it!"

We boldly gathered my wife and child while Archie, Max and Juliana just stared blankly, not imagining what plans we had in mind. We left the house in Victoria Park and headed north towards Boca Raton. I followed Red who was driving an old model Chrysler station wagon. We had agreed that I would stop at the Holiday Inn off Glades Road to leave Cristina and Lisa while we went to get the cocaine.

The guards inside my house aid not react when I announced my entrance. Cucho had met Red on several occasions and knew he was our number one pilot so, there was nothing to fear. I explained to Cucho that I was taking that cocaine and that any resistance from the other men could result in jail for all of them.

"Do whatever you want. I am on your side," he said.

The minute he told the other men of my intentions, one

of them pulled a gun and said to Red, "You fucking gringo take this merchandise out of this house and I have to kill you."

"This is my house" I told him in Spanish, "and if you don t get your ass out of here the federals are coming to put you away for thirty years. He looked at me a then he looked at Cucho who nodded as if to say 'Richard is right.'"

The Colombian trembled and put away his gun and I asked Cucho to drive them back to their hotel after they had put the coke in both our vehicles. In a matter of a few minutes all 1200 pounds of cocaine were loaded into the station wagon and the trunk of the rented car. I followed Red south to Fort Lauderdale and got off at the Oakland park exit. We continued east on Oakland park Boulevard to Dixie Highway to 34th court where men quickly gathered up by Red waited tor our arrival.

They showed us into an open garage at 507 N.E. 34th court, a body shop under the name of R& S Automotive. The cocaine was unloaded by Red's men while we both stood guard outside. Once the load was put away in a secret place our vehicles were driven out of the garage and we returned to the Holiday Inn where I had left my wife and daughter for safekeeping.

My immediate concern was to inform Carlos Lehder of the events that had taken place that day so he would be aware of Archie s underhanded behavior. I needed to speak to him before Archie could give his own distorted account.

I tried calling all the numbers I had, Armenia, Bogota and Medellin to no avail. I didn't want to wait another day, so my only choice was to call Burt Gordon and ask him to fly to Colombia immediately and to locate Lehder for me. I also had a written message from Red demanding payment of at least one million dollars and the immediate firing of Alvaro

Triana, otherwise the cocaine would be sold to the highest bidder.

I sent Lehder a written message separately informing him of the circumstances surrounding Archie, my family and the cocaine and asking him to contact me via Burt on what to do next. Burt left for Colombia two hours after my call. I joined my wife and child and decided to remain in the hotel for the rest of the evening and delay our return home until the following morning. I dreaded going back to that *caleta* which once was a peaceful home. Red gave me a phone number where he could be contacted at any time and then left us at the Holiday Inn.

For the next few days I did not hear from Archie. Red had been threatened by him to return the cocaine, "or else." Red paid no attention to Archie's threats and remained firm in his demands. If Burt did not return with an answer from Lehder by the end of the day, I was advised by Red that the coke would be sold for four million dollars and that he would return to me the balance after he had paid himself up. I intended to do the same, take the $120,000 owed to me and return the balance to Archie.

The present circumstances were driving me to a decision I'd been fighting to make for a long time. The past few days had caused me to reevaluate my life and my relationship with the C.C.Q. No amount of money was worth jeopardizing my family. When my three year old became a pawn in a drug war, I finally came to my senses. It was time to quit the C.C.Q. before I lost all the vestiges of morality along with the ones I loved with all my heart. I waited anxiously for Burt's return to make it official. Cristina was delighted when I shared my thoughts with her. A real new life was about to unfold.

Burt Gordon arrived at my house at six in the evening. He looked exhausted.

"Well, Burt, what's the verdict?"

"No good, I'm afraid."

"I don't understand."

"Joe saw me yesterday. He had already spoken to Archie who apparently told him that you were the one trying to steal the cocaine, and that you were a threat to the whole Colombian cartel."

"But he knows better than that," I complained.

"Archie did a hell of a good brainwashing job. I tried to explain to Joe how things really were, but he believed Archie's version and asked me to pay Red to get the cocaine released. He wants you out of the C.C.Q.."

"So, I am fired?"

"Yes, I am sorry."

"I am not, Burt." I told him of the decision I had already made and {text unreadable}.

"You must see Archie about that."

I paced back and forth trying to digest what Burt had just told me. I was relieved that any temptation to change my mind was gone but I wanted the money that was rightfully due to me and I was ready to accept the terms. "One condition," I said to myself, "I am not through with Alvaro Triana yet."

"Burt, thank you. You have been a perfect gentleman throughout our working relationship. I hope we can continue as good friends." I extended my hand.

"Richard, you have been the best man to work for. Anything I can do for you, just call." We shook hands and said good-bye.

A week later the Colombian Supreme court approved Robert Merkle's extradition request and Carlos Lehder went underground abandoning his resort, his ranches, his planes, his yachts and his senate race.

Red was paid one million dollars in cash the same evening Burt returned from Colombia. The cocaine was released to El Monstruo, and the following day the whole 1200 pounds were distributed among local dealers for sale somewhere in the streets of the United States.

I started to look for a house to live in. I could never afford the rent in the luxurious Boca Raton neighborhood and my cash reserve was getting lower and lower. I swallowed my pride and humbly returned to All-Nation Building Maintenance and moved my family to a-very modest three bedroom house in Tamarac.

PART II

1

WINTER, 1984

Returning to work at All-Nation Building Maintenance required some adjustment after almost two years of association with Carlos Lehder. The routine of an eight hour job behind a desk dealing with the complaints of property owners because their buildings had not been properly vacuumed was quite a change from risking my life as a drug smuggler under the ever increasing demands of Carlos Lehder. But I was thankful to turn my back on the million dollar drug trade and return to All-Nation, especially since the original leave of absence I requested had expired a year back.

Of course I missed the high-class perks that came along with my job with the C.C.Q. The private airplane, the fancy hotel , the VIP treatment, the influence and respect of certain public officials and the clout the Medellin Cartel carried had given me a taste of opulence and a high-flying life style. Nevertheless, I now had one "perk" which made it easy to leave behind all those experiences; I was able to get a full night's rest, and when I left in the morning there was a great possibility I'd be coming back home that evening.

There were a number of items yet to be settled with Archie, and if I wanted a new life away from the dark dealings of the C.C.Q., I had to move fast to settle accounts before grave consequences could take place. For instance, all the houses in operation for the organization had leases under my name, as well as most of the vehicles.

In the event of a traffic violation while one of the employees was delivering cocaine, I would be charged because of my ownership. The same arrest could happen if one of the residences were subject to police investigation. I contacted Jorge Triana, Alvaro's brother, and he assured me that he himself was looking for new houses so I could cancel all the existing leases under my name. I was still living at the house in Boca Raton rented for us by the C.C.Q., but I had already arranged for us to move to an apartment in Plantation. No longer would we enjoy the privacy of a swimming pool and jacuzzi right outside our bedroom, but I had no regrets at leaving our luxurious style of living. A clear conscience was worth the trade-off.

There were outstanding accounts due to me for both salary and expenses. Alvaro had not paid me the last four of my $10,000.00 monthly salary, nor had I been paid my $50,000.00 premium for the last load. The expense account for miscellaneous charges was up to $7,000.00 which I owed to American Express. I prepared a statement with a detailed breakdown of wages due to me up to the date of termination. The bottom line showed $106,000.00.

My creditors were knocking on my door, and in my bank account I had just enough to secure the deposit required to move into an apartment. I had not been back with All-Nation long enough to collect my first salary, so it was imperative that I have a meeting with Alvaro Triana. I dialed his pager and waited impatiently for his phone call. Restlessly I dialed Jorge's pager, again without any results. I was eager to drive to Boca and meet with Archie personally, but to make sure I didn't waste a trip I dialed *El Monstruo's* beeper.

El Monstruo was a Colombian who had been recruited in New York by Carlos Lehder himself. After the transfer of Cesar Londoño, *El Monstruo* had moved to New Jersey away from the duties of the C.C.Q. but upon Archie's appointment he was re-hired to head distribution of the cocaine in Dade County. My phone rang only a few minutes after I dialed his pager.

"Monstruo, please find Archie and tell him that I must have at least $10,000.00 by the end of this business day." I told him in an imperious tone. I had not yet gotten used to the idea that I was no longer entitled to give orders.

"Yes, Richard, I'll give him the message and I will call you back with his answer in half an hour." That was the end of our conversation. Twenty minutes later *El Monstruo* called to inform me that Archie had ordered him to pick up fifty-thousand dollars to give to me that evening. I was delighted to hear the news and immediately set up delivery of the money to take place at the Carrousel, a local bar a couple of blocks from my office.

At six-thirty that evening I drove to the Carrousel and I found *El Monstruo* waiting for me inside the bar.

"Richard, I have the money inside the van," he said.

"Fine, here is a list of the remaining monies that are due to me." I handed El Monstruo a statement, together with a letter notifying Archie that he had seven days to vacate the three houses his people occupied under my name. We walked outside where one of the C.C.Q.'s Volkswagen vans waited in the parking lot. *El Monstruo* handed me a paper bag with the money. There was no need to count it — it was standard procedure. I drove back to my office at All-Nation relieved to know I could now pay all my bills.

I went inside my office and locked the doors. As I opened the paper bag containing the money I saw a few bundles of cash held with rubber bands. The bundles on the top of the bag seemed to be all one dollar bills. I searched deep and ran my fingers throughout each bundle ... every one of those bundles contained only 150 dollars or so. I couldn't believe what I was seeing. I disbelief, I checked again. There was no doubt, Archie had cheated me. I counted each one dollar bill bundle. There were less that two thousand dollars.

The son of a bitch!!" I raged as I pounded the desk with my right fist. I had to confront him right away. As I got ready to leave Boca Raton, Ernesto Alvarado, one of my trusted employees, walked into the building to pick up some chemicals for his route.

"Luis, I would like you to come with me to run an errand in West Palm Beach." I knew the visit to Archie's house could turn into a very unpleasant experience and I wanted Luis to be nearby in case I needed him. I didn't want to be defenseless if Archie turned nasty. I pulled my .38 caliber revolver out of my desk and put it into a leather case that concealed its contents.[1] Luis drove All-Nation's station wagon. I sat rigidly on the passenger's side. As we approached Archie's house I realized the garage was open and from a distance I could see Juliana in the kitchen. I put the leather case under my left armpit and instructed Luis to park near the front.

"If I am not back in twenty minutes please come and get me or call the police if you see trouble."

"No problem " said Ernesto. "Be careful!"

Something inside warned me that this time Archie and I

were finally ready to have our showdown. I walked cautiously into the kitchen. Juliana noticed my presence and with her usual cordiality told me Archie was in his bedroom. I stalked through the living room passing Maximiliano Garzon who looked at me with surprise. He knew I no longer worked for the C.C.Q., but I guess he did not stop me out of respect for our former relationship.

"What the hell are you doing in my house?" shouted Archie as he saw me striding towards him.

"Your house?" I asked him sarcastically. "This house is in my name, and I can have you thrown out of here any time!"

"Get the fuck out of here!" he demanded making his way to the living room. "You no longer work for us, therefore you have no business here!"

"Wrong Archie—I am here to return this." I threw the paper bag right in his face. Hundreds of one dollar bills flew all over the room. "You underestimated me Alvaro Triana and I am not walking out of here without at least 60,000 dollars. I'll deal with Carlos Lehder for the balance!"

Archie sat on a reclining chair that had ruffles reaching down to the floor. "Get this man out of here!" he ordered Maximiliano.

"Please, Richard leave!" urged Maximiliano gently pulling my arm towards the kitchen.

"No way, Maxi, I think you and Juliana should leave before I have this house raided by the police. It's the least I can do for you." In the moment that I lost eye contact with Archie, he leaned over the reclining chair and pulled out a Uzi automatic machine gun. This time his intentions were not just a threat. I could see in his eyes his determination to end my life.

The noise of the bullets shifting to the chamber triggered the most sensitive of my instincts. I ran my right hand to grab my revolver and in a tenth of a second I had reacted by firing three bullets in a sequence. The very loud noise of my revolver left a whistle in my ears as I saw Archie's heavy body fall against the chair in slow motion. My survival instinct reminded me of the proximity of Maxi who I knew was hired to protect Archie, so I turned 180 degrees to point the gun towards his head...

"Maxi, you try something crazy and you get it too!"

Maximiliano Garzon in unison with Juliana fell on his knees with his arms in the air. "Don't kill us!" they begged.

"Carlos, let's get out of here before the police come," cried Juliana once she understood I wasn't going to shoot anybody else.

"No, he's alive!" said Maxi pointing at Archie's body as the injured man held his hand over a face already covered with blood. Juliana ran to the bathroom and brought towels, pressing them over Archie's entire face. I approached Archie and for the first time realized that I had shot him once in his lower jaw and he had blood on his upper right leg.

"Yes, he is alive!" I shouted when I noticed he was conscious. "I'll go call an ambulance," I offered, but just before I rushed for the car I thought of the repercussions of a police investigation. Juliana sat on the floor with Archie's head in her lap.

"Don't worry Archie, you're gonna be O.K." she told him.

"Archie is calling you!" shouted Juliana looking at me.

I hesitated for a second and then ran to his side.

"Please don't call the police. Get me a doctor, go upstairs and get all the cash you need to get a doctor to fix me here."

In his eyes there was pain, but more than pain there was fear; not of dying but fear of an investigation into the shooting.

"I'll do what I can," I told him holding his hand. I felt

very bad for the man, but there was anger in my heart because I knew he would have killed me if I hadn't shot first.

Ernesto Arango[2], who patiently waited outside the house, had heard the shots and decided to come inside where he found me kneeling by Alvaro's head. The blood-soaked towel grazing my legs.[3]

"Ernesto, do you know a doctor willing to help us who would keep his mouth shut?" I asked him.

"No, but my son works with a Cuban doctor[4] in Wilton Manors; maybe he can guide us to the right person.

"Please, take the station wagon and go the nearest pay phone, call your son and get me a doctor's name and number."

Luis[5] left immediately. Alvaro's bleeding seemed to have subsided although it seemed his pain appeared to be getting worse. With the help of Maximiliano and Juliana, Alvaro was transferred to his bed. As Juliana tried to replace the towel that held his face wound, I saw a huge mass of flesh sort of hanging from his lower lip and particles of facial bone were exposed. The bullet wound on his upper leg had ceased from bleeding once Maxi applied a tight knot with a clean bed sheet.

I decided to go outside and check the street. I was afraid the neighbors would be gathering outside the house anxious to find out where the shots came from. The house right across the street looked empty–thank God! I kept walking down Andora Drive and it appeared that the shooting had gone totally undetected . So far we were safe from the police.

Ernesto had called his son and explained the situation. His son had then spoken to the doctor for whom he worked, who in turn gave him a couple of names for me to call. I left

Alvaro's house and raced to a pay phone near Palmetto Park Road.

It was almost eight p.m., and both names and numbers I was given were operated by an answering service. Needless to say I could not leave a message with the operators except that it was absolutely necessary that one of the doctors call me back at that public telephone. My car was parked right next to the phone and I just sat in torment waiting for the phone to ring. It seemed an eternity before one of the doctors called back.

"Doctor, thank you for calling back. I was given your name by Doctor Sanchez[6] and I hope you can help us!"

"Dr. Sanchez has given me some details of the accident, but I'd like to see the patient before I can give you a solid diagnosis." I couldn't thank him enough for sparing me the task of explaining the situation over the phone.

"Doctor, I am ready to meet you anywhere!"

"Where is the patient?" he asked.

"At his house in Boca Raton."

"Well, I live in Boca Raton myself–I am off A1A and Glades Road."

"Wonderful, can we meet..."

"Go to the Stop-n-go on Glades and San Andros!" [7]he interrupted.

"I am on my way, Doctor, I am driving a white Reliant Station Wagon." I put the phone down and before going to Glades Road, I stopped at the house to notify Juliana that help was on the way.

A yellow Cadillac Eldorado pulled next to my car at the Stop-n-Go station. The doctor, a man in his mid-forties, motioned me into his car.

"There is no need to tell you my name until I have

agreed to treat your patient." The doctor was being cautious. "Tell me what happened!" he insisted.

I explained that the shooting was an incident of pure self-defense[8] and that it was the victim's own idea to call him so as not to get the police involved. I went on to describe the nature of the injuries as best as I could. He listened carefully.

"We'd better get him some help," said the doctor, "it sounds as if the man is in serious condition. Leave your car here," he suggested.

During the drive to the house, I was startled when the doctor looked at me and said: "You should have killed him. How do you know that man is not going to get better and have you killed?" The doctor's knowledge of the underworld reinforced the question which had come to my own mind, but I had fought off that frightening thought.

"I must warn you that if I find your patient in a critical condition, I have no choice but put him in the hospital. Normally that requires reports and police investigation."

"I understand, sir," I told him, "Alvaro can pay you whatever price you require in order to avoid an investigation; we can put him in one of our[9] planes to Colombia as soon as his • condition becomes stable."

As we entered the house we could hear Alvaro's moans of uncontrollable pain.

The doctor asked Alvaro the routine questions regarding allergies and his basic medical history, before injecting him with a pain killer. Then he proceeded to wrap bandages all around his head covering the injury, leaving just a slit for his eyes to peer out.

"I'll have to get some intravenous solutions and a suture kit," explained the doctor, "I'll be back in a half an hour or less. That pain killer is very strong and should put him to sleep in ten to fifteen minutes.

"Is he going to be all right?" I asked anxiously.

"He will need surgery to remove the bullet near his pelvis and of course major plastic work to repair extensive tissue damage to his face, but I believe it'll be all right to fly him to Colombia so long as he is properly transported on a stretcher."

Later that evening Alvaro had temporary surgical sutures to hold his face together. An intravenous tube was placed in his arm with pain killers to keep him under sedation until he arrived at a hospital in Colombia. His pelvic injury was patched with bandages, but the doctor decided not to try to remove the bullet.

Soon after the procedure, Alvaro was in a deep sleep. I gave the doctor an envelope which contained twenty-thousand dollars. He felt the thickness and glanced furtively inside. His mouth tightened, and I asked: "Is that enough for your services, Doctor?"

"Yes, that will be sufficient," he replied and it was only then that I noticed the greedy satisfaction in his eye. The following morning I made all the necessary arrangements to have Burt Gordon fly Alvaro Triana to Medellin. Carlos Lehder was advised by HF radio of Triana's arrival, and he ordered his personal helicopter to stand by so Alvaro could be transferred immediately to a local hospital in Medellin. Once Alvaro had been safely transported out of the country, Juliana, Maxi and I sat down to plan our next move.

"Maxi," I asked him, "I am curious to know why you didn't come to Archie's defense when I shot him."

"Well," he reflected, "Alvaro was going to kill you. He didn't need defense; it was you whom I would have defended if you had failed." He paused. "You're the better man, and we knew that Alvaro had cheated you with the money. You did the right thing, only not as well as I would have done it." Maxi ran his index finger across his throat. "Why didn't you finish the job? He was going to kill you. And now when he recovers your life won't be worth a peso."

"Yes, Richard," said Juliana, "the man does not deserve to live! When it came to a showdown, we were on your side."

I thought for a few seconds. They had a good point—but I knew I couldn't have lived with myself if I had killed Archie.[10]

It was enough of a nightmare to have wounded him so severely. But now I'd made an enemy for life. Our long standing friendship had ended abruptly with Triana's attempt on my life.[11] I guess it hadn't been my day to die...nor my day to kill.

I left Juliana and Maximiliano cleaning up Archie's blood-soaked carpet and never saw them again.

In 1987 I learned Maximiliano had been arrested in Miami on Federal charges of carrying cocaine. Juliana left the United States right after the shooting of Alvaro Triana. I wished her well.

The shooting of Alvaro Triana left indelible anguish in my mind. I was not proud of a business which had led to such violence and there were moments when I wondered whether it would have been better not to have defended myself at all. And now I felt like a walking target. Surely even at this moment, Carlos Lehder was hiring someone to avenge the pain of his close associate; or if not Lehder, then the Triana family.

Through reliable sources in Armenia, I learned that Alvaro had been operated on and a complete face build-up had taken place. "You did him a big favor," commented members of my family, "the man looks better with his new face." Their callous remarks didn't erase my regret.

My brother Guillermo one day had run into Alvaro at the Banco de Colombia. With some hesitation he asked how he was. "Fine, Guillermo," Archie answered cordially, acting as if the shooting had never taken place.

*A few weeks later the administration of Belisario Betancourt ordered the arrest of Carlos Lehder with allegations that he was responsible for the brutal assassination of Minister Lara Bonilla. That was Alvaro's chance, even though he had played a very important role in the Lehder organization during this event. Since Lehder now had to go underground, Archie proceeded to defraud him of millions of dollars in assets and cash. Today Alvaro Triana** lives the life of a millionaire, holding title to many of the Lehder properties. He has hired the services of bodyguards, but there is no question in my mind that sooner or later life, or the Lehder forces, will catch up with him. There are also several Federal indictments against Alvaro, and the authorities know it is just a matter of time. I believe Archie knows that, too.

M y withdrawal from the C.C.Q. put a dent in Lehder's activities in the Bahamas. Ramon and Gaviota had money due them from previous flights, and the pilots were worried that the decline in drug runs would leave them with unpaid wages. After a heated but unfruitful argument with Carlos Lehder, the pilots prudently decided to hold on to their last big shipment of cocaine as collateral against Lehder's debt to them. It wasn't long before they contacted me and asked me to help them move that coke, since they were not able to find the right buyer. I had never dealt with sales of any drugs in the past, and I had no desire to start now. I turned them down.

"Richard," coaxed Ramon, "we are wealthy men; we can trust you with this cocaine, and you just turn it into cash at your own pace. Please take it, and call us when you have twenty, thirty or forty-thousand dollars together. We have gotten to know you," added Gaviota, "and we trust you."

"Then you, better than anybody else, know that I have no previous background in the selling of drugs. I thank you for your confidence, but my experience is more like yours, just flying the loads to this country for the wholesalers to distribute it," I protested.

"Come on, Richard, we know Archie and Lehder stole money from you, from me, from Ramon, Pucho and many more. You must be hurting financially, and we thought of you because you're the only one we have faith in!"

They were right. I had worked very hard and I had put my life on the line many times for Lehder and Triana, and at the end walked away with empty pockets. Maybe this could be the opportunity to make up for all the loss, I justified. I had dirtied myself and had nothing to show for it. If a little more dirt could solve my problem, why not?

"O.K., I accept the cocaine, but please understand clearly that right now I don't have the slightest idea of how to sell it. I will hide it in a safe place and if at any time you want it back, just page me and we'll meet. If I haven't been successful in four weeks, I'll return it to you. Is that fair?"

"Fine," said Gaviota, "don't feel pressured, and don't take any risks in an effort to get rid of it. Take your time!" I was instructed to drive to Pompano Fashion Mall at ten a.m. the following morning, and to park next to Sears. A beige Volkswagen passenger van owned by the C.C.Q. would also park near Sears and Monstruo, the driver, would go inside the mall leaving his keys in the ignition.[1] I was supposed to get into the station wagon without being seen by any member of the C.C.Q., and drive the vehicle with the cocaine inside to an undisclosed location. I would then return the wagon to the same location, again carefully avoiding detection, and telephone Ramon or Gaviota to advise them of the situation.

Next morning the mission was accomplished without complications and I drove the Volkswagen van to my hiding place where the cocaine would be safe until I could find a buyer. In total there were six kilos of prime Colombian coke.

When you have six kilos of cocaine that could sell in the street for $240,000.00, you don't just pick up the yellow pages and look under "Coke Users" or "Junkies, Inc."

I cautiously made a few trusted Colombian friends aware of my access to some cocaine, but of course did not disclose how much, or the fact that I already had it under my belt.

When a couple of weeks passed and no one called to express interest in my holdings, I telephoned Ramon to give him the negative news. "It's just not my bag, Ramon, why don't I just return the coke to you and forget all about it?"

"Don't worry," he insisted, "it's safer if you take your time. We'll wait."[2]

I felt better, but I was aware of the seriousness of such a deal, and my nights were getting longer with sleeplessness. Ramon and Gaviota ran a charter aviation service plus a full aviation mechanics shop next door to Associated Air in the youth wing of Fort Lauderdale International Airport. I visited them frequently to keep them up to date on my unsuccessful efforts to sell their coke. In view of my obvious sincerity and honesty, and as an incentive to boost my efforts, they decided to offer me a greater commission if I sold their load.

Instead of the $4,000.00 per kilo, they raised my share to $5,000.00. At last, Ernesto Arango mentioned that someone for whom he worked part time buffing floors had asked him, since Ernesto was Colombian, if he knew anyone who sold good quality cocaine. Ernesto denied knowing anyone, but called me the next morning to pass on the shop owner's request. I told him I knew a very reliable party, but the sale had to be by the kilos and not by ounces or grams as is commonly sold in the streets. I also made it clear to Ernesto that payment had to be made in cash and delivery on a one to one basis; in other words the buyer and seller should be the only ones present at the closing of the deal.

Two days later Ernesto excitedly walked into my office and told me that his friend was ready to buy one kilo for cash, providing I could let him try a sample. I told I would contact the owner of the cocaine and that I would do my best to get him a small sample that same day. We agreed to meet in my office after hours at 7:00 p.m. and I went to the place where the cocaine was hidden, I took one of the kilos that had been vacuum-packed so it felt as hard as a brick, and with the help of a double edge razor blade I carefully made a cut on the surface of the plastic. It was deep enough so that I could, with the tip of a sharp knife, scrape just about a half a gram to take to Ernesto as a sample. By the flaky and glittery look of the cocaine, I had no doubt I was handling the best *perico* from the Colombian kitchens.

Ernesto returned around eleven. I had been on pins and needles thinking that he had been arrested, or possibly even mugged by the same people he went to see.

"They loved it! They've never seen anything so clean and so powerful as this stuff!" Ernesto exclaimed as he sat in front of my desk.

"Did they use it all?" I asked.

"Well, we all did a couple of lines. I had to let them taste it."

I could see in Luis glittering eyes and in his uncoordinated movements that he had had his fair share of the coke, but I made no comment.

"Well, what is their offer?"

I had told Ernesto that if they agreed with the quality, the price would be $38,000.00 and that anything above that price would be his.

"They're ready to buy two kilos at $37,000.00 right now."

I knew that even at that price I could make my $5,000.00 profit per kilo, and still give Ernesto $2,000.00 for delivering both the coke and the money; but the problem was not money at that point.

The problem was making sure his friends were not Federal undercover agents or local county police officers posing as buyers. I decided to investigate the prospective buyers by gathering as much information as possible before meeting them face to face. Ernesto offered to help me find out details of their employment, families, social activities, etc.

Ernesto claimed Eddie and Jeff were a couple of Italians who operated local businesses in Fort Lauderdale, and wanted to multiply their investments by taking cocaine to the streets. Ernesto also commented that he knew a lab technician who could take one of my kilos of cocaine and add an adulterated cut to increase the kilo to 1500 grams. The inferior cocaine would not only cheat the street buyer, it could even be fatal to him[3], but it was a common technique.

It doesn't pay to be naive in the drug business, so I hired a private investigator to follow Eddie and Jeff everywhere they went for a couple of days. The detective was not told the purpose of his assignment. I also spent long hours digging into their backgrounds myself until I felt reassured that the two men were not working for a law enforcement agency. I gave Ernesto the green light to set up a meeting with Eddie and Jeff at a public place; preferably a crowded bar or restaurant. We settled on a small pub, the Alibi, on Powerline Road North of Oakland Park Blvd.

I hated guns, and had only carried mine once since the days of unrest and violence during my tenure as a university teacher in Bogota.[4] Riots against the Colombian government posed a continual danger[5], and guns were a common precaution at that time.

Today I once again pulled my .38 caliber revolver out of the closet. I didn't like to remember the only time I ever used it, against my former friend Archie. I prayed to God that I wouldn't have to use it now.

Country music blasted out of the juke box where booths surrounded a pool table at the center of the Alibi. The time must have been near 6:30 PM, and blue collar workers were coming in by groups of three's and four's to spend some of their hard earned construction dollars. Not wanting to seem out of place, I had taken off my tie and jacket just before I left my car to walk into the establishment. I started a friendly conversation with the waitress but every now and then I glanced nervously around to see if Luis had arrived with the guest of honor.

At last through the smoky window I saw a black Corvette automobile pull to the front of the parking lot. I had never seen Jeff in my life, but I had been told he drove a black Corvette, so I watched carefully as a George Hamilton type entered the bar.

Either by chance or by intuition he chose the stool next to mine and ordered a beer. Jeff, a very clean-cut looking Italian in his forties, started a conversation by ogling the head waitress whom he obviously knew well.

"Isn't that a beautiful piece of tail?...Or isn't that a beautiful piece of tail?" raising his beer to toast her departing figure.

"She looks delicious," I replied.

"Hi, I'm Jeff," he smiled.

"Hi Jeff, I'm Carlos."

"Are we... ahhh...do we ahh," he hesitated.

"I think so, Jeff; let's wait for for Ernesto and for your

partner Eddie so we can move to a quiet table."[6] The moment Jeff discovered my identity and I his, our emotions turned to business and the sexy women might as well have been invisible. Jeff's tone of voice conveyed great deference and admiration for me as he volunteered information about himself.

"I own a beauty salon on Commercial Boulevard. I have never been arrested in my life, but I have saved some money to work with someone like you and start a profitable business relationship. All my buyers are in the Florida Keys. My partners are people whom I have known for many years, but their territory is Michigan and New England."[7]

"Well, I told that I only wanted to meet you and a man called Eddie. I do not have interest in meeting anybody else, not today, not ever!" I spoke firmly. I had learned from previous experiences that when a Colombian owns the cocaine, he always calls the shots and is respected, and I tried very hard to convey that image.

About ten minutes into our conversation, Eddie showed up inside the bar. Eddie, six feet tall with curly short brown hair was wearing jeans and a 'T' shirt; had on the All Nation blue uniform displaying our twenty-four hour emergency number across his chest. Jeff motioned to the newcomers to follow us to a small table away from the juke box and the noise of the pool players.

"Ernesto speaks highly of you, Carlos," said Eddie with a smile.

"Well, he has no choice; otherwise he has to wash windows for someone else." I teased trying to lighten the already tense environment.

Beers were brought up to the table and the waitress asked if we wanted company. "I know four girls who would die to share a good time with you guys!"

"No, Jeanie, maybe some other time," Jeff rebuffed her, "and no more beers unless we call you!"

The girl understood we needed privacy and left meekly.

"O.K., let me explain how we do this," started Ernesto.

"Shut up, Ernesto!" I told him more harshly than was my nature. I had a role to play. "You are just here to keep your eyes open and your mouth shut, understand?"

"Yes, sir," he answered timidly.

"I want this deal fast. You have seen my merchandise; I understand you used it up your noses and you loved it, so it's time you show me your money." I demanded.

"Your stuff is the best and we have the money at my place. You don't expect me to carry $37,000.00 with me, do you?" reasoned Eddie. It didn't smell right to me. I had to be cautious with this very first deal.[8]

"Why not? Don't you drive a car? Or do you think that I just walk up to strangers' houses to pick up cash for drugs?" I was being very stern. I'd heard of traps of that kind.

"I tell you what, you go get the cash, and meet me at the parking lot by Zayre's two blocks south of here. Once we're there we'll find a place to count the cash and deliver the goods."[9]

"It sounds all right," said Jeff.

"No surprises; right Carlos?" Eddie spoke nervously.

"Same goes for you guys...a new face shows up and you might as well kiss this deal good bye."

"When do we meet?" asked Jeff.

"I need at least one hour to pick up the cocaine from Pompano." I was lying, the cocaine was already in my car, but I needed men to protect me in case something went wrong. I went to a pay phone and called Leon, another of my employees, and told him to get me three men just in case. I was a good boss for these men, and they gladly offered their surveillance at no charge.[10]

One hour later I spotted the cars of my "bodyguards" in different positions but all at close range. When Jeff's Corvette approached the parking lot I got out of my car so he could see me.

He parked beside my car and next to him parked Eddie in his Continental. I asked Ernesto to sit inside my car with the cocaine while I used the back seat of Eddie's car to count the $37,000.00.

It took longer than expected since the cash was a mixture of fifties, twenties and a few hundreds. When I had satisfactorily finished the counting I signaled Ernesto to bring the kilo to me by flashing the lights in Eddie's car as previously arranged. I put the kilo in the glove compartment and took the cash inside a shoe box to my car. I had ordered Leon to intercept Eddie or Jeff if they decided to follow me, but later that evening they reported no problems of any kind.

Each one of my three bodyguards made $300.00 for watching me for twenty minutes. The first sale had been completed without incident. I felt great! Three weeks later a second deal took place without difficulties of any kind, and a third followed a few days later. Jeff and Eddie appeared to be 'Honorable Cocaine Dealers' and I was enjoying my share of the sales that complemented my paycheck at All-Nation.

I now could buy the house I wanted and the 36 footer Chris Craft pleasure boat I dreamed of. Every time a sale was consummated, I would drive to Associated Air to make payments to Ramon and Gaviota. They were happy with the efficiency of my sales and even suggested we start our own cocaine importing business by putting all our revenues into cocaine in Colombia.

As appealing as the offer sounded, I wanted out of that relationship and the selling of cocaine as soon as I had entirely paid for my house, my boat and all my bills. I figured the sale of four more kilos would provide me with cash flow to put in my bank at a high yield interest, and then I could continue working for All-Nation and totally abandon the dangerous life of illegal drug sales.

I had already become a co-owner of All-Nation Maintenance Service Inc. I now had a newborn son, Nicolas, and from my personal point of view I thought I had my future under control. What stupidity and what arrogance to believe I could just walk away any time!

I asked Ramon and Gaviota-to get me four kilos, which Eddie intended to sell to a man from Michigan by the name of George. The price to me was set at $39,000.00 per kilo, to net me a profit of $36,000.00 in one day to close my act.

Eddie and I agreed to meet at a neighborhood lounge called Scallies where we would switch vehicles. He would take the four kilos to his friend in Pompano, a twenty minute drive, and I would remain at Scallies waiting for the cash. I had learned to trust Eddie by giving him the cocaine up front before payment, and I never had any problems; besides it avoided my own exposure to the streets. I'd just sit comfortably at home and wait for the cash. It never failed.

This time one hour went by and there was no word from Eddie. I telephoned every number where I might get information of his whereabouts, to no avail. My next move was to return home and to start calling every police station from Miami to Boca Raton, but no precinct had a booking for any drug arrest that evening nor reports of any Eddie Gould or William Ross (his alias) involved in an accident. I kept fighting in my mind the suspicion that Eddie had stolen the cocaine and left town. I paced the house for hours until the phone rang.

"Carlos, I am hurt," his voice sounded as if the man was in pain.

"I was attacked in the parking lot of George's place in Pompano. Somebody hit me on the head when I opened the trunk of the car and they got away with the cocaine."

I listened intently. I did not believe a word he said.

"Did you go to a hospital?" I enquired.

"No, I think I was left unconscious by the side of my car; I just came to and went to a phone booth to call you." The more he spoke the more the heat or anger rose in my veins.

"I want you to meet me at Carousel in a half an hour."

The Carousel was a lounge on Andrews Avenue in downtown Fort Lauderdale. The time was around 7:30 p.m.

I immediately called Ramon and Gaviota and asked them to refer me to a couple of very nasty Colombians, the ones the Cartel used to collect overdue bills. I did not give Ramon the details of what had just happened, but obviously they knew it was related to their cocaine. Right away they assured me they'd send someone to handle the situation. They promised to call me back. Five minutes later the phone rang.

"Listen Richard, this man does not fuck around; he is on our payroll, but he's been instructed to do whatever you order. If you have been cheated on, just let him handle it; that is his field of expertise."

"I'm not sure what happened," I explained to Ramon, "all he says is that somebody hit him on the head, but it sounds fishy to me. I don't want him dead or hurt. I just want your man to give him a scare."

"You tell him what you want done. He'll be at the

Carousel in five minutes. He will be driving a black Chevy Blazer with tinted windows. Wait for him outside the lounge and keep the transaction outside the restaurant."

I listened carefully, I was beginning to feel symptoms of diarrhea. I rushed out of my house on the pretext of attending an emergency at one of the properties I managed. By now I was becoming accustomed to carrying my gun and now I made sure it was loaded.

Just in case, I put another handful of bullets in my pocket. I kissed my wife and kids as if I were going off to war. I felt in my gut that Eddie and Jeff had ripped me off. One hundred and sixty-thousand dollars were lost.

When I pulled in front of the front of the Carousel the black Blazer was already waiting. I left my car and walked towards the "Executioner." He opened the passenger door of his vehicle and invited me in.

"Richard?"

"Yes."

"Get in." I climbed into his vehicle and immediately I saw the Uzi machine gun hanging from his shoulder strap.

"Do you know the circumstances?" I asked the Colombian, a young man about twenty-five, scar-faced and looking very short next to his impressive weapon.

" Nothing! And I don't care. I get paid by the job, the gossip is garbage!"

"Well, let me tell you something; I feel the man you're about to meet has stolen four kilos from me, kilos that actually belong to your bosses Ramon and Gaviota, but as you understand I am accountable for them. I want you to make this man understand that we do not buy his story and that we want the kilos or the cash by midnight tonight. If he doesn't do it, then he is all yours."

I knew I wouldn't let this Colombian animal actually to

harm Eddie, but I needed to show him that I was used to this kind of heat, although I was really shitting in my pants.

The Carousel was half-occupied. We chose a table next to the band to shield the sound of our conversations with the help of the loud country music singer. Eddie sat between the Colombian and me.

"O.K., Eddie, the gentleman sitting next to you was sent by my boss upon my request." I told him. "Once something like this happens, you have to deal with them. But first I would like to ask you some questions."

"Anything you want Carlos," answered Eddie nonchalantly.

"How come you're so calm? Do you know the mess you've gotten yourself into?"

"Well, I'll find the people who did this to me! You don't have to worry."

"You told me an hour ago over the phone that you have been mugged and hurt. I don't see you bleeding or looking bad at all."

"You think I'm lying? Look at the blood on my head!"

He lowered his head so we could see an inch of dry blood under his hair. Apparently he had self-inflicted a minor incision just deep enough to make it bleed; it didn't require a medical examiner to come to that conclusion.

"You're a thief! And you are going to pay for it!" I paused. "I'm giving you until midnight to return the coke or the money; otherwise I turn you over to this gentleman sitting next to you." I pointed to the mean Colombian.

"No, no, please give me a chance. I know who mugged me, I just couldn't fight them all. They knocked me unconscious." Eddie finally had started to shake.

"Take us to the place where you were mugged," ordered the Colombian.[11]

"O.K., but those people are rough!"

"Great. Let's see who's rougher!" threatened the Colombian, then he continued, "do you have any weapons on you?"

"No. I don't carry any when I go on business; besides, I've known these people for years," replied Eddie.

"Are they in a house or an apartment?" asked the Colombian.

"It's a building on the seventh floor, but...ah...are you planning to go there now?" asked Eddie terrified.

"Yes, we are, and you're coming with us if you want to save your life. You see, we don't believe you were mugged. It sounds more like you delivered the goods and you're keeping the money. Isn't that right, Eddie?" sneered the Colombian, this time pressing the tip of his automatic weapon against Eddie's stomach.

I kept silent hoping this technique would force Eddie to come out with the truth. If Eddie did not tell the truth, I knew I could be in deep trouble and maybe that was the reason why I went along with this kind of psychological torture. In any event the man was lying and all three of us sitting at that table knew it.

"O.K., Eddie, let's cut the bullshit and let's go to the building NOW!"

"Why don't you give me a day or two to locate the people, and I'll do the collecting?" His tone of voice was begging. The Colombian looked at me waiting for my reaction. I knew I had to do something to save the poor wretch although I was angry enough to want him to suffer for his dishonesty. My mind raced for any alternative other than turning him over to the Colombian. I knew we could use his "magic" piece and make Eddie's body disappear, and a few months later reappear down the Miami River–if at all.

"I want collateral, right now. I want you to give me all you own to protect my investment and to protect your life," I told Eddie, who was beginning to sense an ugly fate ahead.

"What do you have of value?" I demanded.

"I have my brand new truck, my car, the equity in my house is very little, I just bought that house."

"I want the title to the new Toyota truck, your car, and I want the furniture removed from your house." I paused to take a sip of my drink, "Whatever the balance, I give you 48 hours to have it in cash, otherwise you will not see me again, but instead Mr. Colombian here will deal with you."

I was not going to do harm but I had to take that position. I knew that the Colombian killer would report to Ramon and Gaviota every word that took place in that bar and as much as I hated to put such heavy pressure on the man, I wanted him to understand that to Colombians the drug business is not a casual game of poker.

We all left the bar and followed Eddie to his house where as a bachelor he entertained a different girl every night with champagne and cocaine. I went inside, with my hired man at my heels, to get the title of his new Toyota pick-up truck transferred to my name as well as the title to his Continental.

We left Eddie's house and I ordered the Colombian to go back to Ramon and to tell him that I would take it from this point on. He agreed, but before leaving he turned to Eddie and said menacingly: "You try to leave town, and we'll take care of your plane ticket in a pine box."

Eddie just stared at him expressionlessly. When the Colombian drove off, Eddie looked at me and with tears in his eyes he said: "Sorry, Carlos. I guess I really fucked up this time. Can you help me?"

"I already saved your life." I told him, "Get me that money in 48 hours if you don't want us both to be killed.'

I left his house in inner turmoil over the threat of violence I had just set in motion. No longer could I pretend to myself that I was still a nice guy caught in a temporary unpleasantness. My downward spiral was set in motion when I first let myself listen to Archie's proposition. And now, instead of making a clean break, I was becoming one with the lowest of Colombian dealers. I remembered how my father was persecuted for his firm stand against oppression, and for the first time I realized how ashamed he would be now of his son.

For the next few weeks Eddie kept daily contact, reporting his efforts to collect monies from the alleged muggers, but no progress was made in paying me. At the same time I kept Ramon and Gaviota informed of Eddie's whereabouts.[12]

Suddenly Eddie disappeared from Fort Lauderdale. Our men tried to find him but had no positive clues to work with. Eventually I had to pay the balance of the $120,000 myself, which was the original amount owed on the four kilos to Ramon and Gaviota. I put a lien on my boat, sold my expensive automobile and the Toyota truck, and withdrew sixteen thousand dollars from my savings account at Barnett Bank.

Months passed, and my relationship with Ray Nieto over my partnership in All-Nation was also deteriorating. I offered to sell my share at a very low figure due to the pressing financial situation. A few thousand in cash and a promissory note were my assets on hand.My mortgage was overdue, and I felt lucky to get employment at the Inverrary Hilton as night supervisor for the cleaning crew. My salary was $360.00 per week before taxes.

I knew a lot of people in the cocaine business, and many called to work with at greater salaries, but I was afraid. By now I believed God was warning me of the risk to my life and my precious family if I continued to flout his laws, and that fear made me tremble every time I was approached with a profitable opportunity in cocaine. I kept up my search for Eddie to try to collect the money he owed me, but failed every time. I hoped to collect at least ten or twenty-thousand dollars to move to South Carolina; we had close friends there, and I believed I could start a property management company and cash in on the booming development of a coastal city while leaving my past behind.

Early one evening, driving through a congested Oakland Park Boulevard, I spotted Ed Gould driving an old Ford Sedan. I made an illegal "U" turn to catch up to him. My search had ended! Eddie and I pulled over to a hot dog stand and I listened as he his stories of going to Michigan, Ohio and Missouri in search of the people who had robbed him of the cocaine.

I told him how his treachery had cost me all I owned and kept me working for peanuts to put food on the table. At the end of our conversation he gave me $300.00 which I accepted gratefully since I was literally broke, but he and I knew that $300.00 would not cover 1/8 of a percent of what he owed me. He also knew that now I had found him a phone call was all it would take to have him killed.

"Carlos, I know I owe you more than my life, please give me a few weeks to repay you in full."

I had no choice. I didn't have it in me to call Ramon and have him wasted.

"O.K. Eddie, this is your last chance."

Eddie went on explaining how he was importing some

2,000 pounds of marijuana from Jamaica, and that George, his partner, was due in the States any day now with the load.

"I can pay you in two days with marijuana, or else you can wait a couple of weeks and when I sell it I'll pay you for the inconvenience of waiting."

"I'll tell you what," I responded, "get me a round-trip air ticket to Jamaica and give me the exact location of the place where the load is being set up. If your story stands up, I'll wait for the money. If not, I'll call Ramon and turn you in!"

I was forcing Eddie's hand and I needed to verify the existence of the marijuana. He paced outside the parking lot, then made a call from a pay phone. He came back smiling.

"You're flying tomorrow!"

I went home and told my wife I had to leave for New York to settle some documents with Ray Nieto. The Hilton was informed that I had a very bad cold and I needed two days' rest, fluids and aspirins.

I had met Eddie's partner, George, and his wife Barbara at a casual visit to Eddie's house about eight months back. I also knew the man by the name of Norton who had a reputation as a high seas navigator and was in Jamaica waiting for me.

At twenty past eleven Air Jamaica landed in Kingston, right on schedule. Norton, a petite man with a wrinkled face, greeted me cordially and guided me to a boat that took us to a deserted spot south of the island. During the half hour boat ride, Norton explained to me how the operation was under control, and how they hoped to have the marijuana in Fort Lauderdale in five days if the weather held up.

I was shown three boats loaded with the pot in bales of two hundred pounds each. I made notes of the boat's registration numbers and tried to memorize every detail and every face in that scenario. I managed to get the last flight to the USA that same night. I dreaded an overnight stay in Jamaica.

The following morning I contacted Eddie by means of his pager number and told him I was happy with what I had seen. I also let him know that I was willing to wait for my money the few days he had requested so he could sell the pot in Michigan.

Eddie sounded pleased with my decision, and I even advised him to keep his eyes open for Latin looking men, since I suspected that by now Ramon had a contract on Eddie's life. For the first time in many months I knew we were going to pay our bills, and more than that, I could visualize the name of my new company "CPBM" written with big letters at the office of my new business in Surfside, South Carolina.

One week later Eddie came to my house and asked me to get him one kilo of cocaine to finance his trip to Michigan with the marijuana. I had many sources to get the coke, but hesitated.

Eddie presented me with the cash to pay for it but I told him that I wanted no more part in the cocaine business. I explained how I had been driven to the edge of bankruptcy; I even shared my deepest feelings that God was telling me to get away from cocaine.

He listened with respect, but asked me if I could at least introduce him to someone who could sell him that kilo of cocaine.

I replied that all my sources were Colombians and that a Colombian would never deal directly with a 'gringo.' For the next few hours I could not get off my mind the one or two thousand dollars I would make if I got a kilo of cocaine for Eddie. It seemed to be the only means for him to collect the money that was due him in Michigan, and in turn to me. Though I feared God's anger, I didn't ask Him to show me a way out of my dilemma.[13]

Finally, I thrust aside my conscience again and telephoned Alvaro Suarez who had previously asked me to help him unload some cocaine. In a matter of an hour Suarez was at my house telling me that the requested kilo would be delivered to me the following day and that I could keep it until the sale was consummated. Suarez said he would pick up the cash the following day.

Early on the morning of April 18, 1985, Suarez called to excuse himself for not delivering the kilo personally, but told me not to worry because his sister Sandra would bring it to me to examine it. I had met Sandra at a party a few weeks before, and although I could not picture her clearly, I felt comfortable with the arrangement. Alvaro Suarez gave me Sandra's home and mobile telephone number in case I needed her for any change of plans.

Sandra, perhaps twenty years old, was a thin fragile-looking girl from Medellín, who worked in the cocaine business with her brother Alvaro, supporting her mother and another brother who was at a drug rehabilitation hospital somewhere in the Caribbean. She also attended a small college in Miami for students of English as a second language.

Sandra arrived at our house with her friend Mauricio around eleven p.m., wearing striped jeans and a loose blouse. She had a ready wit that made her very likable. We all sat by the kitchen table while discussing the price of the cocaine and trying to agree on the percentage for my part in the deal.

Sandra asked to use the phone, but did not tell us whom she called. When she returned to the kitchen she said she had to leave for a few minutes to meet a friend who would give her the kilo for Eddie. Both Mauricio and Sandra left and promised to return shortly. Cristina and I did not ask questions, but hinted that we would like to get to bed early. Hardly twenty minutes had passed before they both returned with not one but two kilos.

"I only need one, Sandra," I said to her, holding to the limit I had set for myself.

"Come on, Carlos, help me get rid of them!" Sandra's voice was insistent. "You see, the first one is not so pure as this other one." She was referring to the second kilo wrapped inside a tight plastic yellow tape.

"Eddie is only interested in one, but I'll see if he will take both now that you have come this far." I wavered. The two friends left our house and we agreed to meet early next morning so Sandra could pick up the cash if the deal were put together. I went to Eddie's house so he could judge the quality. Eddie went to a room in the back where he had a 'hot plate' and put some of the cocaine to the test. I noticed that the burning temperature only went up to 82 degrees, so I had to agree with him that the kilo in question was not of prime quality.

I telephoned Sandra and explained the little difficulty we had, she was willing to drop the price a few hundred dollars if her brother agreed, so I decided to go back to my house and wait for him to call me and confirm the new reduced price. Later on that evening Suarez agreed to drop the price eight hundred dollars. After notifying Eddie of the change, I committed myself to deliver the cocaine to him early the next morning, since Sandra was due at my house by 9:00 a.m. to collect her cash.

It was April 19, 1985. At fifteen minutes before nine, the sky had decided to open and give us a view of the sun that had been hidden behind gray clouds for two consecutive days. I had just returned from Eddie's house where I had collected $35,000.00 in cash in a brown supermarket paper bag. I figured that by eleven that morning I would be making my banker a happy man by bringing my mortgage up to date.

Sandra phoned my house from her car and informed me that she was on the Florida Turnpike. I offered to have some coffee ready upon her arrival; she laughed and said to expect her in ten minutes.

The horn of her car went off several times. I motioned her with my cup of coffee to come in, but she insisted on my coming outside to the car. I went around the car to the driver's window.

"Hi!" she said holding a marijuana cigarette, "I have to run to Miami to close another deal," she took another deep puff of the pot, "is the money ready?"

"It's all ready, but I have not taken my commission out of the bag."

"Please, Carlos, give me the money and I'll have my brother bring you your share later today, O.K.?" she insisted in what seemed a very urgent need to leave.[14]

"O.K., have Alvaro call me as soon as possible!" I agreed.

Sandra's car made a "U" turn and she was gone around the curb into Pine Island Road. I had no premonition of the dreadful encounter down the road for Sandra Suarez, nor how deeply it would affect my own life.

3

APRIL 19, 1985

By noon the same day I had tried calling Sandra over and over again on her mobile phone without success. Alvaro Suarez was not at either of the numbers where I normally found him, so I decided to call Mrs. Suarez, Sandra's mother.

"Please Carlos, don't call here." She insisted. "I'd rather have you call her car or her pager, but please don't call this house again. This phone should not be used for her business." I understood her fears, but explained to her that I had been trying both numbers for the past hour and a recorded message only told me that she was not in her vehicle. I left word to please have Alvaro or Sandra call me as soon as possible.

The idea that Sandra had decided to keep my share of the deal herself crossed my mind, but that thought was dismissed every time I considered the quality of people the Suarez family represented. They might be in an evil business, but they would still esteem and deal fairly with fellow Colombians.

By five in the afternoon I began to sense that something

was seriously wrong in regard to Sandra Suarez. At about 6:00 p.m. her brother and Mauricio, her boyfriend, showed up at my house. Alvaro, obviously deeply worried, asked me what Sandra had said after she left my house that morning. I explained in detail our brief conversation, and I suggested we notify the police.

"No!" he said, "Sandra is carrying cocaine in her car. If we notify the police she might be stopped and the cops could arrest her."

Alvaro asked me if he could use the phone. He dialed a number in Miami and in Spanish asked someone to check all the hospitals, police stations or jails. While we waited for any confirmation of his request, we drank some coffee. The phone rang; it was Alvaro's friend. Sandra had not been in any accident or arrested for any reason in the state of Florida. Alvaro began to speak guiltily. "Oh God, just to think that I was such a rotten brother to her. It should have been me, and not her, to disappear this way."

On my own initiative I went ahead and called the police to file a report on a missing person. The police officer at the other end advised me that I had to wait 24 hours before they could officially start a search.

Cristina cooked dinner for all of us. While still at the table, Suarez exploded: "It's all your fault for dealing with gringos she would not be missing if it wasn't for your friend Eddie and his associates!" His voice got louder and more belligerent, and I asked him to control his temper.

Mauricio tried to calm him down but his rage only increased. My daughter, Lisa and our newborn baby, Nicolas, had just gone to sleep, so I ordered him to leave my house. But I feared the worst. It was not at all usual for Sandra to disappear for so many hours. My wife called Sandra's mother to offer some consolation, but needless to say Mrs. Suarez was too gravely concerned to be comforted.

Two days passed without word from Sandra, Alvaro or Mauricio. I decided not to call, thinking that {unreadable} would be most improper under the circumstances. We knew she was deeply involved in the selling of drugs, and a girl of her size and fragile figure, carrying thousands of dollars in cash plus three or four kilos of cocaine was an easy target for anyone who was aware of her activity. There were too many Colombians who knew what she did, and the idea of hungry mules assaulting her for a handful of dollars haunted me.

Eddie's phone call came in around noon. He sounded happy, and he asked me to meet him at the Shelter, a small bar near my house in Tamarac.

"I've got the news you've been waiting for," he announced. I felt great. The marijuana had been sold and maybe he finally had money for me. The Shelter was empty. We chose a table at the far end of the bar near the men's room and ordered a couple of drinks.

"I have $15,000.00 for you in my car outside, and if things go well, I'll have another chunk of cash in a couple of weeks!" *

We left the bar, and Eddie handed me a brown supermarket paper bag with a miscellaneous mess of bills. We both got inside his car and went for a drive while I counted the money. We returned to my car and I left for my house to share the wonderful news with my wife.

"We're going to South Carolina next week!" I told her excitedly. "Let's get out of Florida and leave this filthy life behind. We'll rent a small apartment, put this house up for sale, and start our new business."

We were thrilled at the possibility of regaining a normal

life, even though we also knew that we would miss our big city and many close friends.

I booked a flight to Myrtle Beach the following morning to start looking for an apartment. I asked my wife to call Century 21 and list our Florida house for sale. That night I slept like a baby, maybe the most restful night in three years.

In Myrtle Beach I was greeted by dear friends who took the time to drive me around while I looked for a modest place to live. I settled on a small but brand new town-house within walking distance of the ocean. I dreamed of my children growing up in a quiet neighborhood away from the dangers we had gotten ourselves into while living in Florida. It's a new beginning, I said to myself as I signed the lease to our new home. I returned to Fort Lauderdale on the evening flight. I couldn't wait to tell my family about our new place by the ocean!

After breakfast the next morning I drove to Hollywood to return the old car I had leased, because it had some radiator problems. Lisa wanted to come along. I promised to call if the repairs took more than an hour; it was perhaps 9:30 a.m. At ten thirty I was leaving the car shop and I decided to call my wife to let her know if we were on our way home. The phone rang once, then twice, and a man's voice at the other end.

"Who are you?" he asked me.

"Who the hell are you?" I retorted.

"I am with the Broward Sheriff's office, and you'd better get here right away!" he ordered.

A chill ran through my body. "Is my family all right?" I demanded.

"Your wife is fine and your baby is fine, just come NOW!"

"Put my wife on the phone."

"No, I can't do that."

When he said I couldn't speak to Cristina I imagined the worst. Someone had killed her. And what about Nicolas? He was only a few months old. I put the phone down and drove north on the Interstate at 90 miles per hour. My mind spun with frightening possibilities. When I turned into Paradise Place, the street where we lived, I saw approximately ten unmarked cars around the house; in the front, in the back and even parked over the front lawn. I gripped Lisa's hand tightly and hurried inside to find several men with guns, but no sign of Cristina and Nicolas.

"Where is my wife?" I shouted.

"She is in the bedroom with the baby."

I rushed towards them, but I was stopped by one of the detectives.

"They're all right." He said putting a hand over my shoulder to stop me from going in that direction. The house was inside out. Papers, clothes, upside down tables and cushions were scattered everywhere. The police kept on tearing and destroying while I looked on in dismay.

"What are you doing here?" I asked.

"I have a search warrant to inspect your property," said the tall detective by the name of Sgt. Fantigrassi. He produce a pink paper with my name on it.

"Is this related to Sandra Suarez?" I asked him.

"Yes. How do you know?" He jumped on my question {unreadable sentence}

"I know she has been missing for many days now."

"Do you know what happened to her?" He watched my reactions closely while he informed me her body had been found in the trunk of her car, just a few miles from my home. It had been an especially brutal murder. My mind reeled in horror.

While I answered a few questions asked by Sgt. Fanti-grassi, the other six or more detectives continued their "search and destroy" mission. Every now and then they would put small papers, note books, pictures and other personal items inside plastic bags.

"Are you arresting me?" I asked the detective.

"No. You have to come with us to the Sheriff's office for questioning. Your wife will be taken in a separate vehicle; detectives Palmer and Argentine will drive you. I'll stay here to finish my search with the other detectives."

I was not allowed to see my wife and children who were sobbing in the master bedroom. I was not aware this was a direct violation of elementary rules of search and seizure.[1] I was too distraught to protest; nor would it have changed their procedure if I had, I am sure.

The drive to the Sheriff's Office in downtown Fort Lauderdale seemed an eternity. The two detectives played out a "Mr. Nice Guys" farce. Under other circumstances it would have been laughable to watch them trying to earn my trust so I would tell them everything. But I knew nothing.

"So Carlos, you seem like a good fellow–how did you get involved in this mess?"

"I am not involved in the disappearance of Sandra Suarez. I am willing to cooperate with you in all phases of this investigation. But I can assure you I am not involved with her death."

"Are you willing to give us a statement at the Sheriff's Office?"

"You'll have one," I promised.

By the time we got to Fort Lauderdale, my wife had been driven to her mother's house to drop off the children so she could be interviewed by the Sheriff's detectives.

"Well, Carlos, if you do not tell us the truth we will take

your children away from you and your wife and put them in the hands of the HRS[2]," warned detective Argentine.

I held my temper to avoid an argument. Again, later on I learned this kind of threat , was a direct violation of Florida statutes, but nevertheless, was a common technique of police investigations.[3] I knew what would be asked of me, and I felt that for the sake of my family and for myself I would have to tell them the truth about the sale of cocaine through Sandra. I was willing to open that can of worms if it would mean my freedom and the finding of the person who stabbed Sandra Suarez to death.

The Broward County Sheriff's office is a one story building occupying a whole acre of land near Old Dixie Highway. I was asked to enter through a side door that led to an office with rows of seven desks lining the walls. It was called the Homicide Division. The small interrogation room was like a cubicle; no more than six feet wide by twelve feet long, with an old wooden desk in the center and a metal chair, on each side.

"Where is my wife?" I asked as I sat down in one of the metal chairs.

"She'll be here shortly, but you won't see her because she will be interviewed at a different office in this building. We would like to make a tape recording of your interview, is that all right with you?"

"No problem," I answered. I should have known better. I had never been under these circumstances before and I had the naive and stupid belief that the more truthful one was with the police, the better things would go. I was promised my freedom if I cooperated with the homicide investigation, and I was offered amnesty for my previous drug activities so long as I did everything they asked in their efforts to solve the murder of Sandra Suarez. I believed in their promises and I started telling them nothing but the truth.

I gave them a lengthy account of my relationship with Ed Gould, from beginning to end. I told them in detail how Alvaro Suarez had sent Sandra to deliver the cocaine, up to the last minute when I saw her drive away. They recorded all my words.

At one point I asked:

"Should I get an attorney?"

"No, there will be no need for one; if you want one you can call right now, but you'll be going home very soon so what's the use? Besides, we do not care about your past history of drug selling, we are homicide detectives. We're not interested in your cocaine dealings. So, Carlos, you just help us solve this murder and no one is going to touch you."

So I continued to tell the truth, with no thought of self-preservation in describing my activities. My mind was on Sandra Suarez, and I was feeling satisfaction in helping to find her murderer. Detectives John Palmer and Nick Argentine skillfully led me on, alternating between threats and promises. I wasn't thinking about my Miranda rights as I confessed my drug dealings. That was a big mistake.

After many long hours of questions I was asked to go with them to point out the house where Ed Gould lived. I agreed, and it was nearly midnight when I was finally driven back to our once neat and pretty home. There I found my wife crying as she tried to put together all the pieces of our memories and bring some order back to our possessions. But we felt violated. The unnecessary trampling of two frustrated police detectives had destroyed more than the outward appearance of our home; it had destroyed any warmth and comfort we felt there.

4

MAY, 1985

More than ever we were relieved to be relocating to South Carolina. The moving van was ordered, and the Broward Sheriff's Department was notified of our plans and new address. They added all the information to their files without comment.

Carolinas Professional Building Maintenance was our new business, ready to take advantage of the endless opportunities of property management offered by the booming development of the coastal city. My first jobs were after-construction clean up of some new units built by the Myrtle Beach Resort. Both my wife and I, with the help of friends and hired personnel, worked until the early hours to meet the deadlines and build a reputation in our new town. Our lives seemed to be returning to a peaceful and productive normalcy. We had great hopes of succeeding in South Carolina, and for the first time the money due me by the C.C.Q. no longer mattered.

The morning of July 9th I dressed carefully to leave the house for a meeting with executives of Coastal Bank, who were ready to sign a cleaning contract with me. I felt confident and happy that my business was getting off to a great start. I was totally unaware that a utility truck had been following me for the past few weeks. It blended into the background of my consciousness.

My wife was cooking breakfast when there was a loud knock on the door. I opened it to find a man in his late forties standing in front of me.

"Are you Carlos ?"

"Yes, I am, what can I do for you?" I answered unsuspectingly. Suddenly, behind him I saw two South Carolina State Troopers pointing rifles at my head. Before I could react I was pushed against the door, grabbed by the arm and twisted around in a wrestling hold.

"I am arresting you for the murder of Sandra Suarez in the state of Florida!"

Just then detectives Nick Argentine and John Palmer of the Fort Lauderdale police[1] arrived, also armed with pistols.

"This time we've got you, Carlos!" they announced with smug satisfaction. In their hands they held an arrest warrant charging me with the murder of Sandra Suarez.

Without probable cause, either to arrest or to request extradition, a judge in Horry County had given them the green light to proceed.

I was speechless. I could hear Cristina fighting with the two Florida detectives.

"He hasn't done anything! Leave him alone!"

My face was pressed against the wall so I could not utter a word. Once I was handcuffed, they rushed me into a state trooper's car. I tried to console Cristina as she ran behind me, clinging to my arm and spitting at the two detectives who had already made our lives impossible in Florida. They shook her off and the car drove away. The sight of Cristina screaming by the parking lot of the apartment faded away as we turned onto Highway 17 towards Conway.

The pain in her face was unbearable. It could not be possible.

I wanted to wake up from that awful nightmare. But the nightmare continued, and went on to become the worst reality of my entire life. I was taken to the Conway County Jail to await extradition to Florida. Detectives Argentine and Palmer came to the jail cell later on.

"O.K., Carlos, why don't you just waive extradition and tell us how you killed Sandra Suarez?"

"You know better than that. Why did you arrest me? You and I both know I didn't kill her."

"We have hard evidence my friend. The electric chair is waiting for you in Florida. But of course, if you give us a taped confession right now, we can convince the judge to give you life in prison instead."

I knew the seriousness of the charges, and I shuddered to realize that if I could not prove my innocence their statements could end my life.

I didn't know a criminal attorney in South Carolina, but a friend of ours was a civil lawyer in a neighboring town. Robert, our friend, contacted other criminal attorneys and after some investigation into the arrest I was notified that detectives Palmer and Argentine had obtained the warrant with the false allegation that I was a fugitive from the state of Florida.

Had they not told the Horry County judge that I had escaped from Florida, the arrest warrant could not have been issued on first degree murder charges for lack of probable cause. But it was I who had kept the Florida detectives informed of my move to South Carolina, and had voluntarily given them my home address and phone number in Surfside Beach before I left Florida. What a fool to be so trusting!

"Carlos," advised Robert when he came to the jail to see me, "if you really do not have anything to do with this murder case, sign a waiver of extradition. You will be cleared someday."

The words "someday" sounded too far away, and the thought of extradition meant leaving my wife and children for who knew how long. That first night in Conway I spent pacing back and forth trying to decide whether I should waive extradition.

I had once hired Frederick Graves in Florida to retrieve some documents which had been seized[2] from my house there, but I knew I could not afford a lawyer of that caliber for a case of such magnitude. The idea of falling into the hands of a public defender, who would go perfunctorily through the motions, was worse. I needed a good lawyer to prove my innocence and I didn't have a penny for one. I had to face the charges and pray and believe I would be cleared, so finally I agreed to sign the extradition papers.

At one thirty in the afternoon of the following day I was on a Piedmont Flight to Fort Lauderdale. On my right leg were two iron bars running from my waist to my feet. It was a device used by the Florida detectives so my knees could not bend, nor my toes. My hands were cuffed. I concealed the hand cuffs with my jacket as I boarded the plane in humiliation. During the flight I was unresponsive to their false overtures of friendship. Argentine once again insisted on my taped confession.

"Carlos, you don't want to die in the electric chair. It'll be better for you to get it over with and just tell us how you killed Sandra Suarez."

"I didn't kill Sandra Suarez, Nick." I responded, "I am ready to prove that in court!"

"Well, Carlos, we've found blood stains at your house in Tamarac—those fiber samples are being analyzed now."[3]

That evening I was booked in the Broward County Jail on charges of first degree murder, and put on the maximum security floor. While I awaited preliminary hearings, Cristina and the children flew to Davie, Florida to stay close. The furniture and all our belongings were hurriedly put up for sale in Surfside Beach in order to raise cash for my defense attorney. Cristina contacted several lawyers whom I had met in the past, but they all wanted $50,000.00 as an initial retainer before they would accept my case.

In front of Circuit Judge Mark A. Speiser, I pleaded not guilty to the charges brought in by the State of Florida, and the judge gave me a week to retain proper counsel before a public defender would be assigned to my case.

Three days before the hearings Frederick Graves strode into the jail on his own initiative.

"Why didn't you call me?" he asked angrily.

"Mr. Graves," I explained, "I cannot afford to have you represent me."

"Well, Carlos, I am your attorney on[4] record, so there is no need to go shopping for lawyers all over town!"

"How much will you charge me?" I asked.

"I have not seen the files on this case, but before I take the job I demand an answer to one question. Did you kill Sandra Suarez?" His eyes penetrated mine.

"No, I did not!"

"O.K., I believe you, Carlos. I need fifty-thousand dollars to start." He got up from the chair.

"I'm sorry, Mr. Graves, I don't have that kind of money. Thank you anyway for coming."

"I want you to call Cristina and tell her to bring you a suit and tie for tomorrow. We're going to court." He walked out and left me stunned. I had an attorney, perhaps the best in Broward County.[5]

Fred Graves hired a private investigator to contact Cristina and to tell her that he was the attorney in charge and not to worry about finding another. He also instructed her not to discuss the case with anyone else at all. Later that evening Fred Graves returned to the jail.[6]

"I have great news!" he exclaimed.

"There is no case against you!" Fred pulled a sheet of paper from his briefcase, in which the State of Florida stated its position.

"There is no evidence of your doing any wrong to anyone," he continued, "and there is no way the State can keep you in jail without probable cause. I have asked the judge to hear our case next week. It'll be like a little trial, but I guarantee you that you'll be a free man after the hearings."

Fred explained how both detectives Palmer and Argentine had failed to produce a suspect, and he believed they had decided to arrest me just to close the books. Even the so-called blood stains on the carpet in my house had turned out to be Raspberry Kool-Aid.[7]

The following seven days in jail didn't seem that bad.

I believed I would be a free man in a short time, and knowing the ordeal was almost over made the discomfort of jail life bearable.

The day of the Probable Cause hearing I was taken to the courthouse early in the morning. The judge called my case. Fred Graves was present, and so were Argentine and Palmer. The State called detective Argentine to take the stand. Argentine stated that he assumed I was responsible for Sandra's death because I was the last to have seen her alive. Obviously the statement was stricken from the record once Fred objected to such an accusation based on pure speculation.

5

OCTOBER 21, 1985

The rest of the hearing went on with the testimonies of detective Palmer, the medical examiners, other detectives involved in the investigation, photographers at the scene of the crime and the manager of the Zayre store where the death car was parked.[1] When Fred Graves' turn to cross-examine the State's witnesses came, he virtually destroyed each and every testimony, by arguing the invalidity of their findings.

The judge listened carefully and once the litigation was over, he asked the District Attorney for closing statements. The DA refused. When the defense was asked for closing arguments, Fred simply said: "Your Honor this case speaks for itself; I trust your Honor will find my client 'Not Guilty'[2] of any wrongdoing."

The judge looked at the arresting officers and with a look of concern and authority said: "The State has failed to show probable cause in the arrest of Mr. Stier, there is no evidence that points to him as the responsible party in the death of Ms. Suarez. Motion for the defense is granted;

therefore I order Mr. released from custody immediately and all charges dropped."

I was a free man. I embraced Fred Graves in gratitude.

The judge was getting up from his bench when Assistant State Attorney Jack Coyle strode in.

"Your honor, if the Court pleases, the State of Florida wishes to file charges in this court against Mr. Stier."

I looked at Fred in shock. "What is this all about?" I asked him. "I don't know, but don't worry."

"Your Honor," continued the D.A., "we have a taped confession that was given to Mr. Argentine a few months ago, where Mr. Stier admits having conspired to sell cocaine to Ed Gould."

"OBJECTION!!" shouted Fred Graves in a rage, "the State is bringing up those charges only because my client is now a free man and they screwed up in their investigation!"

"Mr. Graves, let me remind you that this is a court of law and there is no need to shout or use abusive language," replied the judge. "Let me hear your allegations Mr. Coyle."

Jack Coyle produced the cassette tape in which I admitted having had a meeting with the victim and the victim's brother to sell a kilo of cocaine to Ed Gould. That confession was part of a deal with the Broward Sheriff's Office by which I agreed to cooperate in their murder investigation, provided I was given immunity.

Judge Speiser listened carefully to the tape and without hesitation charged me with two counts; one of conspiracy to traffic in cocaine and the second for the possession of cocaine.

"The guidelines call for immediate incarceration and a bond set at half a million dollars."

I collapsed in the chair next to Fred's. Only two minutes ago the bailiff had removed my handcuffs by orders of the judge, and now that same bailiff returned and took me into custody.

Nick Argentine and John Palmer snickered derisively as they walked out of the courtroom.

"Your Honor, this man's rights have been violated, and I won't rest! This court has been prejudicial to my client's constitutional rights, therefore I ask your Honor to excuse yourself from this case." Now Fred had gone too far, but his anger was uncontrollable.

"Motion denied." The judge got up from his chair and stamped away into his chambers.

On October 21st of 1985 I sat in my jail cell frustrated and looking at the ceiling, talking to a God who seemed to have forgotten my existence. At the same, time Cristina sat at her terminal at Proxy Communications, an answering service, trying hard to provide our children with three meals a day and a roof over their heads. She worked intense hours for a salary that barely covered these necessities. And she would need $50,000.00 if she were to meet the bail bond agency's demands.

During a brief bail reduction hearing Judge Mark A. Speiser had agreed to reduce the State of Florida's demands to that amount. In only three months the District Attorney's calling for half a million dollars bond had been reduced to a mere $50,000.00 through the defense filings of strong argumentative motions based on my background, ties to the community and character profile. That morning Gary Perkings, representing the State of Florida, tried diligently to taint the defense's arguments, but to no avail.

As the bailiff escorted me back to the holding cell, Fred approached me and with a warm gesture grabbed my right hand. "I'll get you out today," he whispered in my ear. But even though only 10% of the $50,000.00 had to be paid in cash, and the rest could be secured with property as collateral, it was still totally impossible for Cristina to raise that amount. I appreciated Fred's efforts in the court room, but I also felt his promises to get me out were empty words to keep my spirits high.

My hopes to spend Christmas at home were getting slimmer, and I tried hard to accept that sad reality.

The corrections officer came to my cell around eleven thirty. Most of the inmates were waiting impatiently for the second feeding of the day, which normally arrived by eleven.

"Yo! Deputy!"

It was a loud voice, coming from the black inmate nicknamed "Killer," as the officer walked into the pod. The guard unlocked the thick metal door that separated the inmates from the control room, where the corrections officers observed through thick glass windows every move the accused offenders made.

"Yo! Fuckhead! Where the fuck is the chow?"

Since the opening of the new Broward County jail a month before, the meals had been late and the inmate population had grown angry, not only because of the delays but for the quality of the food. From a hot dish every day, lunch had deteriorated to a slice of bologna between two pieces of day-old bread. Numerous complaints had been filed with the office of Nick Navarro, the County Sheriff, but the inmates soon learned how futile written complaints became.

The corrections officer ignored the insults of the inmates. Standing in the middle of the room and carefully trying not to step over the men who slept on the floor, he proceeded to take a piece of paper from his shirt pocket.

"Carlos! Carlos!"

'Not another change of cell,' I shuddered when I heard my name called. In the last three days they had moved me several times and each time it meant I had to sleep on the floor before I could find a bed.

"There is someone to see you on the second floor."

"The second floor?" I asked, "Why the second floor?"

No inmate went to the second floor unless he was to be released, and because I had just returned from court an hour ago I knew as a fact that there was a mistake. I had no way of posting a $50,000 bail.

"There is a bail bond agent with some papers for you to sign. Congratulations! It seems like you've been bailed out!"

I froze. I just looked at him in disbelief and walked back to my cell to digest his words. Where Cristina got $5,000.00 in cash to pay for bail and what kind of collateral she produced was a mystery to me; all that mattered right then was my freedom. I fell on my knees and gave thanks to God.

"All right , let's go!" shouted the waiting deputy, holding the heavy door half open.

Downstairs on the second floor I was told that Fred Graves, my attorney, had posted bail by putting his own house as security, and had paid the bondsman five thousand dollars cash out of his own pocket. At the same time I signed the papers, Ted Crespi, Fred's associate attorney, notified Cristina of my release that morning. By three in the afternoon of a glorious day for me, I walked out of the Broward jail to find Cristina waiting for me. I held her in my arms ever so lovingly. In my mind I prayed that we never be separated again.

The following weeks I spent close to my children, trying to make up for the days we were apart. Cristina was working harder than ever while I went through the newspapers looking for employment. Fred Graves had explained to me how strongly he felt about bailing me out.

"It is a travesty of the law that you had to sit in jail for three months. Judge Speiser had indicated that he would not grant us another bond reduction so I went ahead and got you out. I just hope you will not disappoint me, because if you do I'll lose my house."

I was overwhelmed that a lawyer would put his family's welfare on the line for me.

Fred Graves believed beyond a reasonable doubt that my case would never go to trial because we could prove to the courts that my statement to detectives Palmer and Argentine was given under duress and I had been cheated with false promises.

"We are going to file a motion to suppress the evidence. All the District Attorney has is a tape of your confession in which you state that you had conspired to sell cocaine to Alvaro Suarez and Edward Gould and I can prove that you were promised immunity of prosecution if you cooperated with the investigation into the murder of Sandra Suarez."

Fred was right and I had a lot of faith in him. I had seen him as an eloquent advocate in a court of law and he had earned his reputation as a stubborn fighter for the rights of his clients.

We were given six months by the courts to prepare for pretrial motions. In the interim Fred offered me a job in his law firm helping him in assisting with the families of many Hispanics he represented who did not speak English. The crimes ranged from shoplifting to first degree murder, with of course quite a few drug offenses. Graves had always been a very difficult person to work for, and although most judges and fellow attorneys spoke highly of his capabilities, no lawyer in his right mind ever associated with his firm. His office had the latest state-of-the-art computer system, but several legal secretaries, law clerks, investigators and others who had worked under him warned me of his moody personality.

"He is a bastard. He talks down to people and insults them without regard for human dignity. He will abuse you."

Those were common characterizations from the lips of most people who knew Fred Graves and wanted to warn me. One thing was very peculiar: after the insults they all agreed that "he is a gruff but loving man" or "he wants things done his way—but if you can stick around long enough, you'll discover he is always right."

I learned from personal experience that Fred Graves could never utter the words "I am sorry," but in his own special way he always made up for his aggressions.

I didn't need to be told about his loving and caring qualities. He had saved me from sitting in jail for another year when I had not even paid for his legal fees, and now he was offering me a job with the opportunity to learn about law research, investigations and litigation. I was delighted. "I'll give it a shot." I told his firm, "Maybe he'll make me quit after the first week, but I'll give him my best shot."

My first assignment was to go to the jails to visit a number of Hispanic inmates who did not speak English. Fred would brief me on their case and give me their files. I would see them with attorney privileges and update them on case status. I knew by experience how it felt when weeks went by without hearing from an attorney and for the first time those clients began to feel recognized instead of neglected.

Fred had gotten me a license to visit them as often as I felt necessary. The results were very positive. More referrals came in and soon Fred offered me a percentage of the fees of those new clients I brought in.[3] I began to repay the fifty-thousand dollars from my own case. My daily exposure to murder trials, drug offenses, conspiracy, divorces, depositions and to the legal terminology opened an appetite for the law and one day I confessed to Fred that I would love to become an attorney.

"That is wonderful. .. I think you'll make a hell of a good lawyer." Fred was always honest[4] and I knew that he was the only person to help me achieve my goals.

As Fred noticed my interest in matters of the law he began to discuss all his cases with me and after the clients had left the office he would answer any questions that I had. He was tough and demanding, and easily would lose his patience, but his lectures on law taught me much. The books in his library were at my disposal, but he would select those that I should read first in order to have a smooth understanding of the world of criminal litigation and federal laws.

Fred and I worked long hours into the night and early morning as he prepared for a jury trial the following day. He trusted my judgment in the courtroom when it came to jury selection, and I learned to signal to him if I felt he had overlooked a small detail during cross examination. During questioning of police officers and detectives he would ask me to be very attentive and not to hesitate to call him to the defense desk if I felt he had not mentioned or brought up an important point that could discredit the testifying witness. My job with Fred took me to trials all over the United States. Many of the clients were people I had met during my years as a drug smuggler.[5]

My studies under Fred's tutelage even enabled me to pass the LSAT of Florida University, achieving a score of 47 out of 49! That assured me a scholarship at Nova University Law School.[6]

My relationship with Fred became profitable[7], and I developed a very special affection for him. The turnover of the secretarial staff was incredible. No one could last more than a month. Fred was often rude, and because of his temper and demanding attitude his aides would resign or just walk out without notice.

Not many people understood how I survived in that working environment, but our stormy father and son relationship[8] lasted almost two years.

Then Judge Speiser refused to grant us the pretrial motion to suppress evidence, and my full jury trial was set to start in July of 1986.

Jury selections and opening arguments filled the hours of the first three days in the trial. John Gallagher, representing the State of Florida, addressed the jury, emphatically telling them that he could prove that I had indeed conspired to sell more than 400 grams of pure Colombian cocaine:

"Ladies and Gentlemen of the Jury, this is an open and shut case. The State will prove beyond any reasonable doubt that this man did willfully and unlawfully try to sell one kilo of cocaine to a man by the name of William Ross, a.k.a. Edward Gould."

6

EARLY FALL, 1986

E dward Gould had been arrested a year back and was serving consecutive sentences for possession of cocaine, assault and battery and other minor misdemeanors. Fred Graves had taken depositions of Gould in which he indicated no interest in testifying against me.[1]

"The Sentencing Guidelines in the state of Florida for the offense of Conspiracy to Traffic in Cocaine carries a mandatory time of fifteen years[2], and it is your responsibility to put this man away for at least fifteen years, once the State proves its case." Gallagher was not an eloquent attorney, but his anger and appetite to win this case were very visible.

It was Fred Grave's opportunity to address the jury. He advanced towards the bar that separated him from the twelve jurors and looked into each jury-member's eyes before returning to the podium.

"Ladies and Gentlemen of the jury: You have heard the State's argument, as you can see it was brief and simple. All Mr. Gallagher told you is that my client should go to jail for fifteen years because there is evidence that he conspired to sell cocaine. Well, it's more complicated than that, and I will take more time than he did, only because he did not tell you all about the constitutional rights we all as Americans have.

It is true that Mr. Stier gave a recorded statement but before you make judgement on his life you must see and understand why he did it and whether or not you would have done the same under the circumstances. It is your obligation and duty to find this man not guilty of wrong-doing if there is any room in your minds to believe that my client acted under duress.

Mr. Stier believed the false promises of two Broward County detectives who tried to nail my client because of their desperate frustration in a murder investigation too big for them to handle. They were just too embarrassed to face their superiors without an arrest. Now, remember that all Mr. Gallagher has is a tape—but it is not a video tape where we can see who, where and how. I think our case will speak to you on its own merits. Thank you."

The members of the jury were carefully screened in an effort to find objective and fair-minded individuals. We looked for jurors who were not prejudiced because of nationality or speech accent. The group we chose was made up a young cocktail waitress who admitted to smoking mari-juana in the past, a homemaker and mother of five who did not believe a person was necessarily a drug dealer just because of association with Colombians, and others who shared the most important element for our defense: a belief that law enforcement officers can be deceitful, and that many of them use their badges to get away with prosecuto-rial misconduct.[3]

During the first three days of testimony, and after the jury had heard the tape in which I confessed trying to sell a kilo of cocaine to Edward Gould, it became increasingly clear to Fred Graves and me that I could easily be found guilty. "Ask for a recess," I urged Fred. I needed to discuss other avenues in order to avoid a guilty verdict. The idea of a *nolo contendere*[4] plea had crossed my mind since the beginning of the trial, but I was not sure of the judge's position if I tried to work a deal with the State Attorney. Fred asked the judge; "Your Honor, at this point I would like to request a thirty minute recess to review this case with my client."

"Mr. Graves, this court has been more than flexible with your tardiness and I have given you ample time to prepare for this trial; there will be no more continuances or recesses. Your motion is denied." Judge Speiser's patience had run out.

"Your Honor," this time Fred approached the bench, "this recess may be the answer to saving the State of Florida thousands of dollars—it is quite possible that my client will accept a plea negotiation."

The judge's face lit up. He wanted this case over and done with, and a plea negotiation was just the right answer to close a file that had been sitting on his desk for over a year.

"Well, if the State agrees to consider a plea in this case, I order a recess until tomorrow at 9:00 a.m." Judge Speiser got up, and so did everyone present in the courtroom. The jury was escorted through a door that led into the Judge's chambers. Fred Graves immediately approached John Gallagher to discuss the conditions of our plea agreement.

The District Attorney's office agreed to a lesser sentence only if I would agree to a polygraph examination regarding the homicide of Sandra Suarez. The Broward Sheriff's office believed that I had some knowledge about the murder and that perhaps I was concealing information. I readily agreed to take the polygraph as soon as possible. Here was a chance to clear myself of the stigma of murder. John Gallagher committed himself not to fight a request for a sentence of probation only, provided the lie detector cleared me of any involvement.[5]

I returned to Fred's office and continued my paralegal work. I felt very optimistic about my future, and now all we had to do was wait for the Sheriff's office to call me for the test.

Judge Speiser had given us the date of September 9 for sentencing. I felt very confident; at least I knew I wasn't going back to jail, and once and for all this ordeal would be over. On August 29, 1986, I was notified to be in the Sheriff's office for the polygraph.

The mode of questioning for the first part was based on identity. "Are you Carlos? Were you born on September 5th, 1950? Do you live in Davie, Florida?" The questioning then moved to the area of the murder investigation. "Did you see Sandra Suarez in April of 1985?" Did you kill Sandra Suarez?" My answers were truthful to every question and I could see the mounting frustration of the Sheriff's detectives as they began to realize they had made a cardinal error in believing I had committed that crime.

Back in July of 1985, when I was in front of Judge Speiser for the hearings to determine Probable Cause, the State had produced color pictures taken at the scene where the body of Sandra Suarez had been found. Those pictures were introduced as State's evidence during the allegations. It was in those grim pictures that I discovered the details of the horrible death of Sandra Suarez. The polygraph examiner was aware that I had knowledge of how ruthlessly she had been murdered, not only because of the photographs, but by the medical examiner who had issued copies of his report to the defense attorneys.

"Mr. Stier, do you know how Sandra Suarez was put to death?" The examiner's question brought back flashes of the unpleasant pictures I had seen a year ago during the Probable Cause hearings. Because I had seen those images of the bloody mutilated body, I should have been careful in answering that question.

I had not been present at the time of her killing, but I felt I was being tricked.

"No, I do not know how she was put to death." I answered, giving way to the sick feeling those photographs brought back to my mind. The results of my answer were disastrous.{Illegible}

intimidate me. "You know something about Sandra's death. I believe you did not kill her, but I also strongly believe you know who did, and you are afraid to reveal names."

"No, no. I do not know who killed her," I protested.

"If I knew, why would I go to jail and have my whole life ruined, instead of telling you?"

"Because you're afraid of retaliation. You know you would be targeted by your fellow Colombian scum."

They were wrong, but in their faces I could clearly see that now they had all it took to put me away. All they needed was one single failed answer—they had finally managed to get something to show for their negligence in the murder investigation.

I walked out of the Sheriff's building full of rage at the way the questioning had been conducted. I went to see Fred immediately and told him what had just happened.

"Those sons of bitches! They were supposed to call me!"

"I am your attorney of record, and they had no right to question my client without my presence." Fred was furious, and he was right in regard to attorney-client privileges violated in this case.

"Don't worry, Carlos," reassured Fred, "the judge will never accept the results of that polygraph once I explain to him how unethically it was handled." I felt better.

"I have a good friend who works for the Drug Enforcement Administration," said Fred Graves as we prepared for my sentencing hearing in two weeks. "He is someone I trust very much, we can meet secretly to see if some of the information you have on Carlos Lehder is of interest to the government."

This was the height of the well publicized Miami River case where police officers of the City of Miami had been indicted and brought to trial in one of the most sensitive cases of police corruption in the country. Michael McManus was a young but well-experienced agent working for the DEA in Fort Lauderdale. He had met Fred Graves years back and Fred had a special respect and admiration for McManus.

His reputation as a police officer for the City of Plantation in the organized crime unit and later as a federal agent for the Drug Enforcement Administration had gained him a respected image among his superiors. His ethical behavior in the prosecution of his cases had earned him a well-deserved reputation among many law enforcement officers in today's court-rooms. John Gallagher and Michael McManus had been friends since early childhood when they attended the same elementary school, and Mark Speiser had been a District Attorney in cases where McManus was the arresting officer in charge.

I told Fred I would like to meet with Special Agent McManus providing we could choose the meeting place and so long as he, Fred, would be present. A few days later Fred asked me to come to one of his properties in Coral Ridge. The house was vacant. I felt relieved when I saw Fred's Mercedes Benz parked in the driveway. A red sports car was parked behind Fred's car. The red car was Michael McManus. Because of past experiences with Broward County detectives, I had lost all trust in any and all members of law enforcement. I felt I had been cheated, and for trusting their promises I had ended up in jail. Now this time I was skeptical and nervous. Could this be a trap again? I trusted Fred Graves with my life, but in spite of all his recommendations about the honor and trustfulness of Michael McManus, I was uneasy.

I rang the bell. Fred opened the door and brusquely asked me to follow him into one of the bathrooms for our private talk. As I passed the living room I saw a man in his mid-thirties sitting next to a red haired lady.

"Michael is here with his partner," Fred explained. "He has to have his partner with him because that is the way the DEA operates. Now, I do not trust anyone but Mike–it is up to you if you want to go through with the meeting. I person-ally have been told by Mike that his partner will keep this conversation off the record, so it's entirely in your hands." I listened carefully as Fred warned me and instructed me how I was to release the information.

"You give them only a little bit, just enough for them to check the validity of that information. Don't give any names, dates or items of information that they haven't got in their files." Fred Graves knew how to play his cards and I was impressed that during this negotiation his clients interests were priority one. Michael McManus was no longer a close friend but an adversary to match wits with.

I was introduced to McManus and his partner, Jane Angelstad. We shook hands formally and sat down.

"Carlos, I am here upon request of Fred. I am here to listen to whatever you have to offer that may be of interest to my agency. I cannot make you any offers unless what you tell me today is fully documented and double-checked by DEA in Washington." McManus was relaxed but genuinely concerned that I understand his position. "I have been told about what happened to you with some detectives of the Broward Sheriff's office, and all I can tell you is that I have a reputation for being ethical, and hope that Fred has informed you of my track record."

"Yes, he has. I wouldn't be here otherwise."

"All right, I must inform you that DEA in Washington has a lot of information about Carlos Lehder and what you have to offer us has to be considered as new and important intelligence information in order for us to consider any kind of negotiation."

"My client will only give you one or two items today," was Fred's answer to Michael's. "You go back, and if it checks, out, we'll meet again for a full debriefing."

"O.K.," said Michael, "tell us what you know."

I proceeded to tell Michael McManus Lehder's date of birth, his mother's and father's name and detailed information that only someone very close to Lehder would know. McManus didn't make any written notes, he seemed to be clicking off my disclosures, in his brain. Jane listened carefully.

Michael McManus then explained how I could work with the government agency once they investigated and corroborated the information I had just given.

"After a complete debriefing and thorough examination you will be working closely with the government in an investigative capacity. Believe me, you will be scrutinized to the nth degree; there's no room for laxity in our operations."

Our meeting ended with Michael's assurance that he would check my information immediately and then contact Fred.

The morning of September 9, 1986, I took my daughter to school completely unaware that in just two hours I would be sentenced to fifteen years in a State penitentiary. I had failed that one question on my lie detector test by Broward Sheriff's Office.

Michael McManus was present at the sentencing hearing together with his partner Jane.

They explained to Judge Speiser the importance of the intelligence information I had, but John Gallagher argued that I had failed a question in the polygraph that was part of the plea agreement, Gallagher asked the judge to order I be sentenced to thirty years. The judge, ignoring the recommendations of the two DEA agents and the arguments of my attorney didn't hesitate to rule for the State Attorney. A sentence of fifteen years of mandatory time was handed down and within minutes my life again collapsed.

This time I saw no reversal. Cristina sat in the courtroom and listened as the judge ruled. I saw her tears, but I was no longer allowed to comfort her. I was taken away by the bailiff to the county jail where I sat for a couple of weeks waiting for the State of Florida Department of Corrections to transfer me to Lake Butler, the infamous state prison to begin serving a sentence that I knew would destroy my life.

The second week of October I was visited in Lake Butler by Richard Rendina, an attorney who once shared office space with Fred. Richard had a case at a federal court in Jacksonville and had taken the time to drive to Lake Butler to visit me. His call surprised me and I was filled with anxiety when I was notified there was an attorney who wanted to see me.

"Haven't you heard the news?" asked Richard as he discovered how upset I felt over the outcome of my sentencing hearing.

"Fred has filed a Motion to Vacate Sentence and Judge Speiser has indicated to him that your sentence will be reviewed in a couple of weeks." My heart soared as I listened to the news.

"I am not sure yet what the judge will do in this case, but it is my understanding that the judge has admitted to making a mistake and is willing to reduce your sentence to five years or maybe even put you on probation." I could hardly believe what Richard was telling me. Perhaps there was a chance for my life after all.

"O.K., Carlos, I have to go and catch a flight back to Fort Lauderdale. You will be transferred to Broward County jail in a week or two to attend the hearings in front of Judge Speiser."

I thanked Richard for his kind effort of visiting me with the good news and went back to the tent in the open air which forty inmates and I shared due to the over-populated prison system. The cold nights of late October pushed the wind right through the canvas. The new facilities were under construction and we were to share a tent until the new buildings were available for occupancy three or four months later.

My transfer to Broward County came a couple of weeks later. I had to sit in jail until on November 21 Judge Speiser put our case on his docket. When I entered the courtroom I saw John Gallagher representing the State of Florida, but Fred Graves was not present. Judge Speiser moved on to hear the arraignments of the day to give Fred enough time to appear, but once again my attorney was late and the Judge lost his temper.

"Mr. Stier, I have given you and your attorney an opportunity to review your sentence but I can see you have no representation in this courtroom. Because I feel sorry for you, I am going to re-schedule this case for tomorrow at 9:00 a.m., but let me warn you, if Mr. Graves does not show up tomorrow I will send you back to State Prison for fifteen years!"

I was very angry at Fred. This was the only chance we had and I felt inclined to waive my attorney and confront Gallagher myself, then I hoped that the next day Fred would show up.

"Your Honor, I thank you for your courtesy and all I can say is that I will make sure Mr. Graves appears tomorrow." After those words I was escorted back to the jail. The rest of the day I spent on the phone, frantically trying to locate Fred. I left messages for him at his house and his office. If by five in the afternoon he had not acknowledged my calls, I thought of calling Richard Rendina to fill in for Fred.

At around seven p.m. that evening Fred came to the jail to see me. Fred explained how the court's clerk had failed to notify his office about the hearing.

"We might not want to accept any reduction of sentences at this point." Fred had a thick manuscript in his hands. It was the writ of his appeal in Appellant Court in West Palm Beach.

"This appeal is going to reverse the judgment and if you're willing to wait in jail for another six months, you will be a free man and then we'll have a counter suit against the State!"

I believed we had a strong case in the appellant court but I wasn't sure I wanted to wait for the slow process of the judicial system. I had been told that appeals could go as long as 18 months. I had placed several calls to Michael

McManus at DEA hoping to see him concerning the possibility of my cooperating with the government.

The following morning Fred was present in front of Judge Speiser but the greatest surprise was to see Michael McManus in the courtroom. This time his partner was Maria Ciociola with whom he had been working with for the last few months. The hearing was very brief. Michael had already met with the judge in his chambers and had explained in detail the importance of the information I had in connection with Carlos Lehder. The judge agreed to release me from jail under the responsibility of Michael McManus so I could be taken to a place already arranged by DEA to have me debriefed.

On December 2nd of 1986, the initial debriefing began at a hotel suite. I was escorted out of Broward County Jail by DEA Special Agents McManus and Ciociola. I was handcuffed as part of the security measures since my information had to be corroborated before the government could officially make an offer and work a deal with the courts. Later in the afternoon we were joined at the hotel suite by Michael Kane, Group Director for DEA in Fort Lauderdale. Mr. Kane had lived in Bogota, Colombia, and was very knowledgeable of the modus operandi of members of the Medellin Cartel.

The questioning was meticulous and in detail. After six hours of debriefing, Michael McManus and Maria Ciociola had to return me to the county jail as part of the agreement with the judge. The next morning the same procedure took place for a second day of exhaustive questioning. I had given DEA a very valuable package of information. There were several ways in which I could work with DEA in an undercover capacity, but the capture and extradition of Carlos Lehder became our first goal. The information I had just given had to be sent to Washington and then I had to be polygraphed on every item before an operational plan could be put together.[6] Approval from DEA in Bogota and the Colombian Government were also necessary before an undercover operation could be executed.

During the days that followed my full debriefing I was ordered released from jail to begin a ninety day discipline and preparation into the DEA's philosophy and way of thinking in order to carry out undercover operations in Miami and Fort Lauderdale as well as in Colombia and the Bahamas. Michael McManus and Maria Ciociola became the agents supervising the start of my career as an undercover confidential informant for the Federal Government. Judge Mark Speiser requested an update in 90 days.

Michael McManus knew that. I had been separated from my family for a number of months, so he allowed me a week off from DEA's work. Cristina continued working to support the family while I treasured every second with my two children.

During the first few weeks, Michael and Maria traveled with me through Dade and Broward counties accumulating data on active drug dealers who operated in amounts of one to two hundred kilos of cocaine. Most of them were Colombian individuals whom I had met in the past.

During the time we spent together, I was informed of how DEA's training was structured to deal with even the most dangerous situations. The following brief description of the 13 weeks training academy in Quantico, Virginia:

"They involved real-life situations played on life-size, computer-driven video screens using .357 caliber Magnum revolvers designed to fire electronic bullets–complete with sound effects and recoil. They also involve street scenes in a mock city built on the academy grounds designed to simulate situations the students are likely to encounter on the job. But they are not games. The stakes are high; the students like to say that those who succeed are winners and those who don't are dead.

The academy may be the most intensive training program in law enforcement in the country. Perhaps in the world. But it has to be. Chances are that many of the 160 or so young men and women who graduate each year will be involved in a fatal shooting within weeks–sometimes days–of their first assignment. It has happened before and certainly will happen again."

John C. Lawn, head of the administration and the impetus behind the revamped training program says: "Losing an agent doesn't come easy for us. When someone is lost it is because a mistake was made. What we are trying to do at this academy is to make sure that we learn from those mistakes, to ensure to the best of our ability that the agents we put on the streets are safe."

With some 3,000 agents stationed throughout the United States and 44 other countries, the Drug Enforcement Administration is responsible for the detention and apprehension of drug traffickers. In 1986 the Agency arrested more than 20,000 suspected dealers and confiscated controlled substances with a total street value of about $500 million.

Today's Drug Enforcement Administration is quite aware of the danger the Colombian Cocaine Cartel poses for their agents. They have stepped up security all around the world with special emphasis on Bogota and Medellin and are now more than ever trained and prepared to combat the evil empire of the Cartel.[7]

I had made a U-turn, and I was happy that I passed all DEA criteria with flying colors. I had a clear understanding of, and now shared wholeheartedly in their goals.

As Michael one day put it to me, "We must identify, arrest, prosecute and successfully destroy drug organizations." I wanted to become part of that effort. I offered Michael McManus my undivided commitment. There was no doubt in my mind that as of that moment I wanted to fight back against the powers of those with whom I had been associated, causing irreparable damage to my life and family. The dangers were great and inevitable but the idea brought an immense peace to my heart.

The Cessna 410 was built in 1975. Its instrumentation looked awkward, but none-theless all its gauges appeared to be functional. It was important to look for any small details that some day could help me identify the aircraft, and to my surprise,

I noticed the letter N on its tail, contrary to the G registration of the Commonwealth of the Bahamas. I prepared myself to be cordial, cool and sporty. With what I hoped was charm I initiated the conversation towards fact-finding, trying hard to sound politely curious rather than nosy.

"I am glad you finally got your own wings," I told Robert Treco, amiably.

"You didn't know I had this plane?"

"No, as a matter of fact last time we saw each other you didn't even know how to fly."

"No shit! Has it been that long?"

"Indeed, almost three years since we flew the last load to Nicholls Town. Boy was that tough!" His attitude was warm as he spoke with the pride of his accomplishments.

"I have a friend at Opa Locka who instructed me, and I

managed to get my pilot's license in a matter of weeks. Now I own this plane and another one in Nassau. I intend to establish my own charter service. Right now I run back and forth to Nassau, Freeport and most places in Andros. I clear roughly two thousand dollars a week. Of course the overhead expense to keep these birds is high, but I still believe it could be bloody profitable."

I was not really interested in his investments or business endeavors. I forced myself to pay attention to his tales while in the back of my mind I prepared my next move. I went straight into a daring question:

"Are you guys running coke loads right now?"

To my relief, his answer was immediate and he seemed comfortable sharing details of his present undertakings.

"We're no longer landing on the island. Since you left the heat came upon us, especially the scandals surrounding Nigel Bowe.[1] Our island was pinpointed as a smuggler's paradise, so we decided to put it to rest for about a year. Only about a year ago we started to bring loads straight from La Guajira, then we air drop them on one of the many lakes on the island."

As I listened to him carefully my adrenaline began to run wild. I could not believe my ears. I had actually broken the ice and we were talking drug business.

"Why air drops?" I asked with genuine curiosity.

"There have been changes in Nassau's way of dealing with the drug situation, because it reflects on the image of the Bahamas. They are now cooperating with the American DEA, making it very dangerous to land a big load. Besides we have not been able to get a set up like the one you used to have with radio communications, people and reliable airplanes."

"I understand how difficult it must be to operate under

such circumstances," I sympathized putting my arm over his shoulder to reassure him of my admiration and approval. I thought it was time to offer my services.

"There is great risk doing air drops. I mean, don't you lose some merchandise in the process?" I carried on before he could reply, "I can give you the answer in going to regular landings with almost infallible results, but in any event we'll discuss it when we all meet later."

I knew that by planting a cryptic seed I would whet his appetite to come to me for more information. The game of gaining control is all important, and I hoped this strategy would give die an edge. I moved to a new subject of conversation, and for the rest of the flight we shared a pleasant exchange of anecdotes of girlfriends, flying and a little gossip.

The green waters that wash the coast of Andros Island were more transparent and calm than in many previous visits. The winds were gentle and the temperature in the mercury reading of the Cessna showed 87 degrees. It had been three years since my last trip to San Andros. Unhappy memories of my last visit crowded my mind, but the sight of the island reminded me of my childhood faith in God's creation in the Western Hemisphere.

The airport in San Andros had not changed a bit. In contradiction to the beautiful surroundings it looked old, deteriorated and neglected. The police wore the same faded blue uniforms and there were the same familiar few natives fighting to help with your bags for small change in return.

Keith descended from the pilot's side of the aircraft; I did the same from the co-pilot's door. A short walk away was the pick up truck that would take us to the heart of the island. We passed the house where I had my headquarters for radio communications and weapons storage a few years back. The outside of the house looked just the same, but I could see some improvement in the landscaping next to the porch as we drove past its driveway a dozen yards away.

"Why are we not going in?" I asked as we went by.

"We sold the house to a British priest some time ago," explained Keith without much expression. I was somewhat disappointed. I had been looking forward to spending a night in that place. It would have been an opportunity to relive those days of tension and nights of sleeplessness, when we would sit next to the HF radios waiting for the whistle code of the C.C.Q. to advise us with progress reports about the departure of our Turbo Commanders loaded with cocaine from Los LLanos.

The roads leading to the center of town were deserted as usual, and only the occasional passing of a vehicle on the opposite direction induced me to keep my eyes on the road. For a while I had forgotten that driving on the left side of the road was mandatory. The few cottages neighboring the Andros Beach Hotel looked empty. A few natives wandered around on bikes, while barefooted children played mirthfully. The unpaved driveway leading to the liquor store was crowded with a motorcycle, a Jet Ski and an old Toyota. We managed to park right next to the front door where Keith's brother was trying to get a conch out of its shell with the help of a wire coat hanger.

"Hey Richard, welcome," he said as he handed me a juicy raw slice of healthy conch.

Laura Treco, my old friend, the daughter of Harry Treco, rushed to greet me with a sweet smile, showing her bright white perfect teeth and looking marvelously pretty. Keith ordered her to bring a bottle of scotch and four glasses. We walked across the store towards the opposite end of the building, right by the water front. A few rocking chairs under a canopy, the warm breeze and the sun setting on the horizon, were all the necessary ingredients to make me forget I had other reasons for coming to this paradise. Laura appeared holding a tray with a bottle of Johnny Walker and a few plastic glasses. The ice box had been on the blink, so it was warm scotch served straight up.

Our conversation went from Bahamian politics to trafficking, airplanes and women. Laura just listened and giggled every now and then, not taking part in many issues.

A few drinks and I felt light headed. I stood up with a little stumble, and excused myself politely.

"Well, it has been a delightful evening. I've had a rough day, so if you will kindly show me to the cottage, I am ready to turn in."

"Sure, Richard," said Keith with a tight hand shake,

"I'll have one of the employees from the hotel cook you a nice breakfast. Good night."

As we all walked towards the front door, I noticed that Laura had gone ahead of us and had already started the motorcycle.

"Get on Richard.... .I'll drive you!" she invited.

"No thanks, I'd rather walk. Isn't one of those the cottage where I am supposed to sleep tonight?" I asked pointing to the few huts with straw roofs.

"It's better that I drive you," she insisted, "it's very dark out there, and besides you are not in the best of shape to walk."

I wasn't so much hesitating about going with her, it was the motorcycle ride that scared the shit out of me; she'd had just as many drinks as I'd had.

I mounted the rear of the bike, holding tight to her waist as she accelerated with a loud roar, and we were off, leaving only a cloud of dirt behind. The cottage was indeed across the street, but Laura wanted to show off her daring capabilities by taking me on a tour of the island, all at 75 miles per hour.

Laura was about twenty-five years old, about five feet eight inches, and weighed maybe 130 pounds. She was taller than I, and her figure was without question well put together. Her breasts were not large but looked firm and she was perhaps one of the best looking Bahamian women I had ever seen. Educated in London and holding an executive job for Air Bahamas in Nassau, she was the town's most outstanding girl. Her father and brothers were very proud of her and she always gave them motherly care and attention, since Ophelia, her mother, had died in an automobile accident three years back.

I had met Ophelia just a few months before her death; a distinguished lady who lived only for her family's interest and the well being of her children. Her widower refused to remarry; he had a lot of women catering to him, so he seemed contented with his lifestyle.

Albert was the richest man on the island, and in spite of his old age he preserved a sprightly posture and a charming, outgoing personality.

Many times in the past I had dealt with Laura, always keeping a distance due to the strict business relationship I had with her family. As much as I saw in her a beautiful woman, desirable and with charisma that attracted my most animal instincts, I had treated her with respect and platonic friendship. This night it was different. Three years had passed since I had last seen her, and a new woman with a more liberated attitude was giving me a great time driving through the winds of San Andros. She had become more independent, more sophisticated, and sexier than ever.

The drive from San Andros to Nicholls Town is at a

considerable distance, but this night we went back and forth in a matter of two hours, stopping at Mr. Tracy's. The fat, friendly Chief of Police was happy to see me and pledged his services if I needed to work in his territory at any time in the future. It was easy for me to understand his liberal offer. It was I who not long ago paid him almost a quarter of a million dollars to protect my operations in that island.

I decided not to pursue his hospitality and offer, because I had more stimulating ideas to share with Laura; however, I marked his conversation for possible future benefit.

How somebody can actually fall asleep riding the back of a fast moving motorcycle beats me, but somehow, I have no idea how, I ended up sitting on a waterbed inside my cottage at the San Andros Hotel in my underwear. It had to be early morning; maybe four or five. The door leading to the beach was open, and there by the water was Laura seated on the sand and letting the waves wash her legs. Careful not to disturb her I let her know of my close presence from a few feet away.

"Come over Richard, let's watch the sunrise."

"What time is it?" I asked her.

"Close to five-thirty." It always amazed me how most Bahamians can give you the exact time of the day or night by looking up to the sky.

"Are you ready for breakfast...?"

"No, let's watch the sunrise," I hesitated with embarrassment, in case she volunteered to refresh my memory about my incurable amnesia.

"Well, Richard, you certainly gave me a good scare last night on our way back from Nicholls Town."

"Wait, Laura—I apologize."

"Don't worry; luckily we were only a few miles from

Tracy's and I managed to turn around and get some help before I lost you. My goodness, you went far out!"

"How in the world did we get here?" By this time I was sitting next to her. She had not noticed how inviting she looked wearing a mesh-like blouse that made her breast totally visible. Obviously she had earlier removed her brassiere. Her nipples looked beautiful against her drying top.

"Well," she started with a very sarcastic tone, "I was told you Colombians could handle good alcohol and a pretty woman, my dear friend. What the hell happened to you last night?"

She then went back to explain how I had collapsed against her on our way back to Nicholls Town, and how she had to pull over immediately not to lose me to a bad fall on the rocky road. Laura then looked for the nearest house, and although at a very improper time, she got an old friend to drive us both to San Andros, leaving the motorcycle behind. As far as I was concerned, she could have made the whole story up, because I didn't remember one-second of it.

I apologized a million times, but the more I did, the more fun she made of me.

As the sun started to show its bright face in the blue horizon, and the temperature felt just right, we both as if pre-planned ran to the water and without taking our clothes off, dove into the cooling Bahamian beach.

Breakfast was tropical. A basket of fresh oranges, fresh coconut, bananas and a loaf of homemade bread and hot tea was served on the table next to my bed. The time was about ten in the morning. I had fallen asleep after half an hour of swimming and playing in the water with Laura. As I ate with a great appetite, Laura helped one of the native employees of the hotel with the making of the bed and the replacement of towels. Robert showed up with a copy of the local news-paper under his arm and sat next to me to have some tea with bread and butter.

"I heard about you last night," he spoke while spreading butter over his steaming slice of bread, "you must feel pretty lousy after all that drinking."

"The Holy waters of San Andros cured all my pains," I replied with a gesture pointing towards the window that gave us a marvelous view of the ocean.

"Well, Richard, when you feel ready, come to my house, the Colombians will be here shortly, their flight arrived in Nassau an hour ago and I already sent Keith to pick them up."

"Great! I am looking forward to this meeting. I'll see you in a half an hour," I told Robert as he walked out of my cottage.

Laura joined me for a cup of tea, then she explained that I would not be able to see her later since she was due in Nassau that day for a meeting with airport security agents. I promised I would look her up the following day upon my return to the States. We said good bye with a tight embrace and a gentle kiss on the lips.

"Thanks for the great ride, Laura."

"You're welcome—we have to do it again, Richard." She walked out with a warm smile.

When I entered the main house I immediately noticed the presence of two Latin men in their mid-twenties. By their appearance I knew right away I was not about to meet the men I had in mind, but I proceeded to greet them in spite of my reservations.

"Good morning, Albert, good morning, Keith, hello, Robert," I shook hands as I moved around the room.

"You must be one of the fellows from Medellin." I said in English to one of the Colombians.

"No comprendo inglés," was the answer he gave me. I knew that, but I wanted to hear it from his lips. I welcomed the second Colombian in Spanish, and then I turned to Albert who sat patiently on a rocking chair by the veranda.

"How in the world do you communicate with these people?" I asked him. He could see how impatient I'd grown since I discovered the two *campesinos*[2] from Colombia.

"We don't, I was hoping you came to help us talk to them," explained the old man with concern.

"These people are not the party I expected to meet." I told him with frustration. "Without even talking to them I can clearly tell you that they are just a couple of mules sent here to convey a message." My disappointment was beginning to be mixed with anger.

"Don't lose your cool," insisted the old man. "Do what you can; you must remember that their boss is a very important man in Colombia. We're talking about five thousand kilos in two months if you provide the right airplane." He was right.

Besides, they didn't know now I was working with the American government. I had to play my cards right.

"O.K., amigos," I started a conversation with the Colombians. "I don't have time to waste. I was told that I would meet your boss here in the Bahamas, but apparently he didn't show up and I am not very happy with that. I know you guys need my services, but he has to understand that I am not interested in running a multi-million dollar operation by sending messages with employees who are not in a position to make any kind of decisions." They listened carefully, not even blinking an eye. I had them under control and they just nodded meekly at my lecture. When I finished they got up from their chairs, and the older one spoke in a very hesitant way.

"Richard, my boss is Ivan Restrepo. He knew about you through Albert, because Albert respects your connections and experience in this business of cocaine. Señor Restrepo is not ready to meet with you until I tell him that we've met here in the Bahamas," he paused for a few seconds. "How many kilos can you bring in one trip?"

"Tell Señor Restrepo that I have access to either a Navajo Panther or a Merlin if necessary, but that in any event I need at least $80,000.00 up front before I send my pilots to Colombia for a pick up. Please also tell him that I must meet him personally either in the Bahamas or in the United States before we embark on any venture of this kind." I shook their hands and walked out of the house without turning back.

The act had been played to perfection. It was not hard to play that role. I knew I had behaved exactly like the professional drug smuggler I used to be.

I crossed the street to one of the cabanas of the Andros Beach Hotel. Robert followed me and I asked him if I could use the phone in his apartment to call my wife in the States.

"Of course, let me take you there to make all the calls you need."

I followed him to a little one story brick structure with large glass windows and vertical blinds. The simple but modern place stood out in the middle of the old fashioned huts with straw roofs and clay facades. The first room as we entered looked sleazy, decorated with shag carpeting, leather furniture and glass tables. A wall unit with a full size stereo, VHS, Television set and every pornographic magazine ever published, occupied the rest of the space on its shelves. Right next to the living room was the "pleasure cage" as Robert called it; a smaller room with just enough space for a queen size waterbed and a couple of night stands. Mirrors from the floor to the ceiling on all four walls were sufficient testimony to the lifestyle of the rich Bahamian bachelor.

"I have to go back to the store, then fly the Colombians back to Nassau before dark, so help yourself to anything you want." Robert pointed to a kitchen incorporated inside a walk-in closet. A mini-microwave oven, a small refrigerator and a sink with enough room for a few dishes made the total inventory of the kitchen. The best part of that little apartment was the shower which stood outside the building among three walls, but with no roof over it.

First I called Bahamas Air in Nassau and asked Laura to please get me a ticket out of the Bahamas later that day. She promised to take care of my travel plans. "Just look me up at the airport when you arrive," she offered kindly.

My second call was to my wife to advise her that I would be going back to the United States that evening. As I prepared to leave Robert walked in.

"Richard, why don't we fly to Miami together, I have things to do there!"

"You mean in your plane? I just made arrangements with Laura to go via commercial." I told him.

"Good! I want to take B.A. too, I am not in the mood to fly tonight, besides, there is a Colombian pilot in Nassau who wants to go with me. He is the one that flew the Colombians from Medellin to Andros. Maybe we can have dinner in Nassau together before we take the late flight to Miami."

Those words were music to my ears. I was glad for the chance to get to know the pilot.

"Great!" I exclaimed. "I am looking forward to meeting him; maybe he has more insight in how we can put this deal together." I needed to contact DEA immediately and inform them of my arrival in Miami that evening with Robert and the Colombian pilot I was about to meet. Fortunately, Robert excused himself and left the house to run some errands before our trip. I dialed the DEA undercover untraceable number in Fort Lauderdale used only for these kind of emergencies. A code was all I needed to have DEA's operator put me in direct line with Michael McManus.

"Hi Mike, this is Richard. I am leaving Nassau tonight on the last B.A. flight to Miami. I'll bring two associates for you to check out."

"We'll be covering the event," said Mike.

I put down the phone without another word.

Special Agent Maria Ciociola followed Robert Treco and the American[3] pilot to a Howard Johnson's in Miami and McManus ordered special surveillance while both men were in Florida. The following day Robert returned to the Bahamas.

On June 18, 1987, following instructions given to me by Michael McManus, I initiated a series of telephone talks with the Treco family. Each conversation was to be recorded logging the date, telephone number dialed and the precise hour. I advised Harry Treco that the airplane he needed was to be ready in the United States for his inspection at any time. He told me Robert was to be in charge of that operation and that he would pass on the message. On July 5th I called Robert Treco, and he informed me that he planned to be in Opa Locka the following day.

"Are you flying your own plane?"

"Yes, Richard, I have to take it to Fort Lauderdale later during the day to have some repairs done by Bradley Aviation at Executive."

Robert gave me a telephone number in Dade County

where I was to contact him around eleven thirty a.m. Immediately I notified McManus and a group of his best men were assigned to cover me during the Treco meeting.

Miguel, the undercover DEA pilot, was to meet us at Executive airport to demonstrate the Navajo Panther I had promised the Trecos. The plane was a superb aircraft with high-tech instrumentation. A color RCA radar and a brand new Bendix HF radio had been recently added to its equipment.

Upon arrival at Bradley aviation I recognized Robert's twin engine Piper. The dark gray and white accented striped plane with tail registration letters N-40601 was parked right outside Bradly's office building, and from a distance I spotted Robert unloading some personal belongings from the cargo compartment since he had to leave his plane for tune-up and repairs for at least two days.

"Welcome, Robert." He jumped as I sneaked behind him.

"You've scared the shit out of me!" he said, as he dropped a cardboard box to the ground.

"I am sorry. Guilty conscience?" I laughed.

I followed Robert to the manager's office and waited at the reception area while he took care of business. I spotted at least five DEA undercover agents in that airport. Maybe the receptionist was one of them and I didn't even know it.

We walked to the runway to wait for Miguel whom I expected to land any minute. Pictures of every move Robert and I made were being taken.

"So tell me about your pilot, Richard."

"Miguel is an expert." I started telling Robert. "I met him in Colombia when he worked for the Ochoa organization. It was in late 1978[4] that I hired him to work for Lehder, and ever since he has been perhaps the most reliable man in air routes of cocaine smuggling."

I was telling a totally fabricated story. I had met Miguel early that morning when Special Agent Dan Anderson introduced us at a Denny's restaurant. I never expected Robert to be asking many questions, so I neglected to prepare Miguel in case he needed to corroborate his background.

Robert listened without comment and I could see satisfaction when I praised Miguel and his expertise.

"Who is the real owner of that Navajo Panther?"

"Michael, I've told you about Mike, haven't I?"

"I think so, your partner from Denver?

"That's right" Now I recalled what I had told Robert. Michael McManus was to play the role as owner of several airplanes and McManus would pay me a percentage of his revenues produced by the leasing of his equipment for transporting drugs. I had portrayed Mike as low profile millionaire who really didn't need the extra cash, but who would allow me access to his airplanes because of our close ties and mutual friendship.

"Maybe someday I'll introduce you to him." I made it sound very conditional as if Robert had to earn that privilege.

"Yes, I'd love to meet the man." Robert had bitten the bait.

For the next thirty minutes our conversation went from drug dealing to women, and other worldly pleasures Robert planned to acquire with the wealth from the loads we would fly in the Navajo Panther. The numbers were very realistic. Each one of us could profit in the millions in only six months. If only Robert knew that I held the key that would lock him up for life.

The bright and shiny Navajo Panther made a smooth landing. Robert and I followed it with our eyes as Miguel taxied and came to a final stop in front of one of Bradley's aviation hangars. I approached Miguel and saluted him in Spanish. My smiling words of welcome were instead informing him of his background. After my quick speech I pretended to be embarrassed that I had forgotten Robert didn't speak Spanish.

"Oh, please forgive me Robert, I got carried away in Spanish. Miguel and I always speak our native tongue. I am sorry."

"I understand," responded Robert. "Does Miguel speak English?"

"Of course I do,"said Miguel cutting in. His English normally did not have a trace of accent, but this time Miguel did a remarkable job forcing that unique Latin touch. After the introductions were in order, we walked around the aircraft. The plane had been seized by DEA and re-titled under the name of Michael McManus for technical and practical purposes of this operation.

"Do you want to fly it?" I offered.

"I don't think I have to, it looks outstanding. Can I just crank the engines without taking off?"

"Please, Robert, be my guest," I insisted warmly.

Robert took the pilot seat, Miguel sat next to him and I sat behind them as both men engaged in a technical conversation about engines, radios, etc. It sounded like a foreign language to me but I was happy to see how well the undercover pilot and the drug dealer got along.

The motors came to life. The small plane shook as Robert Treco pushed the levers giving them full RPM capacity.

"This is the baby we need," said Robert, happily.

"Well, let's discuss some details," I proposed.

We left the plane and walked to a wooden bench under a canvas awning. Miguel indicated he wouldn't take any risks and asked Robert what kind of protection he offered in the Bahamas.

"I have several islands where we can land. The police, customs and immigration authorities are taken care of and I also have alternative routes to get you out in case of emergency."

"Don't worry Miguel," I volunteered, "I've known the Trecos for years and no one in the Bahamas runs a tighter ship."

"O.K., I have to fly back to Miami," said Miguel looking at me, "let me know when I should be available, Richard."

We all shook hands and Miguel left us, taking the airplane with him. I drove Robert to a car rental place in Fort Lauderdale. From there he was followed by other DEA agents to the Howard Johnson's in North Miami.

On October 20, 1987, Robert was introduced to Michael McManus for the first time. The lounge at the Howard Johnson's was beginning to get congested with its regular happy hour crowd. Maria Ciociola and Dan Anderson had taken separate bar stools from where they had a clear view of the table we had chosen. Other DEA agents had been assigned by Michael to keep surveillance right outside the bar. Robert sat timidly waiting for either Mike or me to start negotiating. Finally McManus broke the ice.

"So, Robert, I understand you want to lease one of my airplanes."

"Yes, Richard showed me your Navaho Panther a few weeks ago. I was quite impressed."

"Well," said McManus with a proud smile, "you haven't seen anything yet, I keep all my planes in top shape."

"What other planes do you operate?" enquired Treco.

"Right now I only have a Rockwell 1986 Commander, a 1976 Lear Jet and a couple of Cessna's."

Some modesty, I chuckled to myself as I watched Michael taking control of the conversation.

"I want to move about four hundred kilos to the United States via Bahamas. I want to lease your Navajo and your pilot," said Robert, leaning close to Mike's left ear.

"Fine, I can provide you with two plans. First, I can let you guys use my plane and pilot just for the first leg of the trip to the Bahamas; or I can have Miguel fly you all the way into the United States, but obviously the numbers will be higher."

"No, I already have arrangements to have the load be brought to the States by boat."

"Listen, Robert, Richard has told me a lot about you and your father. I rarely agree to meet people involved in drug trafficking but because of this man," Mike put his arm over my shoulder, "who has been a loyal friend and business associate for years, I agreed to be here. It will cost you $165,000 and believe me it's a steal!"

Robert Treco started to write some numbers on a paper napkin. After multiplying, dividing and subtracting, he spoke up.

"It sounds good. How much money down do you require?"

"Normally I ask for fifty percent down, but because of this old relationship between you and Richard I am willing to take $15,000 just to cover any possible fees in case I have to retain an attorney should if I have to claim my airplane back."

"That sounds fair, I'll have the fifteen in a couple of days, are you going to be in town for a while?"

"Maybe, you can give the money to Richard. We should have a couple of meetings before we materialize our plans."

The meeting was over. We finished our beers and left the bar. Robert told me he would be staying in room 225 for another night and to contact him if I needed anything. Twenty-four hour surveillance was assigned while Treco remained in the States for another day.

On August 27, 1987, Michael McManus, Miguel, the undercover pilot, and I met Robert Treco at 11:45 a.m. in room 475 at the Howard Johnson's on 163rd street in Miami. The meeting was to discuss the coordinates into Colombia to pick up the load in La Guajira and to settle any loose ends of the operation. Robert started by proposing a Colombian co-pilot to fly the load with Miguel.

"NO WAY!" I objected. Everybody turned and looked at me somewhat surprised." I smell something wrong here," I was addressing Robert. "First you indicated you had a Bahamian co-pilot and now he is a Colombian. Since when have you known this Colombian so-called pilot?" I sounded sarcastic.

"I don't know him," confessed Robert, "he is one of the Doc's men with whom he has worked before."

"And who the hell is this Doc?" I was getting angry. It wasn't right for Robert to suddenly, at the last hour, introduce us to all these little surprises. I knew I had nothing to lose by leading him on, but I had a role to play and for the duration of that meeting my mind became that of a drug dealer instead of a DEA undercover man.

"Robert, I think it is better that you tell us who is really involved in this," insisted Michael, "I hate last minute surprises."

Robert looked intimidated and embarrassed. Not only

was he outnumbered, but he had realized and accepted his mistakes.

"I am sorry, Richard, I just forgot to tell you about the Doc. His name is Julio, he is a physician here in Miami. I have been working with him since you left Andros in 1983, and we have been dropping loads. As a matter of fact I just returned from Barranquilla, Colombia not long ago. This man is good. Believe me I wouldn't put you guys in a shaky position."

"What is Julio's role or job description in this operation?" asked McManus.

"He is the financial support. He pays for all expenses including your fees. He is co-owner of the cocaine stored in Colombia."

Although Michael, Miguel and I pretended to be unhappy with the new input. We just couldn't be more thrilled as we listened to Robert Treco unfold his secret information. It was music to our ears. Robert went on to explain how he and a young Bahamian co-pilot had flown loads of marijuana for the Doc. He said he had contacts with Bahamian officials in Nassau providing him with updated data of DEA's operation of its helicopters as well as traffic controllers to help with the flight plans.

"I will be on the island waiting for the Navajo," he said, "I'll have several boats offshore to back up any emergency or an air drop."

I knew, based on expertise and exposure that Robert was good and that his family's connections were infallible. My concern, and that of Mike's, was Miguel's safety. He had to bring in the load with a Colombian co-pilot whom none of us ever met and who could easily do away with Miguel if he suspected anything. On the other hand Michael had yet to deal with deciding when to make the arrest. There are rules and regulations of airspace under different countries and it was not yet clear whether the arrest should be made in mid-air or upon landing in the Bahamas.

There was the alternative of having a DEA helicopter scare the pilots so Miguel could have an excuse to re-route the plane to an island where DEA had pre-arranged backups. That plan was welcomed by Miguel who was to take the most serious risk of the whole plan, however I feared that once the Colombian co-pilot spotted the DEA helicopter he could start shooting at it, putting Miguel's life in serious jeopardy. Another worry for McManus, was the issue of jurisdiction.

The Bahamas was a good place to make the arrest, but its judicial system works differently from the one in this country and we were not sure if DEA could have total control of the seizure and the arrests.

"The only way I agree to fly that load is if the Colombian understands that I am to be the PIC (Pilot in charge) and that he is to take orders from me at any given time." Miguel spoke with authority.

"That's right," I cut in. "and I want to meet that Colombian here in the United States and spend a few hours with him. I have to check him inside and out."[5] Mike's face showed satisfaction hearing my demand.

"Well, I'll explain to the Doc what you guys need in order to have a meeting of our minds, and I'll let Richard know within a couple of days."

"Fine," said Hike. "But, if you cannot iron these little problems by next week, we'll have to postpone it indefinitely because I have a new assignment for the Navajo Panther next month."

He was putting pressure very intelligently.

On August 31, 1987, Robert Treco contacted me by phone

to advise me that he would be in the United States on September 2nd to finalize the plans and to pay us the down payment as agreed. The operation was to occur on September 5th. The phone conversation was recorded for evidence in a court of law.

The weather in the northern jungles of La Guajira had been bad. The heavy rains had caused catastrophic floods in areas near Riohacha where the cocaine waited to be picked up. The weather bureau in Washington informed DEA that there was no relief in sight at least for the next two weeks. Robert Treco called me to let me know that the September 5th project had to be postponed, he had no idea that we had been keeping a close watch on the weather from South America to the United States.

On September 8th, the plan was scrapped. DEA just couldn't have a dozen of its good agents in stand-by indefinitely when there were other priorities that required immediate attention. For the next few weeks I made occasional phone calls to the Bahamas to keep the Trecos aware of my interest in future ventures, while I concentrated on setting up the purchase of cocaine through some Colombian dealers residing in Miami.

I felt as if the Trecos were neglected. They could by now be operating with someone else, so I decided to call them to touch base and to find out about the status of the Doc and his associates. I recorded the conversation.

"So what's happening, Robert?"

"Nothing, last time I heard from the Doc, he was very desperate because he had run out of goods to deliver to his patients."

"And why is that?"

"Since the floods in Colombia, he has not been able to

move anything at all, and his clientele is complaining that they may go to a different doctor."

"How much would it take to keep him in business?"

"Why do you ask? Can you help?"

"Well, I have some old Colombian ties in Miami, I don't know if they have what you need, but I can call you later and let you know."

"Fantastic! That would make the Doc very happy so long as the price is right."

"Well, Robert, I'll make sure we both make some money."

"Call me when you have all the information, price, quality, areas of delivery, terms, etc."

"Don't get too excited, Robert. Let's wait and see what I come up with." We ended the conversation .

On the same day, I contacted Michael McManus and asked him if we could put together a reverse operation.[6] He advised me that he could provide me with all the cocaine I needed to put the deal together, but he had to check with his superiors in Washington to see whether there was danger that this whole deal might backfire on us in a court of law due to entrapment.[7] Later that afternoon Mike gave me the green light to go ahead and start negotiations for the sale of one hundred kilos of pure Colombian coke at $12,000 per kilo to be delivered by us in Miami.

On September 28 1987, Harry Treco called me to let me know that Robert was on his way to Miami to meet with me at the Holiday Inn in Miami Springs to introduce me to the buyers. The next morning Robert told me that he could not convince his buyers to pay more than $9,500 per kilo. I knew the price of cocaine had suffered serious price reductions due to the proliferation of the drug in the streets of Miami, but $9,500 was just too low.[8]

"We won't be making any money Robert" I complained. "I'll be buying this coke for $9,000 per kilo, that leaves hardy enough margin to justify the risk."

"I know," said Robert, "but it will be paid in cash right away."

"I'll check some other sources, keep your people warm. I'll call you back."

I transferred all the information I had to Mike. He suggested I play hard to get for a while then at the end to give in to the $9,500 per kilo providing the money be presented to us before we show the coke. His plan was to make the arrest without us having to transport the cocaine anywhere.

After hours of negotiating over several phone conversations, I gave in to the price and asked Robert to meet me in Fort Lauderdale the following day to set up delivery. He agreed to drive up to State Rd 84 and I-95 and meet Mike and me at the Holiday Inn's lounge. Again, back-up agents were assigned to cover both of us while the meeting took place. I recognized Maria Ciociola sitting by the bar and Dan Anderson having a beer by himself at the table next to us.

"There is only one problem," remarked Robert as he sat comfortably. "The Doc wants to see one kilo before we show you the money."

"The Doc?" asked McManus playing naive and ignorant, "the same Doc who wanted to lease my plane?"

"That's right, you can meet him tomorrow in Miami when you bring the kilo for him to examine the quality."

"I'm sorry Robert, but there is no way in the world that Mike and I would walk into a hotel room to meet a Cuban doctor who might be working for the government and have us all arrested with the kilo in our possession."

"The man is clean," insisted Robert. "I told you before, I've known this man for years."

"I don't like it," said McManus, "it's too risky."

By this time Robert feared he was losing us, but he had no choice. The Doc had valid reasons, to inspect the merchandise he was about to pay $960,000 in cash for. We just gave them a hard time to show how "scared" we were.

"OK, Robert, we'll bring the key... but no surprises."

"Don't worry Mike," reassured Robert.

The next day Michael told me we were going to attend our meeting without the promised kilo. I insisted it was not good to do that, I told Mike that could be the end of the Doc, but he explained how the government insisted in putting more pressure on the Doc to produce the $960,0000 without us taking any risks of being ripped off. I had no saying. Mike was my boss and I would not question his final word.

We had a team of DEA agents inside the hotel positioned at strategic places to cover any possibility of danger. One of the "maids" positioned her laundry cart with an automatic weapon under her towels, right outside room 620, while another agent played bell boy at the front. Before we entered the hotel building, we made sure Mike had no weapons or any other item that could link him to DEA. We were cool and ready.

As we entered the room, Robert said he would call the doctor. After a brief conversation he told us the Doc was on his way. We refrained from telling Robert that we didn't have the kilo until the Doc came in. In a matter of minutes the Doc rang the bell.

The fifty-six-year-old Cuban doctor sat on one of the beds. Michael had taken one of the chairs next to the window, and I stood in front of the dresser.

"I must ask you both a question before we start any business," were the doctor's first heavily accented words.

"Go ahead," Mike and I agreed, sharing the suspense the Doc had created.

"Are you Federal agents working undercover?"

I could not believe my ears. What kind of fool was this man anyway? Did he expect us to tell him the truth? I made a painful effort not to laugh.

"I am not an agent of any kind," said Mike, "are you one?"

"Of course not," responded the Doc.[9] Then he pointed at me to force my reply.

"Me either!"

The Doc thanked us for having been so patient a few weeks back when we had to cancel the Colombian operation, and he reassured us that in the near future he would hire our services to bring the loads.

"Doc, I would like to see the money for the one hundred kilos before we show you our kilo," said Mike anxious to get to the bottom of the deal.

"Well, I have the cash a few minutes away from here. I'd have to make arrangements to have someone bring it over."

I was relieved to know that the Doc had not demanded the sample kilo. "Well, should we come back in one hour or less?" I asked.

"I think so," replied the Doc.

Mike and I left the hotel and went to a restaurant only a couple of blocks from the Holiday Inn to have lunch.

"We got them!" we exulted.

One hour later, after our lunch, we decided it would be appropriate to go back. We didn't see our "bell boy" and went ahead to take the elevator to the sixth floor. No one answered as we rang several times. It was very strange.

Something was wrong. Maria Ciociola was not in place either. I rushed to the front desk and the clerk told me that Mr. Treco had checked out about half an hour back. We were crestfallen. Our "sting" had failed.

A whole week had passed since we lost contact with Robert Treco and his Doc friend. It felt I should not insist by calling then. Robert owed me an explanation and I expected him to call me any time with an account of what has happened. Mike and I felt that maybe the doctor had suspected something and has chickened out at the last minute taking advantage of out absence to make his way out.

On September 29 1987, my pager went off. The Trecos' telephone number in Andros appeared on the screen. Robert explained that nothing serious had happened that the doctor was only waiting for his Colombian partner to go ahead and bring the load of cocaine into the States. I never asked Robert for a further explanation making him believe that I didn't really need that deal in the first place.

It was in late September that the trial of Carlos Lehder in Jacksonville had started with jury selection. I knew my name was among the many witnesses on behalf of the Government, and that any minute now I was to enter the Federal Witness Protection Program. I would be given new identity, a new location to reside in, and total anonymity. I had to part from my past and forget Carlos Stier had ever existed.

I called Robert Treco and told him that I was afraid the Federal government could subpoena me to appear as a witness and that for that reason I was leaving the country to go to Europe for at least a year until Lehder had been tried and sentenced.

"I'll give my pager to Michael," I told Robert, "and keep

in contact with him. You can trust Mike in everything. He's as good as dealing directly through me."

Robert sympathized with my urgency to disappear and assured me that we would renew our relationship upon my return. I knew I would never speak to Robert Treco or any member of his family again. In a very peculiar way I felt sorry for having to end that long relationship with such deception. I had no doubt that in the near future I would face him again as I presented my testimony to a jury to convict him for crimes related to drug smuggling.

I left with my family to an undisclosed location under the protection of the Federal Government.

Every now and then I would telephone Michael McManus and he would tell me about his negotiations with the Trecos. They would ask Mike where I was and he answered that I had taken my family to Barcelona, Spain. Mike continued to pursue the importation of cocaine through the Doc, and by early November Michael had earned both the Trecos and the Doc's trust and close friendship. Michael McManus was always a very likable person. His well-mannered behavior, clean-cut looks and obvious education made him a "prince" anybody could believe in.

The years of exposure to Drug Enforcement had taught him more than any government training seminar could offer. He knew the Colombians, their way of thinking, their weaknesses, their appetites and even their different dialects. He played low profile and knew how to seduce his victims into following his lead. I knew that if I wasn't on his side now, I would had been caught in his net together with many members of the Medellin Cartel.

On November 13 1987, Michael McManus finally managed to put together a deal to import 660 kilos of cocaine with the help of Doc, Robert Treco, Harry Treco and of course the undercover pilots assigned by him to the task.

The following morning, through the Marshal's Service channels, I learned that the Trecos, Dr. Julio Diaz and several Colombian and Bahamians were arrested by DEA under the supervision of Micheal McManus. I was speechless.

8

FEBRUARY, 1988

C asting my lot as an undercover agent[1] for the Drug Enforcement Administration brought me inexorably to the time when I would have to testify against the man whose life had been so intertwined with mine. I dreaded the day when I would have to walk into the crowded courtroom and confront, face-to-face, Carlos Lehder.

Intense emotions built up inside me as I anticipated questions of the press[2] and as I tried to imagine the scornful stares of fellow Colombians who would never understand why one of their own was making a suicidal attempt to destroy a drug empire.[3] For almost a year I had known this date would come, but now I could no longer keep the realization at the fringes of my mind. An army of butterflies arrived, increasing each day as the trial grew closer.

Nevertheless I felt very proud of my decision. I was ready to carry on with my duty in spite of my agony of fright. Our Colombia had suffered through ten years of violence, bloodshed and corruption, and this was my chance to atone for some of the humiliation I had helped heap upon her. For the people of Colombia, for the ministers brutally and cowardly assassinated by the Medellin Cartel, for my family and for the sake of my own soul, I was ready to testify.

US Attorney Robert W. Merkle contacted me through the channels provided by the Marshal's Service. The government had already prepared the routes by which I was to be transported to Jacksonville, Florida. A special task force on 24 hour-detail was immediately assigned to protect me as I traveled from my undisclosed place of residence via: commercial airlines.

I used a different name for each portion of the trip in order to avoid any possibility of being traced. The airlines were notified that I would require the presence of armed men at all times, and special orders were issued to bypass weapons' check-points with no delay. During stop-overs before my final destination, Marshal inspectors were at the arrival gate to reinforce my protection while I waited for a connecting flight. Sometimes the government had prearranged secret passages to whisk me in and out of airports without exposure to the general public.

All these measures made me more than ever aware of the inevitable danger, but in a peculiar way made me feel important. I felt like I was the hero in an 007 movie! Never during my travels under the protection of the federal witness program was I taken from city A to city B in a straight route.

For instance, if I was to be transferred from New York to Washington D.C. the Marshals would fly me first to Tulsa, from Tulsa to Dallas, and only then, if their intelligence division believed it safe, would I get to Washington that same evening. It all represented many exhausting travel hours, not to mention the mental anxiety, but at the end of each trip I was grateful to return home to my wife and two children without a scratch.

The security surrounding my arrival in Jacksonville was unbelievable. Plainclothes detectives were poised with rifles at the ready. I was rushed out of the terminal building to a station wagon waiting to transfer me to the courthouse. A lead vehicle three miles ahead kept our driver informed of any suspicious cars or faces along the route we were to take. Behind us at close distance followed two vehicles containing heavily armed men.

As soon as we pulled away from the curb at the airport terminal, the driver crushed down the accelerator pedal to build speed as fast as possible so that no unfamiliar vehicle could follow undetected. Once we approached the Jacksonville city limits a helicopter hovered overhead to keep constant radio communication with our station wagon and guide our driver into the streets that were clear of any possible roof-sniper.

Starting two blocks away from the Federal Courthouse plainclothes men holding automatic rifles lined the sidewalks at intervals of approximately 50 yards. Our station wagon rolled into the rear parking lot and uniformed police officers surrounded the car to escort me out. My bodyguards rushed me into the building through a rear door where an escalator led to the basement. Inside the building were more heavily armed men than I could count. The kind of SWAT training they had undergone was evident in their alert demeanor and quick reflexes. Those men were not taking any chances. They never underestimated the fury of the Medellin Cartel. Nor did I.

9

MAY 16, 1988

My undercover work with the Drug Enforcement Administration had produced a number of important arrests and indictments of Colombian and Bahamian subjects. Although I had by now officially resigned from the Federal Witness Protection Program, I kept a very careful watch over my family in the new city we had chosen for our place of residence.

The local office of the United States Marshall Service approved of our new location and an agent was assigned to respond to any emergency calls in the event I suspected any danger or considered a relocation to be prudent. During my frequent travels to Florida, measures were taken to protect me in and out of the state, and close detail was established by special DEA agents to ensure my well-being while attending business related to undercover work.

Our greatest hardship, of course, was breaking away from personal friends and the closest of relatives. We were once again strangers in the land of our adoption and we had to be all-in-all to each other. Both my wife and I had learned the hard discipline demanded by our secret lives, and the seven months we spent under federal protection had taught us a few tricks which we adopted in our daily routine.

We arranged a secret post office box where a member of DEA would pick up our mail and forward it to us immediately to keep some contact with our dear families in Colombia. Needless to say, it was hard to assume a new name and to get used to the background history we had manufactured and rehearsed over and over in case anybody asked about our past or origin.

We were fortunate that our children were still young enough to be easily "brain-washed" and soon they were comfortable with our new name. Once I was terrified when my wife blurted out her name as "Cristina," but she smiled girlishly and covered, "oh, that was my maiden name!"

Life took on a normal course. I was happy. My only regret was to have put my family through all the changes and sacrifices. Cristina was stronger and more supportive than I thought any 24 year-old could possibly be. In spite of all the many inconveniences and real suffering she held her faith until we saw a new future unfolding and a promise of a better life.

I still frequently called Fernando, my brother in Colombia, though he had no idea where my calls were coming from. Fernando kept me informed of the events surrounding my children in Colombia, as well as those of my mother, younger brother, sister and their children. They all understood the seriousness of the situation and accepted the fact that I could never disclose to them my new name, my address, nor any remote clue that could allow someone to ferret out our new identity. Of course I trusted their loyalty and love implicitly, but this policy was for their safety almost more than mine. I could not burden them with such a dangerous secret.

Early in May of 1988, during a routine conversation with Colombia, Fernando told me that Alvaro Triana, aka Archie, was to marry in Bogota in a few days.

Alvaro had become the talk of the town when he returned to Colombia after heading up Lehder's interests in the USA His full-size Mercedes-Benz and large holdings of real estate were only a few of the investments that made him an arrogantly rich celebrity. He turned away from the old friends who had once helped him in many ways, and his only so-called buddies had to be those of great wealth associated with the drug industry.

"He forgot about his roots," a once-mutual friend told me. I was not at all surprised. I could not understand how a woman in her right mind would marry a man with such a lurid reputation and unappealing physique but money can also create strange bedfellows. The "victim," Claudia Ximena Uribe, was a very pretty young dentist, daughter of Olga Vargas de Uribe. Archie had fallen madly in love.

The wedding was to take place at Santa Monica, a small Roman Catholic chapel in El Lago, a prominent neighborhood in the capital of Colombia. The new bride and groom were to spend their honeymoon at a number of undisclosed islands in the Caribbean.

"I expect he won't be fool enough to go to countries that have extradition treaties with the United States," I told my brother. I explained how Triana had been indicted in Fort Lauderdale on cocaine trafficking charges and that a court order was out for his arrest.

"He's too smart," agreed Fernando, "he'll never make that mistake."

Nevertheless I mentioned this bit of society news to DEA and on May 13 of 1988 at four-thirty in the afternoon my phone rang.

"Alvaro Triana was arrested in Curacao last night." It was Michael McManus calling me from DEA in Fort Lauderdale, the same man who had notified me a year ago of the arrest and extradition of Carlos Lehder.

"He had a fake passport, but his picture was sent throughout the Caribbean and recognized by Interpol. Special Agent Cindy Schultz will fly to Curacao tomorrow to start extradition proceedings through our embassy."

My emotions surged just as they had at the time of that other call.

"To everything there is a season," I thought again.

In the city of Oranjestad, Aruba, on May 26, 1988, a three-judge panel on that southern Caribbean island ordered Alvaro Triana extradited to the United States on five different counts related to trafficking and conspiracy.

Prosecutor Florencio Wernet told the judges Triana was indicted by a grand jury in Florida. Greg Kehoe, Assistant U. S. Attorney in Fort Lauderdale, informed the press that Triana faced charges involving the smuggling of cocaine between 1980 and 1984.

Triana, who argued that his arrest was a case of mistaken identity, was held under tight security on this self-governing member of the Kingdom of the Netherlands, in the lower Caribbean Sea about 20 miles off the coast of Venezuela. Triana tried to explain that his activities were not related to those of drug smuggling and that he was exporting automobile parts to Colombia.

"I am innocent," he whimpered. "My misfortune was being born in Colombia."

He left the courtroom in tears.

At the end of a two-hour extradition hearing the judges, who had deliberated several hours, recommended to Governor Felipe Tromp that there was sufficient evidence to extradite Mr. Triana. Upon hearing this pronouncement, Archie's mask of piteous purity fell, and he let forth a stream of foul-mouthed Spanish invectives as he was escorted from the courtroom. Mercifully the translator remained silent.

Dutch soldiers were positioned at the prison and Claudia Ximena, his wife, was asked by Dutch officials to leave their country and never return.

She flew to Colombia after her aborted honeymoon, and now with the help of Triana's brother she has taken over management of his wealth. Alvaro Triana was put aboard a private DEA plane and upon arrival in the United States was taken to MCI (Miami Correctional Institution) a federal prison south of Miami.

MAY 19, 1988

T he task force office set up by the Drug Enforcement Administration just for the purpose of the Lehder trial, occupied some two thousand square feet of basement space under the Federal building. It was a fortress. Alarms, barricades, armed guards and metal detectors were just a few of the security devices protect the valuable information kept in that room as well as to protect the lives of attorneys, detectives, special federal agents, secretaries and other personnel who worked around the clock preparing materials, charts and intelligence information to be used by the prosecution during the trial.

The discovery files on the life of Carlos Enrique Lehder Rivas were lengthy, meticulous and detailed to the extreme. Special Agent Doug Driver of DEA in Jacksonville knew more about Carlos Lehder, his past life, background and even personal life than anyone else. The 36 year-old federal agent had spent several years of his life in Colombia and Panama as head of a task force group to investigate Lehder and other chiefs of the Medellin Cartel. Now in Jacksonville he was Robert Merkle's right hand man in directing investigation, background information and other pertinent data in the lives of the more than one hundred witnesses who were to take the stand for the Government.

Statements of bank accounts[1] in Colombia, the Bahamas, United States and Europe were available from as far back as 1970. Articles of corporations[2] chartered in Nassau under the names of Air Montes and Titanic Air had been provided by the Bahamian government as well as evidence of millions of dollars funneled through the bank of Nova Scotia. Pictures of Carlos Lehder since his early life in this country were obtained through special sources, and thousands of depositions, court transcripts and indictments were at hand. High-Tech video and audio systems were installed to review exhibits that would be shown to the jury.

Standing by were official government translators to transcribe and translate documentation that sometimes arrived from Colombia via telex or Fax systems. Cases with pictures, clothes and many miscellaneous personal items confiscated from Lehder's properties in three countries were also ready to be presented as court exhibits. Machine guns, hand guns, grenades and other heavy duty weapons rested next to Doug Driver's desk. Many of those weapons were found in properties in the Bahamas, United States and Colombia. The basement held the results of many years of research, intelligence work and the fruits of thousands of hours of toil by men and women dedicated to bringing a drug kingpin to justice.

U.S Attorney Robert W. Merkle sat at a desk in the middle of the room. FBI, IRS, DEA and Secret Service men sat nearby to provide him with any information at short notice. It was a Sunday but there was hardly time for a coffee break. The telephones would not stop ringing and the activities of law enforcement personnel and office clerks seemed incessant. In an office toward the end of the basement, U.S attorney Ernest Muller, assistant prosecutor in the case, was busy interviewing some potential witnesses. My U.S Marshall's body-guards escorted me to Mr. Merkle.

"Please sit down. I am Robert Merkle in charge of the prosecution."

"How do you do, sir, I am Carlos Stier."

Robert Merkle, wearing jeans and a Polo shirt, stood up to shake my hand. Doug Driver, whom I had met in Fort Lauderdale a year earlier was glad to see me and saluted[3] me with more affection.

I had been warned about Robert Merkle, but no matter how prepared I thought I was his intimidating image and demanding personality put an immediate shield between us. Merkle was an imposing figure of robust stature, shrewd, and with a reputation for bullying witnesses.

He possessed a rhetorical range of operatic dimensions. He could adopt a refined demeanor to obtain his goals, but if that didn't work he would charge at you like a "mad dog"[4] uttering his mind, regardless of consequences, in order to obtain the truth. Frederick Graves had advised me that Merkle's job was not an easy one and that I must stay relaxed and not lose my temper.

I understood Merkle had to be tough in order to prepare me for the toughest cross examination ever by Mr. Edward Shohat, defense attorney for Lehder. I tried to accept his line of questioning as good strategy on his part, but there were moments when I felt as if I were the defendant on trial and did lose my temper, springing from the chair and asking my bodyguards to take me back to the airport.

"Wait, I am on your side," said Merkle, getting up from his desk to stop me from leaving, "but if you are going to react like this upstairs in that courtroom, we're lost."

"Mr. Merkle, I don't like your form of questioning, and I don't have to be here."

"Fine, Carlos, you don't have to do this, but I still believe you are a very important witness in this trial. You have to understand, that the defense attorneys are going to try to destroy you without mercy, and that is why we have to get tough—to stay ahead of them."

I understood his reasoning and returned to the chair in front of him.

"Go get a cup of coffee, you'll feel better."

Merkle proved to be a very aggressive man under fire and I realized after being with him for eight hours non-stop that this case could not have been assigned to anyone else in the country. He had the right ingredients; the charisma, the knowledge, and above all the guts to take on—head to head — the leader of the most dangerous organization in the world.

After several trips to Jacksonville and many long weekend hours of hard work, I began to like Robert Merkle. I felt very grateful to him for the task he had accepted on behalf of the United States government.

The seven long months of the Lehder trial were dominated by the overwhelming evidence presented to the jury. Over one hundred witnesses testified on behalf of the Government, and throughout the long hours of litigation neither Mr. Shohat nor Mr. Quiñon managed to invalidate any of the testimonies presented to the court. The Government had done its homework.

There were descriptions of Lehder's mother transporting cocaine from different points in the United States and laundering money for her son. Others, just as damaging, told of Lehder's unscrupulous ambition for-money and power. There were pictures of his corporations' files and evidence of his wealth.

Most witnesses were credible because they presented the court with detailed personal accounts of the days in Norman's Cay, the loads of cocaine, the orgies, the waste of money, the airplanes and the schemes to defraud the governments of three countries. The IRS had witnesses, as well as the FBI and US Customs agents. There were thick files dating back 1976 of investigations conducted by different Federal agencies. The members of the jury listened for seven months to anecdotes of life styles in which there was no respect for human values.

Money and power were the only denominators in the quest for world domination. The jurors watched video tapes of Carlos Lehder being interviewed in a South American jungle. There he openly announced his alliance with the M-19 terrorist group and he justified the bloody killing of Rodrigo Lara Bonilla, calling it "necessary."

This trial was not based on nationalities, creeds, color or any other prejudice. It was a trial for very serious crimes committed not only under the law of this nation, but under the law of all human kind. This was a trial of the free people against a member of a very evil empire.

On May 14, 1988 I was sitting in front of U.S Attorney Robert Merkle preparing my testimony for the following day.

That same day anonymous phone calls were made to a local newspaper. A Latin male advised the newspaper that if I testified against Carlos Lehder, they would do away with me either before or after my testimony. Merkle did not reveal the threats to me until a couple of days later when he informed me that he was ready to rest his case.

"I'll need you to stand by because the defense will put a

couple of Colombian witnesses on the stand, and I need you to identify them for me." I assented. There was also the possibility that I might be called for rebuttal. Again, I was ready.

The following day Mr. Shohat approached the bench with a petition for sixty days continuance using the excuse that his Colombian witnesses were yet to be found. Motion for the defense was denied and without hesitation Mr. Shohat moved to rest his case. The motion came as a surprise to the judge, the prosecution and the jury. Mr. Shohat had given up! He had thrown in the towel and his frustration was visible to the general public and the press. Lehder looked at him in dismay and sank in his chair, aghast.

The defense attorney walked out of the courtroom to encounter a mass of reporters wanting to know his strategy. Shohat pushed his way through the thick crowd without uttering a word. He was embarrassed, defeated. He had just surrendered his client to the mercy of the courts without a fair fight.

On May 19, 1988 after three days of deliberations, the jurors informed the judge they had reached a verdict. Carlos Enrique Lehder Rivas was found guilty of all eleven counts.[5]

11

JULY 1, 1988

Terri Schubert, the young six-foot-tall US Attorney, was seated behind her desk at the end of a corridor where several other federal prosecutors worked. It was a small office containing only an old wooden desk and a couple of chairs. Files, briefs, writ appeals, motions and other miscellaneous piles of legal paper work filled the top of her desk, but all in orderly fashion. At a glance I could see clearly the typed headings on most of those files:

The United States of America
vs. Alvaro Triana
a/k/a Antonio Jimenez
a/k/a Archie

SINCE TRIANA'S indictments of the previous year, Terri Schubert had spent many late hours of research and study in preparation for this case as well as the prosecution of other defendants indicted together with Mr. Triana. Now the government had him in custody and the time had come for Ms. Schubert to summon all her skills to get a guilty verdict.

As of this date, Mr. Triana had been negotiating legal fees between two prominent Miami attorneys. Edward Shohat, who had represented Carlos Lehder during eight months of exhaustive cross-examination of some 120 witnesses, had at the resting of the prosecution's case simply given up without a fight. This was a surprise to the press, the jury, and to Mr. Robert W. Merkle, the tough US Attorney who prosecuted the case.

On the other hand, Mr. Triana had also been speaking with Oscar Rodriguez, a Latin criminal attorney with a reputation for successfully defending Colombian drug offenders. Based on the charges Alvaro Triana was facing, no attorney would look at the case unless $60,000 was paid up as initial retainer, and a total tag of at least $200,000 was promised for handling the entire case and possible appeal.

Early that morning special DEA agent Cindy Schultz had picked me up at Fort Lauderdale airport. We drove straight to the Federal Courthouse on East Broward Boulevard, left the car in the underground parking lot, and took the elevator to the second floor. Through a glass door we entered the US Attorney's office.

Ms. Schubert, a native of Ohio, had been working for the federal government since her bar exam. Her job had taken her to several states and also to many countries where the United States government has programs to update foreign nations on matters of judicial interest and international treaties.

She had dealt personally with issues of extradition between Colombia and the United States through the

Colombian Embassy in Washington, and was a knowledgeable attorney in matters related to Latin America. Her make-up-free complexion gave her a school girl look although she was 32 years old

As I walked into her office accompanied by Cindy Schultz, Terri put down her half-empty yogurt container.

"Are we interrupting your lunch?" apologized Cindy.

"Not really, I am almost done," answered Terri, setting aside her cup.

"You must be Carlos," she added with a welcoming smile.

"How do you do, Ms. Schubert?" I extended my hand.

I had spoken over the phone to Terri Schubert on a couple of occasions while I was in Jacksonville attending the trial of Carlos Lehder. Somehow I had expected her to be an older woman. She dressed with conservative good taste and from the very beginning I found her to be a most affable and down-to-earth person.

Terri agreed to have a drink with us while Cindy and I had lunch. At the restaurant our conversation focused on the case of Alvaro Triana, his possible sentence, the length of the trial and the expected consequences should he be found guilty of all counts and sentenced. Other plans of my undercover work were also discussed. It was a refreshing meeting.

Terri Schubert offered a very ethical approach to the case. It is difficult to keep from grouping all Colombians under one umbrella marked "guilty," and I was relieved to see that this representative of my adopted country was willing to look at the individual aspects of each case without prejudice.

12

JULY 20, 1988

I   t's July 20, 1988 in this great land. Today America
    celebrates nineteen years since the first men walked
    on the moon, and the Democratic party is nominating
a new man to the White House.

The 20th of July has always been a very special day for
Colombians. It is on this date that the South American
nation celebrates its independence. This is a legal holiday
when the whole country comes to a halt and the three-
striped color flag flies proudly out of every window. Most
families spend this day at leisure.

For the Lehder family this day will not represent independence nor rouse any patriotic feelings. Their only consolation will be that Guillermo Lehder did not live to see the
disgrace of his son.

It is on this day, some four-thousand miles away from
the festivals and parades of his beautiful Colombia, that
Carlos Enrique Lehder faces Judge Howell W. Melton to
hear the final verdict on the rest of his life. Yesterday
Lehder's co-defendant, Mr. Jack Carlton Reed, 58 years old,

was sentenced to fifteen years for one single count of conspiracy.

As I write this last chapter of *The Crippled Mule* I cannot stop to examine the career of a brilliant man; a man with priceless values and respectable family roots, a man gifted with intelligence and wisdom who could have easily ruled his nation if he had controlled his appetite for world dominance through evil means.

What a waste. It saddens me when I imagine myself within his body. Lehder and I, both born on September 5, 1949, both sharing similar backgrounds and both throwing away our chances for a respectable and productive life. Why am I not facing his grim reality of spending the rest of a relatively young life behind bars? How did I escape our interlocked destinies? Is it God who is giving me this second chance? Yes. I am certain of that.

It's now 4:30 in the afternoon and special agent Doug Driver with DEA in Jacksonville has called to inform me that Lehder has been sentenced to life in prison without parole, plus 135 years and $325,000 in fines. I have no comment.

"Thank you for your call." I put the receiver down.

"It's done," I said to my wife, "the crippled mule has fallen.

"But you don't look satisfied," she answers.

It is not a time for personal satisfaction. I feel sorry for the man my age who has been condemned to spend the rest of his life behind bars; for his brothers Guillermo and Federico, his sister Elizabeth and his mother Doña Elena. Into my mind come sudden flashes of the child Carlos Lehder with whom I played marbles and Cowboys and Indians; the young Carlos Lehder with whom I planned to travel to America to become rich and famous. He may have thought he succeeded, but, with no money of my own, I am the rich one now.

The following day in Jacksonville I met with US Attorney Ernest Mueller who told me about the events of the sentencing hearing.

"Lehder gave a twenty-five minute speech before he was sentenced," explained Mr. Mueller, "He asked the judge to deport him either to Colombia or to Germany rather than imprison him in this country. He accused the United States Government and Robert Merkle for his 1987 so-called 'kidnapping' to face charges in Jacksonville," continued Mueller.

"He's part of a very select few who, because they are career criminals, should live and die in jail," Mueller told US District Judge Howell W. Melton.

"The judge fairly, justly and appropriately socked it to a hoodlum who deserves every minute he received!" exclaimed Mueller's boss, acting US Attorney Joseph D. Magri, replacing Robert W. Merkle who was absent at the sentencing hearing because of his bid for the Republican seat in the Senate for the State of Florida.[1]

"The battle against substance abuse will not be won with the conviction and imprisonment of drug barons alone," Melton told Lehder. "This sentence is a signal that our country will do everything in its power to combat the drug problem."

"In a deep, lightly accented voice, Lehder made a speech in which he said he was confused by the US laws under which he could be convicted of having cocaine without ever having been in this country with the drugs," Mueller told me. "Lehder said he felt like an Indian in a white man's court, and that he never intended to come to this country to do any harm to the American people."

"He looked well," continued the US Attorney, "he just began to grow a beard and a mustache, and, reading from some notes, he attacked the Colombian extradition treaty — invalidated four months after his February 4, 1987 arrest under which he was brought to the United States after being denied access to Colombian lawyers and judges. "That treaty was an invitation to violence, and it violated the Colombian Constitution and the United Nations Charter," insisted Lehder. "I have been Mr. Merkle's hostage."

He accused Merkle of directing physical and psychological torture in the condition of his custody and commented on the former prosecutor's political philosophy. He said he had been convicted by the press before his trial and convicted by the jury prejudiced by the barrage of media attention aimed at finding him guilty before any evidence could be introduced.

Have the members of the Medellin Cartel learned something from this case? Has the American justice succeeded in teaching them a lesson? We may never know. But one fact still remains. The war against drugs is not over, and so long as there are Colombians like Attorney General Carlos Mauro Hoyos, Justice Minister Rodrigo Lara Bonilla, Hernando Baquero and police colonel Jaime Ramirez Gomez; Panamanians like Hugo Spadafora, and Drug Enforcement agents like Camarena Salazar who all gave their lives fighting for this cause, there is hope.

Carlos Lehder is not the only "Crippled Mule." There will be others.

THE CHARACTERS

The following is an update on the lives of some of the characters of "The Crippled Mule."

CARLOS ENRIQUE LEHDER RIVAS: Sentenced to serve the rest of his life in a Federal Penitentiary without parole.[1]

ALVARO TRIANA MURILLO, A.K.A ARCHIE, a.k.a ANTONIO JIMENEZ: Arrested in Curacao, Netherlands and extradited to the United States. Faces a jury trial late in 1988 . If found guilty, could be sentenced to 15 to 20 years in a Federal Penitentiary.

HARRY TRECO: Arrested in Chub Cay, Bahamas. His case presently in front of a Bahamian court. If found guilty under the law of the Commonwealth, could serve up to thirty years in. prison. {2018 updated: Harry Treco died at age 80 in 2013.}

ROBERT TRECO and KEITH TRECO: Both face the same fate as their father.

EDWARD GOLDBERG: Convicted in Miami of several charges. Serving an eight year sentence after agreeing to testify against Carlos Lehder and others.

SHEILA GOLDBERG: Filed for divorce and testified against her own husband. For four years kept a daily secret journal which she offered to Fort Lauderdale Organized Crime Unit to help put her husband away. She now lives in South Florida in the company of her new husband enjoying Ed's millions.

NIGEL BOWE: Indicted in the United States, fights extradition and lives in Nassau.[2]

MAXIMILIANO GARZON: Arrested in South Florida for possession of cocaine. Serving a sentence at a Federal Institution.

MICHAEL McMANUS: Active member of the Drug Enforcement Administration in Fort Lauderdale Fla.[3]

DOUG DRIVER: Relocated with The Drug Enforcement Administration somewhere abroad.

ERNEST MUELLER: US State Attorney in Jacksonville, Florida.

ROBERT W. MERKLE: Resigned as U.S Attorney to run for the office of Senator for the Republican party representing the State of Florida.[4]

FREDERICK E. GRAVES: Criminal Defense attorney practicing law in Fort Lauderdale, Fla. [5]

SANDRA SUAREZ MURDERER: The Broward Sheriff's Office has put this investigation on hold after it learned that Sandra's alleged murderer, Mauricio, has moved to Colombia.[6]

JUDGE MARK SPEISER: Still occupies the bench as a county criminal judge in Fort Lauderdale.[7] When the judge asked Michael McManus about Carlos, McManus informed him that still works closely with DEA and has been of vital help in a number of important arrests.

"I had to let him go, but I had great misgivings," Speiser replied. "No other Colombian has ever followed through on his promises to our courts. They disappear across the border and later re-enter to join the drug trade . Tell Carlos I am proud of him; he has renewed my faith in the people of Colombia."

DR. JULIO DIAZ: Dr. Diaz was convicted of drug trafficking but his conviction was overturned on appeal. *See*, U.S. v. Juan Baptista-Rodriguez, 17 F.3d 1354 (11th Cir. 1994). After his appeal was denied, Diaz pled guilty for a lesser sentence.

CARLOS STIER: Carlos Stier, the witness who prepared this statement, is a pseudonym used to protect his identity. Stier continued working as a government informant for many years and is still fearful for his safety.

NOTES

Introduction

1. It is extremely unlikely that Michael Satz' office would have agreed to probation for charges carrying a fifteen year minimum mandatory sentence without substantial cooperation from Stier.

2. Perhaps this is not entirely surprising. South Florida with its many Caribbean and South American immigrants is also home to local versions of santería and palo mayombé from Cuba; Haitian magic and Brazilian macumba.

3. That is, assassins.

4. This interrogation is emblematic of the kind of nonsense defense attorneys have to put up with because they are conflated with their clients.

5. Hearing your attorney threatened by the judge is rarely reassuring.

6. Despite my best efforts, I have not been able to find the source of Wiener's observation.

7. *See*, Executive Order 12333 (1981).

8. "So-called" because these individuals are not employees of the third branch of government, have no relationship to the Southern District of Florida. Instead, they cleared FBI or even CIA agents. The Southern District of Florida maintains its own security employees who guard the various courthouses in the district.

9. *Brady v. Maryland,* 373 U.S. 83 (1963). In this case the Supreme Court required prosecutors to disclose exculpatory information to the defendant's counsel. Prior to *Brady,* a prosecutor had no such obligation.

10. I Gibbon, *Decline and Fall of the Roman Empire* 548, 49 {Modern Library ed.}

11. Quoted by Honoré de Balzac, *Maximes et pensées de Napoleon,* (1838); reprinted by Alma Classics, London (2016) p. 6.

12. The use of a car bomb by Israeli intelligence to murder a political opponent in the heart of Beirut permitted Hezbollah to claim that Lebanese President Rafik Hariri was murdered by Israel the same way.

13. His books, including *Man on a String*, an Edgar Award winner, are enjoying somewhat of a resurgence in these days of Nam-stalgia.

14. For you must explain why you need to bring in the equipment, without giving too much away.
15. Especially when investigators or process servers are required.
16. I happen to believe that the inability of a jury to reach a unanimous verdict ought be, by itself, proof that reasonable doubt exists as a matter of law. But this is not the law. For what it's worth, I also happen to believe that there must be reasonable doubt when after one week of deliberations, the jurors cannot reach a decision. They certainly can pressure the hold-outs to get a verdict, and the chances of this happening are increased the longer they are sequestered for deliberations. A juror should not have to vote against his conscience simply to put an end to his peers haranguing him to change his vote so they all can go home. Liberty is just too precious to be surrendered to peer pressure.
17. Perhaps they didn't want him back because he won.
18. The Bail Reform Act of 1984 imposed severe restrictions on granting bail in federal criminal cases.
19. Hill's *Think and Grow Rich* is a classic text rich with anecdotes promoting a philosophy of positivism and prosperity.
20. The literal translation "narcopenitent" is rare.
21. The Sepam Corporation in New Jersey is the only legal importer of the leaf, which was then denatured, stripped of its methyl benzoyl ecgonine and added to the syrup that makes carbonated water Coca-Cola.

Preface

1. Lehder was certainly a prominent member of the *Medellin* cartel (*a*, but not *the* Colombian cartel) but can hardly be called its leader. That honor goes to Pablo Escobar.
2. Stier was initially arrested for the murder of Sandra Suarez, not for any drug trafficking activity. During police interrogation he admitted to several unrelated drug trafficking crimes in a failed effort to exonerate himself from the murder.
3. Atonement is best left for theological analysis. Stier cooperated with the government to escape the consequences of what would have been at least a fifteen-year state prison sentence for drug trafficking.
4. Stier has since left the Witness Protection Program.
5. Stier enjoyed the benefits of drug trafficking before reaching this conclusion.
6. There is no doubt that the Medellin cartel dealt harshly with its enemies. The murder of Barry Seal and the downing of Avianca flight

203 testify to this fact. Stier surely would have documented an attempt on his life but he did not do so.

1. February 14, 1987

1. Stier's native language is Spanish and his statement often contains non-conventional language such as this. For the most part these have been retained in this version of his statement. "Moment of silence" is most likely intended.
2. Lehder was far from being the "lord and ruler" of Colombia. By seeking to aggrandize Lehder, Stier exaggerates his own role.
3. The United States is always arresting the "biggest drug dealer in the world." In recent memory there was have Roberto Suarez, Carlos Lehder, Jorge Ochoa (who was released), General Manuel Noriega, Pablo Escobar, Gilberto Rodriguez Orejuela and "El Chapo," Joaquín Guzman Loera, all of whom who were claimed to be leaders of the drug world. There seems to be no shortage of "biggest drug dealers in the world."
4. Stier omitted the first names of both defense attorneys. This is a curious omission. Perhaps the DEA agents who worked with him on the statement in Jacksonville were initially unaware of their first names.
5. Stier does not subsequently identify the DEA informant who provided this information, if indeed he ever existed.
6. MAS was created not by Lehder, but by the Ochoa family after the abduction of Marta Ochoa by the M-19 guerrilla group.
7. It is generally accepted that the killing of Rodrigo Lara Bonilla was ordered by Pablo Escober, not Carlos Lehder.
8. This assertion contradicts the previous claim that Lehder formed MAS to go to war against M-19.

2. January 1983

1. This reference to Stier's own nickname for Lehder is not explained in the statement.
2. From this passage it is not clear whether Stier claims to have met Lehder in Colombia as a child or in New York as a teenager. Stier in fact had known Lehder from childhood in Colombia.
3. Given the rapidity with which Stier joined the Lehder trafficking organization, this claim of incredulity is simply unbelievable.

4. At least here Stier recognizes Lehder's actual role in the Medellin cartel. According to Stier, Lehder owned only a fifth of the cocaine.

5. Yet a few pages above, Stier claims that he and Lehder "danced the night away" with the daughters of the wealthy at these parties.

4. March 1983

1. Here Stier clarifies that he knew Lehder in Colombia, before either of them went to New York. His claim that he "ran into" Lehder later in New York and began living with him and two other un-named Colombians is not believable.

5. April 24, 1983

1. Another instance of Stier's native Spanish leaking into the English text. He means "cooperate."

7. May 10, 1983

1. Here is yet another example of Stier's true feelings shining through when describing his fellow lawbreakers.

2. Despite his later condemnations of traffickers as a class, Stier is more likely to praise his fellow lawbreakers.

8. May 13, 1983

1. The DEA believes that Stier's information about the relationship between Fidel Castro is correct but the agency never used this information. Indicting General Noriega was one thing; indicting Castro would be quite another. US In 1983 the Soviet Union had not fallen. These events would play a small part in the subsequent trial of Dr. Julio Diaz.

2. If true, this is an astonishing example of hypocrisy. Castro had General Arnaldo Ochoa executed in 1989 for drug trafficking while accepting a birthday present and maintaining cordial relations with a leading figure of the Medellin cartel.

3. There is an unreadable lacunae in the text here where Stier and Lehder discuss what Lehder, a few minutes before, claimed not to

have time to discuss. Part of the discussion concerned cash payments to Stier's children in Colombia.

9. May 15, 1983

1. This stilted dialog seems lifted from the cult film *The Room* but was not altered.
2. Again Stier's true feelings shine through his confession.
3. By not naming these individuals, Stier protected them from the DEA and state authorities. It is not known whether this was deliberate, or if Stier's impressive memory had merely failed him.
4. The DEA would certainly want to know about a traitor in their midst. Stier leaves the traitor unnamed.
5. According to Stier, there were corrupt FAA employees as well. Stier does not identify them. It is not known whether his allegations are true. Nevertheless, by using Stier as a witness the Department of Justice vouched for his truthfulness.
6. It could hardly be a secret to Laura if she had just received one hundred thousand dollars in cash from Stier.
7. Far from being ashamed of his lawbreaking, Stier was proud of his accomplishments.
8. "Attention, attention, this is the Paisa calling from the capital of the arepa." Paisa is a term for a native of Antioquia, the Colombian province of which Medellín is the capital. An arepa is a flat, round patty made of corn meal and is typical of the region.
9. Stier was fascinated by Laura Treco and in an earlier version of his confession he tried to protect her by giving her a false name.
10. Here, Stier's native Spanish shines through the text of his confession. "Inconveniences" here is Spanish for "difficulties."

10. June 16, 1983

1. A "mule" is a person who smuggles drugs on commercial aircraft, usually by swallowing condoms full of powder. Stier previously did not mention that he had any contact whatsoever with this smuggling channel, but here he admits that he "normally" dealt with drug mules.
2. Stier fails to expand on his allegation that former Colombian president Belisario Betancur was a friend of drug traffickers.

3. No such allegation was made against General Noriega at his trial. Perhaps this was a rumor that Stier heard which he placed in the mouths of the Colombian bankers for greater credibility.

4. This is the first casual mention connecting Stier with a contract killer.

5. Was he only a part-time contract killer? Uncharacteristically, Stier is not clear.

6. Stier would have us believe that this money laundering transaction was his first. He betrays himself with words like "normally." It is unlikely the event he speaks of was Stier's first money-laundering rodeo. Secondly, it is odd that he telephoned Lehder after Lehder told him to use the telephone only in life or death situations.

11. July, 1983

1. The southern plains of Colombia are at a distance of 725 kilometers from the country's northern coast. Perhaps that was the location of a cocaine laboratory but it would not be prudent to add almost five hours of flight time to a journey to the Bahamas. Either Stier was trying to be dramatic, his memory failed him or he was just lying about an inconsequential detail. But if he would lie about an inconsequential detail he could also lie about more materials facts. The problem is that it is impossible to know what else he was lying about.

2. Apparently Stier knows very little about aviation. Landing with engines off is a dangerous maneuver as the landing cannot be aborted if, for example, there is an obstruction on the runway or for any other reason.

3. Despite his professed loathing for the "filthy business" of drug trafficking, Stier no difficulty admiring his fellow lawbreakers and continuing in the business. Sentences like this were added to the statement to counter Stier's multiple statements showing the pride he had for his work as an accomplished trafficker.

4. It is hard to understand how the plane could be "properly" re-fueled when in the previous paragraph Stier complains that "much of the jet fuel was lost."

12. August 25, 1983

1. According to Stier, "It was several months later that I learned that Botero's trip to Germany was to meet with underground terrorist groups to negotiate the purchase of weapons to supply the M-19 revolutionary and terrorist group in Colombia."

2. Stier's narrative does not reveal when he was supposed to have met these other pilots.

3. There is no solicitor named "Turnkuist" in the Bahamas. While this may be a mis-spelling of the surname "Turnquist," there are currently no listings for a solicitor with that surname either. However, there is a law firm called Dupuch & Turnquest, one of the oldest firms in the Bahamas. It is not clear whether Stier is referring to one of that firm's founders or if he simply made up a name.

4. Dupuch & Turnquest's offices are in Freeport, not Nassau.

5. Here Stier's native Spanish slips through: the translation of "to greet" in Spanish is the verb *saludar*.

6. Of course, Stier was not anyone's legal representative as he is not a lawyer.

7. Stier subsequently cooperated against Bowe for the DEA and this statement was written with an eye towards its use in the case against Bowe.

8. Chalk's Airways ran amphibious aircraft from the Port of Miami to the Bahamas. In 2005 one of these planes crashed after taking off from Ft. Lauderdale. The two pilots and twenty passengers were killed. The airline went out of business shortly thereafter.

9. One of the founders of Dupoch & Turnquest was indeed knighted by Queen Elizabeth.

13. September, 1983

1. This is apparently a reference to Stier himself, but the text is not clear.

2. In Colombian slang, a place to hide cash.

1. Winter, 1984

1. The risk of violence is quite high if you take a pistol along to collect a drug debt.

2. Stier seems unsure as to whether one of his "trusted" employees was named Ernest Alvarado or Ernesto Arango.

3. In the original, Stier writes "ruffle" instead of "towel." 'Ruffle' is not a noun.

4. I

This Cuban physician is not identified. By not identifying him, Stier leaves the impression that he is Dr. Julio Diaz, whom Diaz met with extensively during his later sting efforts on behalf of the DEA.

5. Is Ernesto also Luis? Stier's statement is not clear.
6. Dr. Sanchez may or may not be Luis/Ernesto's son. The lack of precision is surprising in a court document.
7. There is still a strip mall at Glades Road and San Andros Street in Boca Raton.
8. Stier may be right in that he had no alternative to shoot, but the case is not one only of "pure self-defense" but armed drug trafficking.
9. "The use of the possessive 'our' suggests that Stier is not being completely honest about having cut ties to the C.C.Q.Q.
10. This evidence of remorse is unconvincing. Stier took a pistol with him to collect a drug debt from a man who had cheated him and who had previously abducted his wife and child.
11. One would think that Triana's abduction of Stier's wife and child would be sufficient grounds for terminating their friendship.

2. Summer, 1984

1. Despite Stier's abandonment of Lehder's organization, he still has access to the organization's vehicles and personnel. Or perhaps Stier had not left at all.
2. With reference to a drug trafficking debt, it is astonishing that Stier can use the phrase "take your time" and expect anyone to believe it.
3. Pure cocaine is usually cut with lactose, a harmless substance.
4. Somehow Stier has forgotten the incident in which he almost shot Alvaro Triana's face off.
5. Bogota could be a dangerous place in the 1970's but the insecurity had nothing to do with student riots opposing the government.
6. Stier had previously stated that only buyer and seller could be present to consummate a transaction but here he has buyer and seller waiting for the arrival of two others.
7. In South Florida, the lure of quick money drew many otherwise respectable citizens into the cocaine business. The fact that South Florida was a major transit point meant that cocaine in large quantities could be found easily.
8. Mysteriously the number of kilos to be sold has been reduced to just one.
9. Sandra Suarez' body was found in the trunk of a car left in a shopping center parking lot.
10. Stier would have the judge and jurors believe that his other janitors would involve themselves in a drug trafficking transaction not only without compensation, but that the matter was so trivial for them that

not only were they able to function in this role but that this was somehow their second nature.

11. This makes no sense. Eddie was mugged in a parking lot.

12. Stier does not explain how a forty-eight hour period was extended to a few weeks.

13. Stier claims never to have heard the proverb, "fool me once…"

14. Stier's claim here, as an experienced drug trafficker and seller who had already been ripped off once, that he would fail to take his commission from the sale is not believable. Clearly there is more to the story. If, on the other hand, Stier was really this naive, how would he react if he was stolen from again?

3. April 19, 1985

1. Keeping witnesses separate is a common police tactic. There is nothing illegal about it. This tactic has nothing to do with the rules governing search warrants.

2. In Florida, the correct acronym is DCF, for the Department of Children and Families.

3. It is a violation only in Stier's imagination. If he and his wife were to be incarcerated, his children would be turned over to the DCF in the interim.

4. May, 1985

1. Both Detective Nick Argentine and Detective John Palmer were homicide detectives with the Broward Sheriff's Office, not the Ft. Lauderdale police. At the time Stier's statement was written, unearthing this information would have been a difficult, though not impossible task. Today, with Google, it is trivial. It is strange that the DEA did not correct this error, unless they were not eager to have the defense attorneys locate the two detectives.

2. There obviously is more to this story if Stier had to hire Fred Graves to recover documents seized by the police on another occasion. Stier provides no details of that episode or even when it occurred.

3. While the issue of matching fibers is more complicated, finding Sandra Suarez' blood at Stier's house would certainly qualify as probable cause for the issuance of a warrant for Stier's arrest.

4. Should be "of record," but at this stage, according to Stier, Graves had yet to file an appearance on behalf of Stier.

5. In Stier's eyes, Fred Graves may have been the best attorney in Broward County, but the Florida Bar did not agree. Graves had been disciplined in 1987 and 1989 and was disbarred in 1991. In 1992 he was charged and convicted of felony theft. After he was disbarred, Graves moved to North Carolina where he worked as an insurance salesman. He died in 2012.

6. Graves did not need to hire a private investigator to make a phone call.

7. Several newspapers report that the files of the Sandra Suarez case are no longer available in Broward County. It beggars belief that three homicide detectives would confuse spilled Raspberry Kool-Aid with human blood stains.

5. October 21, 1985

1. The reader will remember that this same parking lot was chosen by Stier as a venue for his narcotics transactions.

2. A probable cause hearing is not a trial and the concept of legal culpability is never addressed. That a lawyer would ask a judge to find his client 'not guilty' in a probably cause hearing is not believable.

3. It is illegal for a lawyer to share legal fees with a non-lawyer. Doing so can subject the lawyer to disbarment.

4. It is unlikely that Graves' victims would agree with his sentiment. Collectively, it is estimated that Graves stole $450,000 from his clients.

5. This suggests that the real reason why Stier was working in Graves' law office was to obtain clients. According to Stier, he had only been working as a trafficker for two years. The likely truth is that Stier in fact had been involved for years and had developed many contacts along the way.

6. This is hyperbole. Nova University in Broward county does not grant scholarships on the basis of a high LSAT score. Stier's score, if as high as he claims, would only have made him eligible for admission.

7. See note 5, above.

8. Actually, Graves and Stier were contemporaries.

6. Early Fall, 1986

1. Stier presents Gould's reluctance to testify as if it were exculpatory. More likely, Gould did not wish to be branded a cooperating witness while serving time in the Florida state prison system.

2. This cannot be a verbatim account. In state criminal cases in Florida and in federal criminal cases throughout the United States, a lawyer is not permitted even to mention a possible sentence to the jury. The penalty phase in death penalty cases is the sole exception. Otherwise, the imposition of sentence is left to the presiding judge.

3. The DEA surely was unhappy that this opinion was included in Stier's witness statement and it is surprising that it was not redacted.

4. A nolo contendere plea is the equivalent of a guilty plea in the State of Florida and is counted as such for the purpose of calculating a defendant's criminal history. Stier means, "The idea of a *plea bargain had crossed my mind...*"

5. Given that Judge Speiser had already denied Graves' motion to suppress Stier's recorded statement, it is not believable that the prosecutor would agree to probation in a case that provided for a sentence of fifteen years. A period of incarceration would certainly have been required, though less than fifteen years.

6. It is not known whether this second polygraph covered the circumstances of Sandra Suarez' murder. If Stier had passed such a second polygraph he surely would have included this information in his statement. It is therefore likely that Stier was not asked about Sandra Suarez or if he were, he failed again.

7. Here Stier appears to have copied information from a DEA press release.

7. March, 1987

1. Nigel Bowe was arrested in the Bahamas in 1985. He was extradited to the United States in 1993. Stier is not mentioned in the Eleventh Circuit's opinion disposing of Bowe's appeal. Further information about a BBC interview with Bowe after his release from federal prison is mentioned in *The Injustice System: A Murder in Miami and a Trial Gone Wrong*, by Clive Stafford Smith (Penguin 2012). Bowe returned to his office after his release from federal prison and died in 2015 or 2016.

    See, Evil Money: Encounters Along the Money Trail, Rachel Ehrenfield (HarperCollins 1988, 1992) at p. 41; *United States v. Frederick Nigel Bowe*, 221 F.3d 1183 (11th Cir. 2000)

2. That is, "peasants" in Spanish.

3. Stier is inconsistent in the identification of the pilot who accompanied Robert Treco back to the United States. In the previous paragraph he was Colombian but in this one he is American.

4. Stier was drug trafficking with the Trecos in 1983, when he claimed to just have entered the drug business. Here he claims to have been

involved at least since 1978, which would have put him in the middle
of the Lehder 1981 indictment. He says that the story is "totally fabricated," but perhaps this fabricated story was seeded with the truth, as
all good lies are.

5. Presumably, the Colombian pilot would do the same. The date of
Stier's entry into business with Lehder could not easily be hidden.

6. A 'reverse sting' is an operation in which the government agents pose
as sellers, rather than buyers.

7. The use of the defense that the government manufactured the crime,
known popularly as 'entrapment' is rarely successful. A person who
already is in the drug business could not possibly use the defense.
Here Stier suggests to whoever will read his statement that Washington had predetermined that the crime was not manufactured.

8. For all the drug war's interdiction efforts, the American taste for
cocaine and the unrelenting enforcement of the law of supply and
demand caused the price to drop from roughly $40,000 per kilo in
1983 to less than $10,000 in 1987.

9. In fact, Dr. Julio Diaz was as much of an agent as was Stier. The
exception is that Stier worked as an informant for the DEA to work
off a drug trafficking sentence while Dr. Diaz worked as an FBI agent
and before that, the CIA in order to fight for the freedom of Cuba.

8. February, 1988

1. Stier deluded himself into believing that he was a DEA agent. He was
never a government employee but at all time was only a confidential
informant (CI) who was never entitled to any of the benefits of
government employment.

2. Federally-protected witnesses are not made available for press confer-
ences for obvious reasons.

3. Stier's reasons for turning against Lehder had less to do with his
integrity than with his desire to escape a Florida drug-trafficking
conviction.

10. May 19, 1988

1. That is, "bank account statements."

2. Corporate "Articles of Incorporation..."

3. Again, Stier probably means "greeted" here.

4. "Mad Dog" was Merkle's nickname in the press.

5. Stier never testified in Lehder's trial.

12. July 20, 1988

1. Merkle lost his bid for a seat in the United States Senate.

13. The Characters

1. In 1991, Lehder reached a post-trial plea agreement with the government in which he agreed to testify against General Manuel Noriega. His sentence was subsequently reduced. Lehder claims that the government reneged on a deal to transfer him to Germany under the prisoner exchange treaty in force between the two countries.
2. Bowe lost his extradition fight and was sentenced to prison for drug trafficking and money laundering. He also cooperated with the government and returned to the Bahamas to practice law.
3. Special Agent McManus has retired from the DEA.
4. Merkle lost his Senate bid. He died in 2003 when he was only 58 years old.
5. Graves was subsequently disbarred and charged for stealing money from his clients. He never practiced law again. He moved to North Carolina where he sold insurance until his death in 2012.
6. There is no statute of limitations on this cold case. Stier does not give Sandra Suarez' boyfriend's surname in his statement. Stier has also claimed that Suarez was murdered by the Medellin Cartel to frame him.
7. Judge Speiser was a circuit judge, not a county court judge. He now sits in the Probate Division of the 17th Judicial Circuit in Ft. Lauderdale.